THE POWER OF THE BLOOD OF JESUS:

A Scriptural Study

THE

POWER OF THE
BLOOD OF JESUS
A SCRIPTURAL STUDY

The Power of the Blood of Jesus:
A Scriptural Study

Copyright © 2025 Shine International
First edition January 2025
Published by Shine International
Phoenix, Arizona
Email: shinebooksmedia@gmail.com
Website: www.shineinternational.org

ISBN 978-1-962580-05-2

*In Him we have redemption through His blood, the forgiveness of sins,
according to the riches of His grace*

Ephesians 1:7

CONTENTS

INTRODUCTION

The purpose of this study is to open our eyes to the treasure available to us, which is the transformative power of the blood of Jesus. As believers, we need to perceive the vast extent of the work of the blood of Jesus so that it can work in us deeply, transforming us into Christlikeness.

We receive the work of the blood of Jesus in our lives when we understand the biblical truth and proclaim with faith what the Word of God says. Therefore, one essential requirement is knowing what the Bible teaches about the blood of Jesus, which is the purpose of this book.

In fact, the New Testament speaks about 12 acts of the blood of Jesus. As you perceive the biblical truth and continue to proclaim it regularly, you begin to experience its deep work in your life.

If we could grasp what the blood of Jesus has offered us, we would worship God in a totally different way and our inner life, our view of ourselves, and our ministry would completely change! Oh, if we could grasp what is in the blood of Jesus! We have the eternal, uncreated, measureless life of God Himself in the blood of Jesus.

As you read this book, open your heart to the Holy Spirit so that you may enter into a new experience and a new dimension in discovering this great and mystical unending spring of life and healing.

After reading this book and learning the full revelation of the New Testament about the work of the blood of Jesus, you will need to proclaim it over your life by praying the 12 statements of the blood[1] explained in this book daily so that you may practically experience its transforming effect in your life.

The Bible speaks about confessing with our mouth (Romans 10:9). It also speaks about Jesus as the High Priest of our confession (Hebrews 3:1). What is confession? It literally means *saying the same as*. Therefore, for us, confession means we say the same with our mouth as God says in His Word.

---

1 See p.4 for the 12 statements of the blood of Jesus.

We make the words of our mouth agree with the Word of God. You cannot testify as to what the Word of God says about the blood of Jesus unless you know what the Word of God says. This is what you will discover as you read this book.

Proclamation means releasing the authority of God's Word into a situation, into our own lives, into the life of the Church. Proclamation is the most effective way to release the power of God into a situation. Proclamation is the activity of a herald.

We read about this truth pertaining to proclamation in the following verses:

> Seeing then that we have a great High Priest who has passed through the heavens, Jesus the Son of God, *let us hold fast our confession* (Hebrews 4:14).

> *Let us hold fast the confession* of our hope without wavering, for He who promised is faithful (Hebrews 10:23).

What are the benefits of proclaiming the statements of the blood of Jesus over your life?

To mention but a few benefits, proclaiming the statements of the blood of Jesus every day over your life opens the door for the grace of God to work in your inner man. This proclamation strengthens your faith, opens your mind to the Holy Spirit, and protects you from the attacks of the enemy. Turning the Word of God into prayer is the surest way to receive the inspirations of the Holy Spirit.

We need the life of Jesus to come into our inner man. We need to have soft hearts. Sometimes there is hidden hardness within us that shows up at times; it does not glorify God and does not bear witness to the grace of God. Due to this hardness, we sometimes fail to understand the will of God. This is because the will of God is not revealed to our minds, as we may think. The mind of God is actually revealed to our hearts. There is no separation between the mind of God and the heart of God. When man was created, there was no separation between his mind and heart, for he was created in God's image. The separation happened after the fall. The hardness of the heart is like an aggregation of clouds that separates us from the revelation of God's will. These proclamations are a tool that softens our hearts.

Proclamation can also be a tool to cleanse us and work all its acts in us if we understand the biblical truth behind what we proclaim. You can proclaim the blood of Jesus without understanding its acts and find that it does not work in your life. Therefore, it is important to understand the acts of the blood of Jesus, and as we proclaim them with awareness and understanding, we turn the Word of God into a real sword.

Finally, as you read through the book, you will find many scriptural verses. Make sure to read them, not just skim over them, because reading the verses sanctifies the soul and allows the person to experience the presence of God. Learn to love the Word of God and to love to read it.

Also, as you are reading, you may find that some parts are scholastic, involving some theological study. Do not think that it is not for you and is exclusive to theology students, for every believer ought to be a theological student and a student of the Bible to an extent. When this understanding began to be absent from the Church, everything declined. We need to prepare ourselves as a bride of Christ, who is fervent in her love and, at the same time, deep in her understanding because both go together.

Remember also that studying this biblical topic will build your inner man with meat.[2] Many believers have nourished on milk for so long and now they need meat. The body of Christ needs to be nourished with meat in order to be prepared as a bride for the Bridegroom who is coming soon.

Therefore, if you truly care about deep sanctification and spiritual growth, you need to develop some interest in such biblical studies. But, as you study, you ought to maintain a balance between study and prayer to avoid dryness. Studies bring light to our minds, but prayer brings life and spirit. Prayer opens the door for Christ Himself to accompany the person. Through this, we can taste the glory of God. Christ longs to see His glory resting on His people.

---

2 Hebrews 5:14

THE 12 STATEMENTS OF THE BLOOD OF JESUS

1. The blood of Jesus has redeemed me from the hand of Satan.[3]

2. The blood of Jesus has redeemed me from every curse.

   In Christ Jesus, I am free from every curse and blessed with all blessings. I shall be blessed in my place and my affairs shall be blessed. I shall be blessed at my work and the fruits of my labour shall be blessed. I shall be blessed when I come in and I shall be blessed when I go out. The Lord will cause my enemies who rise up against me to be defeated before my face; they will come at me from one direction but flee from me in seven. The Lord will send a blessing on my barns and on everything I put my hand to; and the Lord, my God, will bless me in the land He is giving me. The Lord will establish me as His holy people; then all the peoples on earth will see that I am called by the name of the Lord and they will fear me. The Lord will grant me abundant prosperity. The Lord will open the heavens, the storehouse of His bounty, to send rain on my land in season and to bless all the work of my hands; so I will lend to many nations but will borrow from none. The Lord will make me the head, not the tail and I will always be at the top, never at the bottom.

3. The blood of Jesus has sealed an eternal covenant for me.

4. The blood of Jesus has reconciled me to and granted me peace with God the Father, all people, and all creation.

5. The blood of Jesus has granted me forgiveness of all my sins.

6. The blood of Jesus, the son of God, cleanses me from all sin.

7. The blood of Jesus justifies me from all condemnation, so all the accusations of the devil against me are nullified; He makes me righteous as though I have never sinned.

8. The blood of Jesus sanctifies me and consecrates me so I become belonging to my Lord, dedicated to Him and set apart for His ministry.

---

3 All 12 statements can be repeated three times for proclamation.

9. The blood of Jesus cleanses my conscience from acts that lead to death so that I may serve the Living God.

10. The blood of Jesus makes me enter the Most Holy Place to serve the Holy God.

11. The blood of Jesus grants me victory over Satan and all his principalities.

12. The blood of Jesus is the reason for my everlasting rejoicing.

✳ 3 Prostrations[4]

---

4 Here, you can prostrate once or three times according to your preference.

CHAPTER 1

THE BLOOD OF JESUS
HAS REDEEMED ME
FROM THE HAND OF SATAN

Readings

For even the Son of Man did not come to be served, but to serve, and to give His life *a ransom* for many (Mark 10:45).

In Him we have *redemption through His blood*, the forgiveness of sins, according to the riches of His grace (Ephesians 1:7).

He has delivered us from the power of darkness and conveyed us into the kingdom of the Son of His love, in whom we have *redemption through His blood*, the forgiveness of sins (Colossians 1:13, 14).

Knowing that you were not *redeemed* with corruptible things, like silver or gold, from your aimless conduct received by tradition from your fathers, but with the precious blood of Christ, as of a lamb without blemish and without spot (1 Peter 1:18, 19).

I. The Meaning of the Word *Redemption*

A. The Linguistic Meaning

1a. To buy back (repurchase)

1b. To get or win back

2. To free from distress or harm, including:

  - To free from captivity by payment of ransom

  - To extricate from or help to overcome something detrimental

  - To release from blame or debt, to clear the debt

  - To free from the consequences of sin

3. To change for the better (reform)

4. To repair or restore

5a. To free from a lien[5] by payment of an amount secured thereby

5b. To remove the obligation by payment

5c. To exchange for something of value

5d. To make good, fulfil

6a. To atone for; to expiate (make amends for an error)

6b. To offset the bad effect of

6c. To make worthwhile, to retrieve (rescue)

---

5 A lien is a right to keep possession of property belonging to another person until a debt owed by that person is discharged.

B. The Meaning According to the Hebrew Language of the Old Testament

Several words are used for *redemption* in the Hebrew language, but two main words are commonly used:

- *Padah*

Pronounced *paw-daw* which means *to redeem from slavery*. This word is repeated 50 times in the Old Testament. Refer to Exodus 13:13; Deuteronomy 15:15; Isaiah 1:27; Isaiah 29:21; Isaiah 51:11.

- *Ga'al*

Pronounced *gaw-al* which means *restore/restorer*. This word is repeated 84 times in the Old Testament. Refer to Genesis 48:16; Exodus 6:6; Exodus 15:13; Leviticus 25:25, 26, 30, 48, 49, 54; Ruth 4:1; Job 19:25; Psalm 69:18; Isaiah 51:10; Isaiah 52:3, 9; Isaiah 54:5, 8.

C. The Meaning According to the Greek Language of the New Testament

In the original Greek language, there are three main words that are translated as *redemption* or *ransom*:

- *Agorazo*

This word means *to purchase a slave in the slave market* (used in the following verses):

For you were *bought* at a price; therefore glorify God in your body and in your spirit, which are God's (1 Corinthians 6:20).

You were *bought* at a price; do not become slaves of men (1 Corinthians 7:23).

Those who weep as though they did not weep, those who rejoice as though they did not rejoice, those who *buy* as though they did not possess (1 Corinthians 7:30).

But there were also false prophets among the people, even as there will be false teachers among you, who will secretly bring in destructive heresies, even denying *the Lord who bought them,* and bring on themselves swift destruction (2 Peter 2:1).

And they sang a new song: "You are worthy to take the scroll and to open its seals, because you were slain, and *with your blood you purchased men for God* from every tribe and language and people and nation" (Revelation 5:9, NIV).

Notice the use of the verbs *buy, bought,* or *purchased* in these verses.

- *Exagorazo*

This word means *to purchase a slave out of the slave market* (used in the following verses):

Christ *has redeemed us* from the curse of the law, having become a curse for us (for it is written, "Cursed is everyone who hangs on a tree") (Galatians 3:13).

To redeem those who were under the law, that we might receive the adoption as sons (Galatians 4:5).

- *Lutro (or apolutrosis)*

This word means *to set free a slave by a price.* It is repeated nine times in the New Testament. Examples are:

Who gave Himself for us, that He might *redeem* us from every lawless deed and purify for Himself His own special people, zealous for good works (Titus 2:14).

Knowing that you were not *redeemed* with corruptible things, like silver or gold, from your aimless conduct received by tradition from your fathers (1 Peter 1:18).

II. A Comment on the Meaning of the Word *Redemption*

Based on the above meanings, the word *redemption* biblically signifies and highlights the following:

- We were slaves and needed to be purchased and delivered from slavery:

But God be thanked that though *you were slaves of sin*, yet you obeyed from the heart that form of doctrine to which you were delivered (Romans 6:17).

- The idea of being sold to sin:

We know that the law is spiritual; but I am unspiritual, *sold as a slave to sin* (Romans 7:14, NIV).

- There is a debt that needs to be paid on our behalf so that we may become free.

- There is something that was lost and needs to be restored. There is a need for a Restorer.

III. Important Highlights

- What is this debt?

There are many interpretations in this respect. However, recent studies brought back the interpretation and conviction of the early Church fathers. Man was granted the gift of being created in the image and likeness of God. When man disobeyed God and obeyed Satan, he lost this gift; thus, man fell into debt.

Jesus paid our debt with His blood so that our debt would be cancelled; thus, we would be able to restore the original image and be Christlike. In other words, Christ ransomed us to restore to us this gift:

> For whom He foreknew, He also predestined *to be conformed to the image of His Son*, that He might be the firstborn among many brethren (Romans 8:29).

- After the fall, Satan gained authority over man, and hence, man needs to be delivered from the slavery caused by *the dominion of Satan, sin, and the world*, as we see in the following verses:

- Deliverance from the dominion of Satan:

> He has *delivered us from the power of darkness* and conveyed us into the kingdom of the Son of His love, in whom we have redemption through His blood, the forgiveness of sins (Colossians 1:13, 14).

- Deliverance from the dominion of sin:

> But God be thanked that though *you were slaves of sin*, yet you obeyed from the heart that form of doctrine to which you were delivered (Romans 6:17).

- Deliverance from the dominion of the world:

> Who gave Himself for our sins, that He might *deliver us from this present evil age*, according to the will of our God and Father (Galatians 1:4).

- Biblical verses that highlight that the price—the blood of Jesus—by which we were purchased was paid:

Before His crucifixion, Jesus proclaimed this truth, saying:

For even the Son of Man did not come to be served, but to serve, and to *give His life a ransom for many* (Mark 10:45).

The apostles understood this truth, and they proclaimed it clearly and openly.

- Apostle Paul said:

For *you were bought at a price*; therefore glorify God in your body and in your spirit, which are God's (1 Corinthians 6:20).

For he who is called in the Lord while a slave is the Lord's freedman. Likewise he who is called while free is Christ's slave (1 Corinthians 7:22).

- Apostle Peter said:

Knowing that you were not redeemed with corruptible things, like silver or gold, from your aimless conduct received by tradition from your fathers, *but with the precious blood of Christ*, as of a lamb without blemish and without spot (1 Peter 1:18, 19).

IV. God's Economy to Redeem Man

1. Out of His Mercy and Love (Mercy Seat)

Being justified freely by His grace through the redemption that is in Christ Jesus, whom God set forth *as a propitiation* by His blood, through faith, to demonstrate His righteousness, because in His forbearance God had passed over the sins that were previously committed (Romans 3:24, 25).

The Greek origin of the word *propitiation* is *hilasterion* or *hilasterios*, meaning *Mercy Seat*. The Mercy Seat is the cover for the Ark. Thus, the word denotes *covering*, which is *kofer* in Hebrew, meaning *cover of sins*.

But God, *who is rich in mercy, because of His great love with which He loved us,* even when we were dead in trespasses, made us alive together with Christ (by grace you have been saved) (Ephesians 2:4, 5).

Out of His love and mercy, God planned to grant us the blood of Jesus to enable us to receive the cleansing of sin, meaning the covering of sin. When we believe in Jesus and repent, we receive this cleansing and covering. Thus, Satan cannot accuse us, for our sins will not be seen again.

God's love and mercy led to the incarnation of the Son of God, His death, and His resurrection, which brought life to us.

2. Putting an End to the Dominion of Satan, Sin, and Death (The Passover Lamb)

This truth is expressed in the Old Testament in a simple way through the story of the Passover lamb. The blood had to be sprinkled on the door so that the destroyer would pass without destroying. Thus, the blood of the lamb put an end to the destroyer:

Then Moses called for all the elders of Israel and said to them, "Pick out and take lambs for yourselves according to your families, and kill the Passover lamb. And you shall take a bunch of hyssop, dip it in the blood that is in the basin, and strike the lintel and the two doorposts with the blood that is in the basin. And none of you shall go out of the door of his house until morning. For the Lord will pass through to strike the Egyptians; and when He sees the blood on the lintel and on the two doorposts, the Lord will pass over the door and not allow the destroyer to come into your houses to strike you" (Exodus 12:21–23).

The Passover lamb refers to Jesus, the Lamb of God. When the blood of Jesus that has been shed on the cross is sprinkled on the lives of the believers by the Holy Spirit, it puts an end to the destroyer, meaning it abolishes the authority of Satan and sets us free. It is written, 'You shall know the truth, and the truth shall make you free' (John 8:32).

3. Restoring the Image of God

There is therefore now no condemnation to those who are in Christ Jesus, who do not walk according to the flesh, but according to the Spirit (Romans 8:1).

And for this reason He is the Mediator of the new covenant, by means of death, for the redemption of the transgressions under the first covenant, that those who are called may receive the promise of the eternal inheritance (Hebrews 9:15).

After we are freed from condemnation, the Holy Spirit works in our lives, restoring to us the gift of God that we have lost—His image.

Therefore, it would be inappropriate if, after having been saved, we neglect *working out our salvation* as the Scriptures command us:

Therefore, my beloved, as you have always obeyed, not as in my presence only, but now much more in my absence, *work out your own salvation with fear and trembling*; for it is God who works in you both to will and to do for His good pleasure (Philippians 2:12, 13).

If we work out our salvation, we will please God by becoming Christlike:

He shall see the labour of His soul, and be satisfied (Isaiah 53:11).

V. Our Responsibility Towards God's Complete Redemption That Has Been Offered to Us

Our responsibility in this respect lies in faith, fellowship with the Holy Spirit, and the Church life.

1. Faith

Our responsibility is to exercise our faith by believing in what Christ has accomplished for our salvation and receiving His redemptive work in our spirits (Romans 3:24, 25).

> For by grace you have been saved through faith, and that not of yourselves; it is the gift of God (Ephesians 2:8).

2. Fellowship With the Holy Spirit

God's redemptive work should flow continuously in our lives to keep us free and to enable us to restore God's image in us. This can only be achieved through the fellowship of the Holy Spirit:

> In Him you also trusted, after you heard the word of truth, the gospel of your salvation; in whom also, having believed, you were sealed with the Holy Spirit of promise, who is the guarantee of our inheritance until the redemption of the purchased possession, to the praise of His glory (Ephesians 1:13, 14).

> And do not grieve the Holy Spirit of God, by whom you were sealed for the day of redemption (Ephesians 4:30).

3. Church Life

Through fellowship with the believers (the Church) and the means of grace, we are accounted as the body of Christ, which is connected with the Head—the Person of Christ; thus, His redemptive power will continuously work in our lives:

And He put all things under His feet, and gave Him to be head over all things to the church, which is His body, the fullness of Him who fills all in all (Ephesians 1:22, 23).

But of Him you are in Christ Jesus, who became for us wisdom from God— and righteousness and sanctification and *redemption* (1 Corinthians 1:30).

The word *redemption* here is *apolutrosis*.

These three factors are channels that bring the redemption of Christ to our lives. We need to keep these channels open so that the power of redemption may continue to come to our lives again and again. We need the continuous covering of our sins, a continuous process that puts an end to the destroyer, and a continuous process to restore our image.

VI. Final Concluding Points

1. Redemption is God's provision through:

   Jesus (Person) + His Blood + the Holy Spirit (God's Power)

2. The results of redemption are:

   - New relationship
   - New life
   - New hope
   - New purpose
   - New witness (testimony)

CHAPTER 2

THE BLOOD OF JESUS HAS REDEEMED ME FROM EVERY CURSE

Readings

For as many as are of the works of the law are under the curse; for it is written, "Cursed is everyone who does not continue in all things which are written in the book of the law, to do them." ... *Christ has redeemed us from the curse of the law, having become a curse for us* (for it is written, "Cursed is everyone who hangs on a tree"), that the blessing of Abraham might come upon the Gentiles in Christ Jesus, that we might receive the promise of the Spirit through faith (Galatians 3:10, 13, 14).

He who sins is of the devil, for the devil has sinned from the beginning. For this purpose the Son of God was manifested, *that He might destroy the works of the devil* (1 John 3:8).

Introduction

Curse is one of the most important topics in the Bible that is not properly understood. We need to know what the Bible says about it and what the blood of Jesus has done regarding it, and hence worship God appropriately for all He has done for us!

I. The Meaning of the Word *Curse*

A. The Linguistic Meaning

1. A prayer or an invocation for harm or injury to come upon a person

2. Something that is cursed or accursed

3. Evil or misfortune that comes in response to retribution

Generally speaking, it is something bad and harmful, coming from a person to a person or the devil to a person.

B. The Meaning According to the Hebrew Language of the Old Testament

Three main words are used in the Hebrew language of the Old Testament to mean *curse*:

- *Qalal*

It describes the *curse* from the aspect of its *utterance or pronunciation*. This word is used in Genesis 8:21:

> And the Lord smelled a soothing aroma. Then the Lord said in His heart, "I will never again *curse* the ground for man's sake, although the imagination of man's heart is evil from his youth; nor will I again destroy every living thing as I have done."

- *Arar*

It describes the *curse* from its *operational aspect* (the action). This word is used in Genesis 12:3:

> I will bless those who bless you, and I will curse him who curses you; and in you all the families of the earth shall be blessed.

- *Killel*

It describes a wide range of injurious activities varying from verbal abuse to material harm. It basically means *to take lightly and with disrespect*. This word is used in Isaiah 8:21:

> They will pass through it hard-pressed and hungry; and it shall happen, when they are hungry, that they will be enraged and *curse their king and their God*, and look upward.

This word describes the effect of the curse (the results). The reference says they will disrespect God.

- There is another important Hebrew word that is used in the Old Testament, which is *charom*.

This word refers to complete destruction, hence indicating that a curse can bring complete destruction. It occurs in Zechariah 14:11:

> The people shall dwell in it; and no longer shall there be *utter destruction*, but Jerusalem shall be safely inhabited.

C. The Meaning According to the Greek Language of the New Testament

Some believers maintain that since we are redeemed, no curse can affect us. If this were the case, the word *curse* would not be mentioned in the New Testament. But, in fact, there are seven different Greek words in the New Testament that refer to a curse. This indicates that there are different channels through which a curse can reach the believers. However, in the New Testament, we have the tool to deal with the curse. Therefore, we need to understand the work of the blood of Jesus in this respect.

Seven Greek words in the New Testament that mean *curse*:

- *Anathematizo*

This word occurs once in the New Testament in Mark 14:71:

> Then he began *to curse* and swear, "I do not know this Man of whom you speak!"

- *Katathematizo*

This word occurs once in the New Testament in Matthew 26:74:

> Then he began *to curse* and swear, saying, "I do not know the Man!"

- *Ara*

This word occurs once in the New Testament in Romans 3:14:

> Whose mouth is full of *cursing* and bitterness.

- *Blasphemio*

This word occurs three times in the New Testament in the following references:

> And men were scorched with great heat, and they *blasphemed* the name of God who has power over these plagues; and they did not repent and give Him glory (Revelation 16:9).

> They were seared by the intense heat and they *cursed* the name of God, who had control over these plagues, but they refused to repent and glorify Him (Revelation 16:9, NIV).

> They *blasphemed* the God of heaven because of their pains and their sores, and did not repent of their deeds (Revelation 16:11).

> And *cursed* the God of heaven because of their pains and their sores, but they refused to repent of what they had done (Revelation 16:11, NIV).

> And great hail from heaven fell upon men, each hailstone about the weight of a talent. Men *blasphemed* God because of the plague of the hail, since that plague was exceedingly great (Revelation 16:21).

> From the sky huge hailstones of about a hundred pounds each fell upon men. And they *cursed* God on account of the plague of hail, because the plague was so terrible (Revelation 16:21, NIV).

- *Epikataratos*

This word occurs twice in the New Testament in the following references:

> For as many as are of the works of the law are under the *curse [katara]*; for it is written, "*Cursed [Epikataratos]* is everyone who does not continue in all things which are written in the book of the law, to do them" (Galatians 3:10).

> Christ has redeemed us from the curse [katara] of the law, having become a curse [katara] for us (for it is written, "Cursed [Epikataratos] is everyone who hangs on a tree") (Galatians 3:13).

- *Katara*

This word occurs five times in the New Testament. It occurs in Galatians 3:10 and twice in Galatians 3:13, as well as in the following references:

> But if it bears thorns and briers, it is rejected and near to being *cursed*, whose end is to be burned (Hebrews 6:8).

> Out of the same mouth proceed blessing and *cursing*. My brethren, these things ought not to be so (James 3:10).

- *Kataraomai*

This word occurs six times in the New Testament in the following references:

> And Peter, remembering, said to Him, "Rabbi, look! The fig tree which You *cursed* has withered away" (Mark 11:21).

> But I say to you, love your enemies, *bless those who curse you*, do good to those who hate you, and pray for those who spitefully use you and persecute you (Matthew 5:44).

> Then He will also say to those on the left hand, "Depart from Me, you *cursed*, into the everlasting fire prepared for the devil and his angels" (Matthew 25:41).

> Bless those who *curse* you, and pray for those who spitefully use you (Luke 6:28).

> Bless those who persecute you; bless and do not *curse* (Romans 12:14).

> With it we bless our God and Father, and with it we *curse* men, who have been made in the similitude of God (James 3:9).

II. Types of Curses

- Curses from the country we belong to (the curse of the land)

- Curses from the family line (spiritual heritage from the family and ancestors)

- Curses from repeated sins of which we do not repent

III. Causes of Curses

In Proverbs 26:2, we read:

Like a flitting sparrow, like a flying swallow, so a curse without cause shall not alight.

This indicates that if there is a curse, there is always a cause behind it, and there must also be a cure for it: Curse, Cause, Cure.

There are seven main causes of curses:

1. God Himself

- Genesis 12:1–3

Now the Lord had said to Abram: "Get out of your country, from your family and from your father's house, to a land that I will show you. I will make you a great nation; I will bless you and make your name great; and you shall be a blessing. I will bless those who bless you, and *I will curse him who curses you*; and in you all the families of the earth shall be blessed."

God protected Abraham and said to him that whoever curses him shall be cursed.

- Deuteronomy 27:11–26

And Moses commanded the people on the same day, saying, "These shall stand on Mount Gerizim to bless the people, when you have crossed over the Jordan: Simeon, Levi, Judah, Issachar, Joseph, and Benjamin; and these shall stand on Mount Ebal to curse: Reuben, Gad, Asher, Zebulun, Dan, and Naphtali.

"And the Levites shall speak with a loud voice and say to all the men of Israel: 'Cursed is the one who makes a carved or moulded image, an abomination to the Lord, the work of the hands of the craftsman, and sets it up in secret.'

"And all the people shall answer and say, 'Amen!'

'Cursed is the one who treats his father or his mother with contempt.'

"And all the people shall say, 'Amen!'

'Cursed is the one who moves his neighbour's landmark.'

"And all the people shall say, 'Amen!'

'Cursed is the one who makes the blind to wander off the road.'

"And all the people shall say, 'Amen!'

'Cursed is the one who perverts the justice due the stranger, the fatherless, and widow.'

"And all the people shall say, 'Amen!'

'Cursed is the one who lies with his father's wife, because he has uncovered his father's bed.'

"And all the people shall say, 'Amen!'

'Cursed is the one who lies with any kind of animal.'

"And all the people shall say, 'Amen!'

'Cursed is the one who lies with his sister, the daughter of his father or the daughter of his mother.'

"And all the people shall say, 'Amen!'

'Cursed is the one who lies with his mother-in-law.'

"And all the people shall say, 'Amen!'

'Cursed is the one who attacks his neighbour secretly.'

"And all the people shall say, 'Amen!'

'Cursed is the one who takes a bribe to slay an innocent person.'

"And all the people shall say, 'Amen!'

'Cursed is the one who does not confirm all the words of this law by observing them.'

"And all the people shall say, 'Amen!'

From this passage, we notice the following:

- Disobedience brings curses.

- There are 12 different curses mentioned.

- The people should refrain from worshipping idols and false gods (which is equivalent to the occult), from dishonouring their parents, and from having any illegitimate or unnatural sex, for all these matters bring curses.

- Jeremiah 17:5, 6

Thus says the Lord: "*Cursed is the man who trusts in man and makes flesh his strength, whose heart departs from the Lord.* For he shall be like a shrub in the desert, and shall not see when good comes, but shall inhabit the parched places in the wilderness, in a salt land which is not inhabited."

Man is cursed when he turns away from God and seeks the strength of people.

- Zechariah 5:1–4

Then I turned and raised my eyes, and saw there a flying scroll. And he said to me, "What do you see?" So I answered, "I see a flying scroll. Its length is twenty cubits and its width ten cubits." Then he said to me, "This is the curse that goes out over the face of the whole earth: 'Every thief shall be expelled,' according to this side of the scroll; and, 'Every perjurer shall be expelled,' according to that side of it." "*I will send out the curse,*" says the Lord of hosts; "*It shall enter the house of the thief and the house of the one who swears falsely by My name.* It shall remain in the midst of his house and consume it, with its timber and stones."

Stolen things and false oaths bring curses.

2. Men Representing God

- Joshua

Then Joshua charged them at that time, saying, *"Cursed be the man before the Lord who rises up and builds this city Jericho; he shall lay its foundation with his firstborn, and with his youngest he shall set up its gates"* (Joshua 6:26).

In his days Hiel of Bethel built Jericho. He laid its foundation with Abiram his firstborn, and with his youngest son Segub he set up its gates, according to the word of the Lord, which He had spoken through Joshua the son of Nun (1 Kings 16:34).

As clear from these two references, Joshua cursed Jericho in 1300 B.C., and then 500 years later, the curse was fulfilled.

- David

O mountains of Gilboa, let there be no dew nor rain upon you, nor fields of offerings. For the shield of the mighty is cast away there! The shield of Saul, not anointed with oil (2 Samuel 1:21).

David cursed these mountains in 1000 B.C. Today, 3000 years later (1000 years B.C. + A.D. 2000 years), the mountains of Gilboa are still barren.

- Jesus and His disciples

Now the next day, when they had come out from Bethany, He was hungry. And seeing from afar a fig tree having leaves, He went to see if perhaps He would find something on it. When He came to it, He found nothing but leaves, for it was not the season for figs. In response Jesus said to it, *"Let no one eat fruit from you ever again."* And His disciples heard it (Mark 11:12–14).

Compare the verses above with Matthew 21:20, 21:

And when the disciples saw it, they marvelled, saying, "How did the fig tree wither away so soon?" So Jesus answered and said to them, "Assuredly, I say to you, if you have faith and do not doubt, *you will not only do what was done* to the fig tree, but also if you say to this mountain, 'Be removed and be cast into the sea,' it will be done."

Jesus cursed the fig tree and He gave His disciples the authority to also curse.

This is the only reference in the New Testament indicating that believers have the authority to curse; however, this ought to be exercised carefully and with a purpose.

Once, a missionary went to the jungle and saw a lion coming upon him; thus, he said, "In the name of Jesus, I order you to die", and the lion died. He was directed by the Holy Spirit at that moment to curse the lion. The lion is God's creation but it was cursed in this instance because it was driven by the devil to kill this missionary. This verse above tells us that sometimes we can curse creation for a purpose.

Jesus cursed the fig tree prophetically because it represented the nation of Israel, but also practically to teach His disciples that there is a time when creation will not fulfil the purpose for which it was created and therefore, can be cursed because Adam was created to have authority over creation.

3. People With Relational Authority

These can be people such as:

- A father with his children

- A pastor with his congregation

- A teacher with his disciples

Many times, negative words come out unintentionally from a father or a teacher and these words bring a curse and negatively affect those spoken to.

4. Self-Imposed Curses

- Rebecca

"Perhaps my father will feel me, and I shall seem to be a deceiver to him; and I shall bring a curse on myself and not a blessing." But his mother said to him, "*Let your curse be on me, my son*; only obey my voice, and go, get them for me" (Genesis 27:12,13).

In fact, a great deal of trouble came later on Rebecca because of the wives of Esau:

And Rebecca said to Isaac, "I am weary of my life because of the daughters of Heth; if Jacob takes a wife of the daughters of Heth, like these who are the daughters of the land, what good will my life be to me?" (Genesis 27:46).

- The Jews during Christ's trial before the crucifixion

When Pilate saw that he could not prevail at all, but rather that a tumult was rising, he took water and washed his hands before the multitude, saying, "I am innocent of the blood of this just Person. You see to it." And *all the people answered and said, "His blood be on us and on our children"* (Matthew 27:24, 25).

As we know, many troubles came upon the Jews throughout history.

- The Jews who plotted to kill Paul

They came to the chief priests and elders, and said, "*We have bound ourselves under a great oath* that we will eat nothing until we have killed Paul" (Acts 23:14).

[They] went to the chief priests and the elders and said, "*We have bound ourselves under a curse* to partake of nothing until we have killed Paul" (Acts 23:14, LEB).

- Peter when he denied Jesus

Then he began *to curse* and swear, "I do not know this Man of whom you speak!" (Mark 14:71).

The original Greek word shows that Peter had actually put a curse on himself.

5. Men Representing Satan

This refers to witchcraft which is condemned in both Testaments:

> You shall not permit a sorceress to live (Exodus 22:18).

> There shall not be found among you anyone who makes his son or his daughter pass through the fire, or one who practises witchcraft, or a soothsayer, or one who interprets omens, or a sorcerer (Deuteronomy 18:10).

> ... idolatry, sorcery, hatred, contentions, jealousies, outbursts of wrath, selfish ambitions, dissensions, heresies (Galatians 5:20).

Witchcraft is the primary cause of family breakdowns.

6. Soulish (Sensual) Utterances

> But if you have bitter envy and self-seeking in your hearts, do not boast and lie against the truth. This wisdom does not descend from above, but is earthly, sensual, demonic (James 3:14, 15).

These kinds of utterances refer to:

- Believers speaking negatively against each other—the power of the word/utterance.

- False prophecies that may change the thinking and plans of the listener, leading him into a false destiny or future.

7. Unscriptural Covenants

In Exodus 23, we read:

> You shall make no covenant with them, nor with their gods (Exodus 23:32).

This refers to a husband or a wife who is in a marital bond with a family that has a history of curses or cursed groups such as Freemasons.

In Deuteronomy 28, we read about two lists, one of blessings resulting from obedience to God and another of curses from disobedience.

- Summary of the blessings

  - Being exalted (*'set you high above all nations'*)

  - Good health

  - Productivity in every area of life

  - Prosperity

  - Victory over the enemy

  - God's favour

- Summary of the curses

  - Humiliation

  - Failure to be productive in any area or aspect of life

  - Mental and physical sickness

  - Poverty

  - Defeat

  - Family breakdowns

  - Oppression

  - Failures

  - Lack of favour in God's sight

IV. Possible Manifestations of Hidden Curses

Based on the passage in Deuteronomy 28, we can suggest some manifestations that can help us discover if there is the presence of a hidden curse so that we may deal with it. These manifestations may be:

- Mental and emotional breakdowns
- Recurrent or chronic illness
- Repeated miscarriages and related family problems
- Marriage breakdowns
- Continuous financial insufficiency, especially if the income appears sufficient
- Being accident-prone
- A history of suicide or unnatural deaths in one's family

V. How to Deal with a Curse

The solution is to move from curse to blessing. In Galatians 3, we read:

> Christ has redeemed us from *the curse* of the law, having become *a curse* for us (for it is written, "*Cursed* is everyone who hangs on a tree"), *that the bless-ing of Abraham* might come upon the Gentiles in Christ Jesus, that we might receive the promise of the Spirit through faith (Galatians 3:13, 14).

These verses say that Christ has redeemed us from the curse of the law.

What is the curse of the law?

It is the list of curses in Deuteronomy 28!

Therefore, *Christ has redeemed us from the curse of the law* means that He redeemed us from the list in Deuteronomy 28.

Notice the exchange that Jesus has done for us:

- Jesus was wounded so that we may be healed.
- Jesus died so that we may live and have life.
- Jesus was made sin so that we may be made righteous.
- Jesus was rejected so that we may be accepted.
- Jesus was made a curse so that we may enter into blessings.

Thus, in Christ, God has made provision for every human need, including the need to be freed from curses.

Notice that the word *curse* is mentioned three times in this reference. Therefore, the blessing is assured. However, we should not stop only at the level of being eligible to receive it as it is given to us, but we need to move from this level to the experiential state where we practically experience the blessings in our lives.

VI. The Process of Release

Some Bible scholars suggested the following process of release, which consists of four words, each starting with the affix *re*:

- **Recognise** your problem and its cause.

- **Repent** of any sin that had opened the way to curse because sin is the ground for a curse.

- **Renounce** anything that brings curses.

- **Resist** every attempt from Satan to keep you under a curse.

Through *continuous obedience,* we maintain our freedom from curses and maintain the blessings.

VII. Practical Steps for Releasing Oneself from Curses

It is advisable to follow the practical steps of releasing yourself from any curse after reading this whole book and understanding the complete work of the blood of Jesus.[6]

The practical steps are outlined as follows:

1. Establish a clear scriptural basis and understanding

> Christ has redeemed us from the curse of the law, having become a curse for us (for it is written, "Cursed is everyone who hangs on a tree"), that the blessing of Abraham might come upon the Gentiles in Christ Jesus, that we might receive the promise of the Spirit through faith (Galatians 3:13, 14).

> In Him we have redemption through His blood, the forgiveness of sins, according to the riches of His grace (Ephesians 1:7).

> He has delivered us from the power of darkness and conveyed us into the Kingdom of the Son of His love, in whom we have redemption through His blood, the forgiveness of sins (Colossians 1:13, 14).

> He who sins is of the devil, for the devil has sinned from the beginning. *For this purpose the Son of God was manifested, that He might destroy the works of the devil* (1 John 3:8).

> Behold, I give you the authority to trample on serpents and scorpions, and over all the power of the enemy, and nothing shall by any means hurt you (Luke 10:19).

These five passages are important as our scriptural basis for being released from any curse.

Read these references and pray with them to be sure that you have a solid basis and ground. Focus on Jesus through these references. Jesus has dealt with every curse and has broken them to redeem us from every curse. Tell Him:

---

[6] See Appendix for this practical part in detail.

"I trust You, Lord Jesus, help me to receive from You the power of redemption from every curse. Lord Jesus, let Your redemptive power be released more and more in my spirit. Holy Spirit, please open my inner eyes to understand deeply the meaning of these verses. Holy Spirit, enable me to receive in my spirit this redemptive power over curses. You are the Spirit of faith; enable my faith to be activated to hold fast unto this truth."

2. Confess your faith in Christ

Therefore, holy brethren, partakers of the heavenly calling, consider *the Apostle and High Priest of our confession*, Christ Jesus (Hebrews 3:1).

Pray saying: "Jesus Christ, we confess that You are the Apostle and High Priest of our confession."

3. Commit yourself in obedience

4. Confess any known sin

You may even confess sins on behalf of deceased grandparents.[7]

5. Forgive others

- Lack of forgiveness hinders blessings.
- Forgiveness is a decision and not feelings.

6. Renounce all contact with the occult

Whether this contact is with people, groups, statues, or other things, all should be renounced.

Even if you don't remember, you can say: "I renounce any occult that I came in touch with."

---

[7] Daniel 9:5–8

7. Release yourself in the name of Jesus

The following references remind us that Jesus gave us the authority to release ourselves from any curse:

> Assuredly, I say to you, whatever you bind on earth will be bound in heaven, and whatever you loose on earth will be loosed in heaven (Matthew 18:18).

> And in that day you will ask Me nothing. Most assuredly, I say to you, whatever you ask the Father in My name He will give you. Until now you have asked nothing in My name. Ask, and you will receive, that your joy may be full (John 16:23, 24).

A Prayer to Release Oneself Suggested by Some Bible Scholars

- Lord, Jesus Christ, I believe that you are the Son of God and the only way to God, and that you died on the cross for my sins and rose again from the dead. I proclaim Jesus is Risen.

- I renounce all my sins and I turn to You, Lord Jesus, for mercy and for forgiveness. I believe that you do forgive. From now on, I want to live for You; I want to hear Your voice and I want to obey You.

- In order to receive Your blessing, Lord, and to be released from any curse on my life, I confessed any known sins committed by me, by my ancestors, or by other people related to me.

- Lord, I thank You because I believe that You have forgiven everything that I have confessed. Now, I want to say that I also forgive all people who have harmed or wronged me. I forgive them all now as God has forgiven me. In particular, I forgive [...]

- Also, Lord, I renounce any contact (whether through myself or anyone related to me) with Satan, any occult power in any form or any kind of secret society. I also commit myself, Lord, to renounce from my house any kind of occult objects that honour Satan and dishonour Jesus Christ. With Your help, Lord, I will remove them all.

- And now, Lord Jesus, I thank you further that You were made a curse on the cross so that I may be redeemed from curse and may receive blessings. Because of what You did for me on the cross, I now release myself from every curse, every evil influence and every dark shadow over me or my family from whatever source.

- I release myself now, in the name of Jesus. Amen.

Breaking the Curse: A Prayer Said by the Lord's Servant

- Now, Lord, because of this person's prayer, we break every curse that has been over his life. We revoke those curses now and we release him/her from them in the name of Jesus, the Son of God. In His all-prevailing name, we declare this person released.

- Satan, I declare to you that you have no claims and no more access to this person's life, his/her family, or his/her business. They have all been lifted out of the domain of darkness and transferred into the Kingdom of God's Love.

- Thank You, Lord Jesus. We praise You. We give You the glory. We give You thanks. Amen.

CHAPTER 3

THE BLOOD OF JESUS
HAS SEALED AN ETERNAL COVENANT
FOR ME

Readings

And as they were eating, Jesus took bread, blessed and broke it, and gave it to the disciples and said, "Take, eat; this is My body." Then He took the cup, and gave thanks, and gave it to them, saying, "Drink from it, all of you. *For this is My blood of the new covenant,* which is shed for many for the remission of sins" (Matthew 26:26–28).

Because finding fault with them, He says: "Behold, the days are coming, says the Lord, when *I will make a new covenant with the house of Israel* and with the house of Judah—not according to the covenant that I made with their fathers in the day when I took them by the hand to lead them out of the land of Egypt; because they did not continue in My covenant, and I disregarded them, says the Lord. For this is the covenant that I will make with the house of Israel after those days, says the Lord: I will put My laws in their mind and write them on their hearts; and I will be their God, and they shall be My people. None of them shall teach his neighbour, and none his brother, saying, 'Know the Lord,' for all shall know Me, from the least of them to the greatest of them. For I will be merciful to their unrighteousness, and their sins and their lawless deeds I will remember no more." In that He says, "*A new covenant,*" He has made the first obsolete. Now what is becoming obsolete and growing old is ready to vanish away (Hebrews 8:8–13).

And for this reason *He is the Mediator of the new covenant,* by means of death, for the redemption of the transgressions under the first covenant, that those who are called may receive the promise of the eternal inheritance (Hebrews 9:15).

Now may the God of peace who brought up our Lord Jesus from the dead, that great Shepherd of the sheep, *through the blood of the everlasting covenant,* make you complete in every good work to do His will, working in you what is well pleasing in His sight, through Jesus Christ, to whom be glory forever and ever. Amen (Hebrews 13:20, 21).

From these references, we understand that the covenant is sealed by the blood of Jesus.

Being in a covenant relationship with God is an important and essential matter in the Christian life. Understanding the covenant relationship with God can deeply change the whole life of the believer.

Introduction

We first want to understand God's mind concerning the word *covenant* as used in both the Old and New Testaments. Then, we want to understand what it means to be in a covenant relationship with God, which is essential and foundational in understanding the relationship between man and God.

Therefore, we have three main sections in this topic:

  I. The Meaning of the Word *Covenant*

 II. Important Points Related to the Covenant

III. Practical Considerations

I. The Meaning of the Word *Covenant*

A. The Linguistic Meaning

1. An agreement between two parties

But they said, "We have certainly seen that the Lord is with you. So we said, 'Let there now be an oath between us, between you and us; and *let us make a covenant with you*'" (Genesis 26:28).

And at the end of some years they shall join forces, for the daughter of the king of the South shall go to the king of the North *to make an agreement*; but she shall not retain the power of her authority, and neither he nor his authority shall stand; but she shall be given up, with those who brought her, and with him who begot her, and with him who strengthened her in those times (Daniel 11:6).

2. The purpose of the covenant is:

- Establishing friendship

Then Jonathan *made a covenant* with David, because he loved him as his own soul (1 Samuel 18:3, ESV).

- Obtaining assistance in war

Then Asa took all the silver and the gold that were left in the treasures of the house of the Lord and the treasures of the king's house and gave them into the hands of his servants. And King Asa sent them to Ben-hadad the son of Tabrimmon, the son of Hezion, king of Syria, who lived in Damascus, saying, "*Let there be a covenant between me and you*, as there was between my father and your father. Behold, I am sending to you a present of silver and gold. Go, break your covenant with Baasha king of Israel, that he may withdraw from me" (1 Kings 15:18–19, ESV).

- Mutual protection

But they said, "We have certainly seen that the Lord is with you. So we said, 'Let there now be an oath between us, between you and us; and *let us make a covenant with you, that you will do us no harm,* since we have not touched you, and since we have done nothing to you but good and have sent you away in peace. You are now the blessed of the Lord" (Genesis 26:28–29).

"If you oppress my daughters, or if you take wives besides my daughters, although no one is with us, see, God is witness between you and me." Then Laban said to Jacob, "See this heap and the pillar, which I have set between you and me. This heap is a witness, and the pillar is a witness, that I will not pass over this heap to you, and you will not pass over this heap and this pillar to me, to do harm (Genesis 31:50–52, ESV).

- Establishing peace

And Joshua *made peace with them and made a covenant with them,* to let them live, and the leaders of the congregation swore to them. At the end of three days after they had made a covenant with them, they heard that they were their neighbors and that they lived among them (Joshua 9:15, 16, ESV).

- Promoting commerce

"Now therefore command that cedars of Lebanon be cut for me. And my servants will join your servants, and I will pay you for your servants such wages as you set, for you know that there is no one among us who knows how to cut timber like the Sidonians." As soon as Hiram heard the words of Solomon, he rejoiced greatly and said, "Blessed be the Lord this day, who has given to David a wise son to be over this great people." And Hiram sent to Solomon, saying, "I have heard the message that you have sent to me. I am ready to do all you desire in the matter of cedar and cypress timber. My servants shall bring it down to the sea from Lebanon, and I will make it into rafts to go by sea to the place you direct. And I will have them broken up there, and you shall receive it. And you shall meet my wishes by providing food for my household." So Hiram supplied Solomon with all the timber of cedar and cypress that he desired, while Solomon gave Hiram 20,000 cors of wheat as food for his household, and 20,000 cors of beaten oil. Solomon gave this to Hiram year by year (1 Kings 5:6–11, ESV).

- Selling land

Ephron answered Abraham, "My lord, listen to me: a piece of land worth four hundred shekels of silver, what is that between you and me? Bury your dead." Abraham listened to Ephron, and Abraham weighed out for Ephron the silver that he had named in the hearing of the Hittites, four hundred shekels of silver, according to the weights current among the merchants (Genesis 23:14–16, ESV).

3. The conditions of the covenant are:

- Clearly specified

Then Nahash the Ammonite came up and encamped against Jabesh Gilead; and all the men of Jabesh said to Nahash, "Make a covenant with us, and we will serve you." And Nahash the Ammonite answered them, "*On this condition I will make a covenant with you*, that I may put out all your right eyes, and bring reproach on all Israel" (1 Samuel 11:1–2).

- Confirmed by oath

Now therefore *swear to me here by God* that you will not deal falsely with me or with my descendants or with my posterity, but as I have dealt kindly with you, so you will deal with me and with the land where you have sojourned (Genesis 21:23, ESV).

Therefore that place was called Beersheba, because there *both of them swore an oath* (Genesis 21:31, ESV).

Then they arose early in the morning and *swore an oath with one another*; and Isaac sent them away, and they departed from him in peace (Genesis 26:31).

- Witnessed

So the field of Ephron in Machpelah, which was to the east of Mamre, the field with the cave that was in it and all the trees that were in the field, throughout its whole area, was made over to Abraham as a possession *in the presence of* the Hittites, *before all who went in at the gate of his city* (Genesis 23:17, 18, ESV).

Then Boaz said to the elders and all the people, "*You are witnesses* this day that I have bought from the hand of Naomi all that belonged to Elimelech and all that belonged to Chilion and to Mahlon. Also Ruth the Moabite, the widow of Mahlon, I have bought to be my wife, to perpetuate the name of the dead in his inheritance, that the name of the dead may not be cut off from among his brothers and from the gate of his native place. You are witnesses this day." Then all the people who were at the gate and the elders said, "*We are witnesses.* May the Lord make the woman, who is coming into your house, like Rachel and Leah, who together built up the house of Israel. May you act worthily in Ephrathah and be renowned in Bethlehem" (Ruth 4:9–11, ESV).

- Written and sealed

And because of all this, we make a sure covenant and *write it*; our leaders, our Levites, and our priests *seal it* (Nehemiah 9:38).

Now those who *placed their seal* on the document were: Nehemiah the governor, the son of Hacaliah, and Zedekiah (Nehemiah 10:1).

4. God is often called to witness

"If you oppress my daughters, or if you take wives besides my daughters, although no one is with us, see, *God is witness between you and me*" ... "The God of Abraham and the God of Nahor, the God of their father, judge between us." So Jacob swore by the Fear of his father Isaac (Genesis 31:50, 53, ESV).

5. When the covenant is confirmed, it is unalterable

Brethren, I speak in the manner of men: Though it is only a man's covenant, yet *if it is confirmed, no one annuls or adds to it* (Galatians 3:15).

6. The covenant is made by passing between the pieces of the divided sacrifices

He said to him, "Bring me a heifer three years old, a female goat three years old, a ram three years old, a turtledove, and a young pigeon." And he brought him all these, cut them in half, and laid each half over against the other. But he did not cut the birds in half. And when birds of prey came down on the carcasses, Abram drove them away. As the sun was going down, a deep sleep fell on Abram. And behold, dreadful and great darkness fell upon him. Then the Lord said to Abram, "Know for certain that your offspring will be sojourners in a land that is not theirs and will be servants there, and they will be afflicted for four hundred years. But I will bring judgment on the nation that they serve, and afterward they shall come out with great possessions. As for you, you shall go to your fathers in peace; you shall be buried in a good old age. And they shall come back here in the fourth generation, for the iniquity of the Amorites is not yet complete." When the sun had gone down and it was dark, behold, a smoking fire pot and a flaming torch *passed between these pieces* (Genesis 15:9–17, ESV).

And the men who transgressed my covenant and did not keep the terms of the covenant that they made before me, I will make them like *the calf that they cut in two and passed between its parts*—the officials of Judah, the officials of Jerusalem, the eunuchs, the priests, and all the people of the land *who passed between the parts of the calf.* And I will give them into the hand of their enemies and into the hand of those who seek their lives. Their dead bodies shall be food for the birds of the air and the beasts of the earth (Jeremiah 34:18–20, ESV).

7. A covenant of salt, which is a sign of perpetuity

All the heave offerings of the holy things, which the children of Israel offer to the Lord, I have given to you and your sons and daughters with you as an ordinance forever; *it is a covenant of salt forever* before the Lord with you and your descendants with you (Numbers 18:19).

Should you not know that the Lord God of Israel *gave the dominion over Israel to David forever, to him and his sons, by a covenant of salt?* (2 Chronicles 13:5).

8. The covenant is ratified (approved or enacted) by joining hands

Though they join forces, the wicked will not go unpunished; but the posterity of the righteous will be delivered (Proverbs 11:21).

Since he despised the oath by breaking the covenant, and in fact gave his hand and still did all these things, he shall not escape (Ezekiel 17:18).

9. It is followed by a feast

So he made them a feast, and they ate and drank (Genesis 26:30).

Then Jacob offered a sacrifice on the mountain, and called his brethren to eat bread. And they ate bread and stayed all night on the mountain (Genesis 31:54).

10. Presents are given as tokens

So Abraham took sheep and oxen and gave them to Abimelech, and the two men made a covenant. Abraham set seven ewe lambs of the flock apart. And Abimelech said to Abraham, "What is the meaning of these seven ewe lambs that you have set apart?" He said, "These seven ewe lambs you will take from my hand, that this may be a witness for me that I dug this well" (Genesis 21:27–30, ESV).

Then Jonathan and David made a covenant, because he loved him as his own soul. And Jonathan took off the robe that was on him and gave it to David, with his armour, even to his sword and his bow and his belt (1 Samuel 18:3-4).

11. Pillars are raised in token of the covenant

So Jacob took a stone and set it up as a pillar. Then Jacob said to his brethren, "Gather stones." And they took stones and made a heap, and they ate there on the heap (Genesis 31:45–46).

12. Names are given to places where the covenant is made

Therefore he called that place Beersheba, because the two of them swore an oath there (Genesis 21:31).

Laban called it Jegar-sahadutha, but Jacob called it Galeed. Laban said, "This heap is a witness between you and me today." Therefore he named it Galeed, and Mizpah, for he said, "The Lord watch between you and me, when we are out of one another's sight" (Genesis 31:47–49, ESV).

13. A warning for the children of Israel

- The children of Israel were forbidden to make a covenant with the nations of Canaan

You shall make no covenant with them, nor with their gods (Exodus 23:32).

And when the Lord your God delivers them over to you, you shall conquer them and utterly destroy them. You shall make no covenant with them nor show mercy to them (Deuteronomy 7:2).

- The children of Israel frequently made a covenant with other nations

So the Lord gave Solomon wisdom, as He had promised him; and there was peace between Hiram and Solomon, and the two of them made a treaty together (1 Kings 5:12).

And the king of Assyria uncovered a conspiracy by Hoshea; for he had sent messengers to So, king of Egypt, and brought no tribute to the king of Assyria, as he had done year by year. Therefore the king of Assyria shut him up, and bound him in prison (2 Kings 17:4).

- The children of Israel were condemned for making a covenant with heathen nations

Who set out to go down to Egypt, without asking for my direction, to take refuge in the protection of Pharaoh and to seek shelter in the shadow of Egypt! Therefore shall the protection of Pharaoh turn to your shame, and the shelter in the shadow of Egypt to your humiliation. For though his officials are at Zoan and his envoys reach Hanes, everyone comes to shame through a people that cannot profit them, that brings neither help nor profit, but shame and disgrace (Isaiah 30:2–5, ESV).

Ephraim feeds on the wind, and pursues the east wind; he daily increases lies and desolation. Also they make a covenant with the Assyrians, and oil is carried to Egypt (Hosea 12:1).

- The children of Israel regarded the covenant as sacred

At the end of three days after they had made a covenant with them, they heard that they were their neighbours and that they lived among them. And the people of Israel set out and reached their cities on the third day. Now their cities were Gibeon, Chephirah, Beeroth, and Kiriath-jearim. But the people of Israel did not attack them, because the leaders of the congregation had sworn to them by the Lord, the God of Israel. Then all the congregation murmured against the leaders. But all the leaders said to all the congregation, "We have sworn to them by the Lord, the God of Israel, and now we may not touch them" (Joshua 9:16–19, ESV).

In whose eyes a vile person is despised, but he honours those who fear the Lord; He who swears to his own hurt and does not change (Psalm 15:4).

14. The covenant is violated by the wicked

But to the wicked God says: "What right have you to declare My statutes, or take My covenant in your mouth" (Psalm 50:16).

For thus says the Lord God: "I will deal with you as you have done, who despised the oath by breaking the covenant" (Ezekiel 16:59).

Those who do wickedly against the covenant he shall corrupt with flattery; but the people who know their God shall be strong, and carry out great exploits (Daniel 11:32).

15. The covenant is illustrative of the following:

- Of the contract of marriage

Yet you say, "For what reason?" Because the Lord has been witness between you and the wife of your youth, with whom you have dealt treacherously; yet she is your companion and your wife by covenant (Malachi 2:14).

- Of God's promises to man

And as for Me, behold, I establish My covenant with you and with your descendants after you, and with every living creature that is with you: the birds, the cattle, and every beast of the earth with you, of all that go out of the ark, every beast of the earth. Thus I establish My covenant with you: Never again shall all flesh be cut off by the waters of the flood; never again shall there be a flood to destroy the earth (Genesis 9:9–11).

Remember that you were at that time separated from Christ, alienated from the commonwealth of Israel and strangers to the covenants of promise, having no hope and without God in the world (Ephesians 2:12, ESV).

- Of the united determination of a people to serve God

Then Jehoiada made a covenant between the Lord, the king, and the people, that they should be the Lord's people, and also between the king and the people (2 Kings 11:17).

Then they entered into a covenant to seek the Lord God of their fathers with all their heart and with all their soul (2 Chronicles 15:12).

These joined with their brethren, their nobles, and entered into a curse and an oath to walk in God's Law, which was given by Moses the servant of God, and to observe and do all the commandments of the Lord our Lord, and His ordinances and His statutes (Nehemiah 10:29).

- Of good resolutions

I have made a covenant with my eyes; why then should I look upon a young woman? (Job 31:1).

- Of carnal security (covenant with death and hell)

Because you have said, "We have made a covenant with death, and with Sheol we have an agreement, when the overwhelming whip passes through it will not come to us, for we have made lies our refuge, and in falsehood we have taken shelter" … Then your covenant with death will be annulled, and your agreement with Sheol will not stand; when the overwhelming scourge passes through, you will be beaten down by it (Isaiah 28:15, 18, ESV).

- Of peace and prosperity (a covenant with stones of the field and beasts of the earth)

For you shall have a covenant with the stones of the field, and the beasts of the field shall be at peace with you (Job 5:23).

In that day I will make a covenant for them with the beasts of the field, with the birds of the air, and with the creeping things of the ground. Bow and sword of battle I will shatter from the earth, to make them lie down safely (Hosea 2:18).

B. The Meaning According to the Hebrew Language of the Old Testament

In the Hebrew language, the word *covenant* means *a contract or an agreement between two parties*. The Hebrew word used in the Old Testament for *covenant* is *berith*.[8] *Berith* is derived from a root which means *to cut*.

What is the relation between the word *cut* and the covenant?

> And the men who transgressed my covenant and did not keep the terms of the covenant that they made before me, I will make them like *the calf that they cut in two and passed between its parts*—the officials of Judah, the officials of Jerusalem, the eunuchs, the priests, and all the people of the land who passed between the parts of the calf (Jeremiah 34:18,19, ESV).

Refer also to Genesis 15:9–18.

A covenant is made by cutting or dividing animals into two parts while the contracting parties pass between them.

We will look at some examples of references in the Old Testament to understand the use of the word *covenant (berith)* and understand the main principles in God's mind about the *covenant* as revealed in the Old Testament.

The word *berith* is used to refer to the following:

1. Covenant in general

   - A covenant or agreement between man and man (two persons)

   So they made a covenant at Beersheba. Then Abimelech and Phicol the commander of his army rose up and returned to the land of the Philistines (Genesis 21:32, ESV).

---

[8] The corresponding word in the Greek language used in the New Testament is *diatheke*. It is, however, generally translated *testament* in the Authorised Version (AV). Yet, it ought to be translated as *covenant* as the word *berith* used in the Old Testament is translated.

- A covenant between tribes or nations

Then Nahash the Ammonite came up and encamped against Jabesh Gilead; and all the men of Jabesh said to Nahash, "*Make a covenant with us*, and we will serve you" (1 Samuel 11:1).

And they went to Joshua, to the camp at Gilgal, and said to him and to the men of Israel, "We have come from a far country; now therefore, *make a covenant with us*" ... So Joshua made peace with them, and made a covenant with them to let them live; and the rulers of the congregation swore to them (Joshua 9:6, 15).

- In entering into a covenant, God was solemnly called on to witness the agreement

If you oppress my daughters, or if you take wives besides my daughters, although no one is with us, see, *God is witness between you and me* (Genesis 31:50, ESV).

- Based on this, it was called a *covenant of the Lord*

Therefore you shall deal kindly with your servant, for you have brought your servant into a *covenant of the Lord* with you. Nevertheless, if there is iniquity in me, kill me yourself, for why should you bring me to your father? (1 Samuel 20:8).

The phrase *a covenant of the Lord* is repeated many times in the Scriptures.

- The marriage agreement was called *the covenant of God* because marriage was made in God's name

In God's mind, marriage is a kind of covenant between husband and wife; therefore, we ought to take it seriously. It is not a simple matter to break this covenant because God is part of it. Proverbs 2:17 highlights this point:

... who forsakes the companion of her youth, and forgets the *covenant of her God.*

- Sometimes the word is used in an unusual way: *a covenant of death*

For example, in Isaiah 28, wicked men are spoken of as acting as if they have made a *covenant with death* not to destroy them or with hell not to devour them:

Because you have said, *"We have made a covenant with death, and with Sheol we are in agreement.* When the overflowing scourge passes through, it will not come to us, for we have made lies our refuge, and under falsehood we have hidden ourselves." ... Your *covenant with death* will be annulled, and your *agreement with Sheol* will not stand; when the overflowing scourge passes through, then you will be trampled down by it (Isaiah 28:15, 18).

2. Covenant with God

- The covenant usually reflects God's promise to His people

For example, God's promise to Noah after the Flood is called a covenant:

Then God said to Noah and to his sons with him, *"Behold, I establish my covenant with you and your offspring* after you, and with every living creature that is with you, the birds, the livestock, and every beast of the earth with you, as many as came out of the ark; it is for every beast of the earth. *I establish my covenant with you,* that never again shall all flesh be cut off by the waters of the flood, and never again shall there be a flood to destroy the earth" (Genesis 9:8–11, ESV).

- We have an account of God's covenant with Abraham (refer to Genesis 17)

Refer also to Leviticus 26:42:

Then I will remember *My covenant with Jacob, and My covenant with Isaac and My covenant with Abraham* I will remember; I will remember the land.

- God made a covenant with the priests of old because they were the tribe set apart to serve the Lord

Therefore say, 'Behold, I give to him My covenant of peace; and it shall be to him and his descendants after him *a covenant of an everlasting priesthood,* because he was zealous for his God, and made atonement for the children of Israel' (Numbers 25:12, 13).

Who says of his father and mother, 'I have not seen them'; nor did he acknowledge his brothers, or know his own children; for they have observed Your word and *kept Your covenant* (Deuteronomy 33:9).

Remember them, O my God, because they have defiled the priesthood and *the covenant of the priesthood* and the Levites (Nehemiah 13:29).

- A covenant was made in Sinai

This is an important and a well-known covenant. It was made with the whole nation of Israel:

Then the Lord said to Moses, "Write these words, for according to the tenor of these words *I have made a covenant with you and with Israel.*" So he was there with the Lord forty days and forty nights; he neither ate bread nor drank water. And He wrote on the tablets the words of the covenant, the Ten Commandments (Exodus 34:27, 28).

And if you despise My statutes, or if your soul abhors My judgments, so that you do not perform all My commandments, but break *My covenant* (Leviticus 26:15).

- The covenant of Sinai was later renewed at different times in the history of the people of Israel

Refer to Deuteronomy 29; Joshua 24; 2 Chronicles 15, 23, 29, 34; Ezra 10; and Nehemiah 9.

Notice that God was training humanity in the concept of being in a covenant. There was first a covenant between two persons, two nations, two tribes, or husband and wife. Then, God made a covenant with the tribe of Levi—a tribe set apart for the Lord as priests—and then with the whole nation of Israel, which was the covenant in Sinai.

God knew the weakness of human beings, which is the lack of trust and disbelief. He wanted to help them to trust Him; thus, He brought the idea of a covenant. Despite this, He knew that human beings could still not trust Him fully.

Therefore, He began to use their ways. Usually, when one wants another person to trust him, he uses an oath. Thus, God began to use an oath to help us trust Him as if He wanted to say to us, "I am serious; trust Me". We thus notice that the Bible began to use the word *swore* about God. God was lowering Himself to our level and using our means of relating to one another to help us trust Him.

- Therefore, in conformity with human custom, God's covenant is said to be confirmed with an oath

For the Lord your God is a merciful God, He will not forsake you nor destroy you, nor forget the covenant of your fathers which *He swore to them* (Deuteronomy 4:31).

I have made a covenant with My chosen, *I have sworn to My servant David* (Psalm 89:3).

We see here that God swore to the fathers of the nation of Israel and He even swore to one person—David.

- God's covenant is also accompanied by a sign

Refer to Genesis chapters 9 and 17.

We now understand that a covenant can be linked with a promise and an oath to help us perceive its meaning and significance.

- Thus, the covenant is called *God's counsel, oath,* or *promise*

I have *made a covenant with My chosen*, I have *sworn to My servant David*: "Your seed I will establish forever, and build up your throne to all generations" (Psalm 89:3, 4).

He remembers His covenant forever, the word which He commanded, for a thousand generations, the covenant which He made with Abraham, and *His oath to Isaac*, and confirmed it to Jacob for a statute, to Israel as an everlasting covenant, saying, "To you I will give the land of Canaan as the allotment of your inheritance" (Psalm 105:8–11).

For when *God made a promise to Abraham,* because He could swear by no one greater, *He swore by Himself,* saying, "Surely blessing I will bless you, and multiplying I will multiply you." And so, after he had patiently endured, he obtained the promise. For men indeed swear by the greater, and an oath for confirmation is for them an end of all dispute. Thus God, determining to show more abundantly to the heirs of promise the immutability of His counsel, *confirmed it by an oath,* that by two immutable things, in which it is impossible for God to lie, we might have strong consolation, who have fled for refuge to lay hold of the hope set before us. This hope we have as an anchor of the soul, both sure and steadfast, and which enters the Presence behind the veil, where the forerunner has entered for us, even Jesus, having become High Priest forever according to the order of Melchizedek (Hebrews 6:13–20).

Blessed is the Lord God of Israel, for He has visited and redeemed His people, and has raised up a horn of salvation for us in the house of His servant David, as He spoke by the mouth of His holy prophets, who have been since the world began, that we should be saved from our enemies and from the hand of all who hate us, to perform the mercy promised to our fathers and *to remember His holy covenant, the oath which He swore to our father Abraham:* to grant us that we, being delivered from the hand of our enemies, might serve Him without fear, in holiness and righteousness before Him all the days of our life (Luke 1:68–75).

- God's covenant consists wholly in the bestowal of blessing

"As for Me," says the Lord, "this is My covenant with them: My Spirit who is upon you, and My words which I have put in your mouth, shall not depart from your mouth, nor from the mouth of your descendants, nor from the mouth of your descendants' descendants," says the Lord, "from this time and forevermore" (Isaiah 59:21).

But this is the covenant that I will make with the house of Israel after those days, says the Lord: I will put My law in their minds, and write it on their hearts; and I will be their God, and they shall be My people. No more shall every man teach his neighbour, and every man his brother, saying, 'Know the Lord,' for they all shall know Me, from the least of them to the greatest of them, says the Lord. For I will forgive their iniquity, and their sin I will remember no more (Jeremiah 31:33, 34).

- The word *covenant* is also used in the Old Testament to refer to matters other than the relationship with God:

  - The term *covenant* is used to designate the regular succession of day and night

  Thus says the Lord: 'If you can break *My covenant with the day and My covenant with the night*, so that there will not be day and night in their season …' (Jeremiah 33:20).

Again, God is dealing with the main sickness of humanity, which is disbelief. He is saying here, "Can you see the succession of day and night? It never changes. This is My covenant with the day and night. Because I made this covenant with the day and night, their succession never changes. In the same way, I want to make a covenant with you that will never change."

When humans trust God, they often worry that things may change. However, if one is in a covenant relationship with God, he ought to be sure that things will never change and will always be in his favour as God is always on his side. We will come back to this point later.

  - The regular succession of the Sabbath

  Therefore the children of Israel shall keep the Sabbath, *to observe the Sabbath* throughout their generations *as a perpetual covenant* (Exodus 31:16).

  - The regular succession of circumcision

  And God said to Abraham: "As for you, you shall keep My covenant, you and your descendants after you throughout their generations. *This is My covenant which you shall keep*, between Me and you and your descendants after you: *Every male child among you shall be circumcised* (Genesis 17:9, 10).

  - The regular succession of any ordinance of God in general

  Thus says the Lord, the God of Israel: "I made a covenant with your fathers in the day that I brought them out of the land of Egypt, out of the house of bondage, saying, 'At the end of seven years let every man set free his Hebrew brother, who has been sold to him; and when he has served you six years, you shall let him go free from you.' But your fathers did not obey Me nor incline their ear" (Jeremiah 34:13, 14).

- A *covenant of salt* signifies an everlasting covenant where salt is used in the agreement as a symbol of perpetuity

Salt has a distinct taste and preserves things from decay. Thus, God says that He wants to have a covenant of salt with us so that we may trust Him.

> All the heave offerings of the holy things, which the children of Israel offer to the Lord, I have given to you and your sons and daughters with you as an ordinance forever; *it is a covenant of salt forever before the Lord with you and your descendants* with you (Numbers 18:19).

> And every offering of your grain offering you shall season with salt; you shall not allow the salt of the covenant of your God to be lacking from your grain offering. With all your offerings you shall offer salt (Leviticus 2:13).

> Should you not know that the Lord God of Israel gave the dominion over Israel to David forever, to him and his sons, *by a covenant of salt*? (2 Chronicles 13:5).

C. The Meaning According to the Greek Language of the New Testament

The Greek word for *covenant* used in the New Testament is *diatheke*, pronounced /dee·ath·ay·kay/.

It occurs in the New Testament 33 times; the Authorised Version (AV) translates it as *covenant* 20 times and as *testament* 13 times.

It has the following two meanings:

1. An arrangement of any sort which one wishes to be valid; the last arrangement which one makes of his earthly possessions after his death; a testament or will.

2. A covenant, a testament

Thus, according to the Greek origin, the word *covenant* means *a will*, indicating that God is giving us a specific thing and that receiving it depends on the death of a person or that it will be released after the death of a person.

Notice here that another idea is introduced concerning the covenant, which is death. Of course, the reference is to the death of Jesus.

God does not change His mind; therefore, all the principles we mentioned about a covenant in the Old Testament still apply. The Book of Jeremiah helps us understand that there is a new covenant in the New Testament related to Jesus (Jeremiah 31:34).

An overview to connect and highlight significant points before moving to the comparison between the two testaments:

In the Old Testament, God was helping humanity to understand what a covenant was. In Sinai, God made the covenant with the nation of Israel (Exodus 24:8). Because of this, the whole of the Old Testament is called the old covenant (covenant and testament have the same meaning).

From the days of Moses until Jeremiah, the nation of Israel was known to be in a covenant relationship with God. However, they kept breaking the covenant as they were unable to trust God nor obey His commandment. We will see how God dealt with this problem in the New Testament. But it is important to understand first what happened in the time between Moses and Jeremiah.

Exodus 24:8 speaks about the covenant at the time of Moses and Jeremiah 31:31–34 speaks about the covenant at the time of Jeremiah.

Jeremiah began to speak prophetically about a new covenant that was to come. Why did this happen specifically during the time of Jeremiah and why was this a significant landmark?

This is because, during the time of Jeremiah, the people of Israel went into captivity, and Israel was no longer a nation ruled by a king, for when they returned from captivity, they became a state under the leadership of an emperor. Since the nation of Israel had ended and God had made a covenant with them as a nation, this meant the covenant was no longer active.

Jeremiah knew prophetically that the covenant was coming to an end; thus, he spoke about a new covenant that was to come. This is why during the Last Supper, Jesus said that it is the new covenant.

These points are further elaborated on in the comparison below.

D. Comparison Between the Two Covenants or Testaments With a Comment by Saint Augustine

1. The *Old Testament* was first called *the covenant* in Moses' days:

   And Moses took the blood, sprinkled it on the people, and said, "*This is the blood of the covenant* which the Lord has made with you according to all these words" (Exodus 24:8).

2. Later, Jeremiah announced that God would make a new *covenant* with His people:

   Behold, the days are coming, says the Lord, when *I will make a new covenant with the house of Israel and with the house of Judah*—not according to the covenant that I made with their fathers in the day that I took them by the hand to lead them out of the land of Egypt, My covenant which they broke, though I was a husband to them, says the Lord. But this is the covenant that I will make with the house of Israel after those days, says the Lord: I will put My law in their minds, and write it on their hearts; and I will be their God, and they shall be My people. No more shall every man teach his neighbour, and every man his brother, saying, "Know the Lord," for they all shall know Me, from the least of them to the greatest of them, says the Lord. For I will forgive their iniquity, and their sin I will remember no more (Jeremiah 31:31–34).

3. This new covenant is what Jesus established in the Last Supper:

   For this is My blood of the *new covenant*, which is shed for many for the remission of sins (Matthew 26:28).

For I received from the Lord that which I also delivered to you: that the Lord Jesus on the same night in which He was betrayed took bread; and when He had given thanks, He broke it and said, "Take, eat; this is My body which is broken for you; do this in remembrance of Me." In the same manner He also took the cup after supper, saying, "This cup is the *new covenant* in My blood. This do, as often as you drink it, in remembrance of Me" (1 Corinthians 11:23–25).

But now He has obtained a more excellent ministry, inasmuch as He is also Mediator of *a better covenant*, which was established on better promises. For if that first covenant had been faultless, then no place would have been sought for a second. Because finding fault with them, He says: "Behold, the days are coming, says the Lord, when I will make a *new covenant* with the house of Israel and with the house of Judah" (Hebrews 8:6–8).

4. Hence, the former part of the Bible is called the *Old* Covenant (Testament), and the latter is called the *New* Covenant.[9]

The relationship between the two covenants is well summarised by the famous statement of St. Augustine the theologian (5th century):

'The Old Testament revealed in the New, the New veiled in the Old.'[10] [11]

Christ is the theme of both covenants as may be seen from the chart on the following page. Refer also to Hebrews 10:7; Luke 24:27, 44; John 5:39.

---

[9] Cf. Hebrews 8:13: *'In that He says, "A new covenant," He has made the first obsolete.'*

[10] Augustine, Expositions on the Book of Psalms, Ps. 106:3, in Philip Schaff, ed., Nicene and Post-Nicene Fathers, 2d series, vol. 8.

[11] In other sources, the same quote of St. Augustine is rendered: 'The New is in the Old concealed; the Old is in the New revealed' (Questions on the Heptateuch, 2.73).

In the Old Testament, Christ is:	In the New Testament, Christ is:
In shadow	In substance

The sacrifices of the Old Testament pointed to Christ and are hence the shadow, but in the New Testament, He came as substance.

In pictures	In Person

Many events referred to Christ in various pictures, such as the lamb of the Passover. Jesus is the Lamb of God, according to the Gospel of John.

In type	In truth Jesus said, 'I am the truth' (John 14:6)
In ritual	In reality
Latent (meaning hidden and not yet manifest)	Patent (meaning overt)
Prophesied	Present
Implicitly revealed	Explicitly revealed (especially when He was incarnated)

II. Important Points Related to the Covenant

In this section, we will discuss three main points:

A. The Use of the Words *Testament* and *Covenant* in the Bible and Their Spiritual Significance

B. The Main Eight Covenants in the Bible

C. Christ and the Covenant

A. The Use of the Words *Testament* and *Covenant* in the Bible and Their Spiritual Significance

- **Testament**

The English word translated from the Greek signifies the *covenantal administrations of God*. Prior to Christ, this covenant is known as the *Old Testament*. Under Christ's administration, it is called the *New Testament*.

The Greek word generally means *last will and testament*. It contains certain legal characteristics that have important theological implications:

- First, a testament was not an agreement between parties (especially equals) but rather was exercised solely by the testator (meaning the person who makes the will).

- Second, the testament became effective upon the death of the testator.

- Third, the testament was irrevocable (unchangeable).

When the Old Testament was translated into Greek, the translators had the option between two words to use to translate the Hebrew word for *covenant*. One term carries the idea of a mutual agreement, and this is often between equals. Since this would blur the divine initiative in God's covenantal dealings with the patriarchs and with Israel, the other word was used. This other word signified the self-determined action of the Sovereign in making the covenant.

The New Testament writers saw additional significance in the word *testament*. Since a testament only becomes valid at the death of the testator, the benefits of the new covenant are given to believers as a consequence of Christ's death:

> And for this reason *He is the Mediator of the new covenant, by means of death,* for the redemption of the transgressions under the first covenant, that those who are called may receive the promise of the eternal inheritance. *For where there is a testament, there must also of necessity be the death of the testator. For a testament is in force after men are dead, since it has no power at all while the testator lives.* Therefore not even the first covenant was dedicated without blood. For when Moses had spoken every precept to all the people according to the law, he took the blood of calves and goats, with water, scarlet wool, and hyssop, and sprinkled both the book itself and all the people, saying, "This is the blood of the covenant which God has commanded you." Then likewise he sprinkled with blood both the tabernacle and all the vessels of the ministry. And according to the law almost all things are purified with blood, and without shedding of blood there is no remission (Hebrews 9:15–22).

> In the same manner He also took the cup after supper, saying, "This cup is the new covenant in My blood. This do, as often as you drink it, in remembrance of Me" (1 Corinthians 11:25).

> Likewise He also took the cup after supper, saying, "This cup is the new covenant in My blood, which is shed for you" (Luke 22:20).

• Covenant

We want to follow God's covenants in the Old and New Testaments.

The covenant was first made with Abraham, Isaac, Jacob, the children of Israel, and David, and it was renewed in the gospel. These were successive covenants between God and humanity.

◆ Covenant made with:

- Abraham

Then He said to him, "I am the Lord, who brought you out of Ur of the Chaldeans, to give you this land to inherit it." And he said, "Lord God, how shall I know that I will inherit it?" So He said to him, "Bring Me a three-year-old heifer, a three-year-old female goat, a three-year-old ram, a turtledove, and a young pigeon." Then he brought all these to Him and cut them in two, down the middle, and placed each piece opposite the other; but he did not cut the birds in two. And when the vultures came down on the carcasses, Abram drove them away. Now when the sun was going down, a deep sleep fell upon Abram; and behold, horror and great darkness fell upon him. Then He said to Abram: "Know certainly that your descendants will be strangers in a land that is not theirs, and will serve them, and they will afflict them four hundred years. And also the nation whom they serve I will judge; afterward they shall come out with great possessions. Now as for you, you shall go to your fathers in peace; you shall be buried at a good old age. But in the fourth generation they shall return here, for the iniquity of the Amorites is not yet complete." And it came to pass, when the sun went down and it was dark, that behold, there appeared a smoking oven and a burning torch that passed between those pieces. On the same day *the Lord made a covenant with Abram,* saying: "To your descendants I have given this land, from the river of Egypt to the great river, the River Euphrates" (Genesis 15:7–18).

"And *I will make My covenant between Me and you,* and will multiply you exceedingly." Then Abram fell on his face, and God talked with him, saying: "As for Me, behold, My covenant is with you, and you shall be a father of many nations. No longer shall your name be called Abram, but your name shall be Abraham; for I have made you a father of many nations. I will make you exceedingly fruitful; and I will make nations of you, and kings shall come from you. And *I will establish My covenant between Me and you* and your descendants after you in their generations, for an everlasting covenant, to be God to you and your descendants after you. Also I give to you and your descendants after you the land in which you are a stranger, all the land of Canaan, as an everlasting possession; and I will be their God." And God said to Abraham: "As for you, you shall keep My covenant, you and your descendants after you throughout their generations. This is My covenant which you shall keep, between Me and you and your descendants after you: Every male child among you shall be circumcised; and you shall be circumcised in the flesh of your foreskins, and it shall be a sign of the covenant between Me and you. He who is eight days old among you shall be circumcised, every male child in your generations, he who is born in your house or bought with money from any foreigner who is not your descendant. He who is born in your house and he who is bought with your money must be circumcised, and My covenant shall be in your flesh for an everlasting covenant. And the uncircumcised male child, who is not circumcised in the flesh of his foreskin, that person shall be cut off from his people; he has broken My covenant" (Genesis 17:2–14).

To perform the mercy promised to our fathers and to *remember His holy covenant, the oath which He swore to our father Abraham*: to grant us that we, being delivered from the hand of our enemies, might serve Him without fear, in holiness and righteousness before Him all the days of our life (Luke 1:72–75).

You are sons of the prophets, *and of the covenant which God made with our fathers,* saying to Abraham, 'And in your seed all the families of the earth shall be blessed' (Acts 3:25).

Now *to Abraham and his Seed were the promises made.* He does not say, "And to seeds," as of many, but as of one, "And to your Seed," who is Christ (Galatians 3:16).

- Isaac

God said, "No, but Sarah your wife shall bear you a son, and you shall call his name Isaac. *I will establish my covenant with him as an everlasting covenant* for his offspring after him ... But *I will establish my covenant with Isaac,* whom Sarah shall bear to you at this time next year" (Genesis 17:19, 21, ESV).

Sojourn in this land, and I will be with you and will bless you, for to you and to your offspring I will give all these lands, and *I will establish the oath that I swore to Abraham your father.* I will multiply your offspring as the stars of heaven and will give to your offspring all these lands. And in your offspring all the nations of the earth shall be blessed (Genesis 26:3, 4, ESV).

- Jacob

And behold, the Lord stood above it and said, "I am the Lord, the God of Abraham your father and the God of Isaac. The land on which you lie I will give to you and to your offspring. Your offspring shall be like the dust of the earth, and you shall spread abroad to the west and to the east and to the north and to the south, and in you and your offspring shall all the families of the earth be blessed" (Genesis 28:13, 14, ESV).

The covenant which He made with Abraham, and His oath to Isaac, and confirmed it to Jacob for a statute, to Israel for *an everlasting covenant* (1 Chronicles 16:16, 17).

- The children of Israel

I have also *established My covenant with them,* to give them the land of Canaan, the land of their pilgrimage, in which they were strangers (Exodus 6:4).

You are sons of the prophets, and of *the covenant which God made* with our fathers, saying to Abraham, 'And in your seed all the families of the earth shall be blessed' (Acts 3:25).

- David

Although my house is not so with God, yet *He has made with me an everlasting covenant,* ordered in all things and secure. For this is all my salvation and all my desire; will He not make it increase? (2 Samuel 23:5).

I have made a covenant with My chosen, I have sworn to My servant David: 'Your seed I will establish forever, and build up your throne to all generations' (Psalm 89:3, 4).

♦ When sin entered under the gospel

For this is My covenant with them, when I take away their sins (Romans 11:27).

Because finding fault with them, He says: "Behold, the days are coming, says the Lord, when I will make a new covenant with the house of Israel and with the house of Judah—not according to the covenant that I made with their fathers in the day when I took them by the hand to lead them out of the land of Egypt; because they did not continue in My covenant, and I disregarded them, says the Lord. For this is the covenant that I will make with the house of Israel after those days, says the Lord: I will put My laws in their mind and write them on their hearts; and I will be their God, and they shall be My people." ... In that He says, "A new covenant," He has made the first obsolete. Now what is becoming obsolete and growing old is ready to vanish away (Hebrews 8:8–10, 13).

Refer also to Jeremiah 31:31–33 (quoted earlier).

◆ The covenant is fulfilled in Christ

"Blessed be the Lord God of Israel, for he has visited and redeemed his people and has raised up a horn of salvation for us in the house of his servant David, as he spoke by the mouth of his holy prophets from of old, that we should be saved from our enemies and from the hand of all who hate us; to show the mercy promised to our fathers and to remember his holy covenant, the oath that he swore to our father Abraham, to grant us that we, being delivered from the hand of our enemies, might serve him without fear, in holiness and righteousness before him all our days. And you, child, will be called the prophet of the Most High; for you will go before the Lord to prepare his ways, to give knowledge of salvation to his people in the forgiveness of their sins, because of the tender mercy of our God, whereby the sunrise shall visit us from on high to give light to those who sit in darkness and in the shadow of death, to guide our feet into the way of peace" (Luke 1:68-79, ESV).

◆ The covenant is confirmed in Christ

And this I say, that the law, which was four hundred and thirty years later, cannot annul *the covenant that was confirmed before by God in Christ*, that it should make the promise of no effect (Galatians 3:17).

◆ The covenant is actualized (formally approved) by the blood of Christ

But Christ came as High Priest of the good things to come, with the greater and more perfect tabernacle not made with hands, that is, not of this creation. Not with the blood of goats and calves, *but with His own blood* He entered the Most Holy Place once for all, having obtained eternal redemption. For if the blood of bulls and goats and the ashes of a heifer, sprinkling the unclean, sanctifies for the purifying of the flesh, how much more shall the blood of Christ, who through the eternal Spirit offered Himself without spot to God, cleanse your conscience from dead works to serve the living God? (Hebrews 9:11–14).

Refer to Hebrews 9:16–23 (quoted earlier).

To sum up, the covenant is *fulfilled in Christ, confirmed in Christ,* and *actualised by the blood of Christ.*

Now, we move to some characteristics of the covenant:

♦ It is a covenant of peace

"For this is like the waters of Noah to Me; for as I have sworn that the waters of Noah would no longer cover the earth, so have I sworn that I would not be angry with you, nor rebuke you. For the mountains shall depart and the hills be removed, but My kindness shall not depart from you, nor shall *My covenant of peace* be removed," says the Lord, who has mercy on you (Isaiah 54:9, 10).

I will make *a covenant of peace* with them, and cause wild beasts to cease from the land; and they will dwell safely in the wilderness and sleep in the woods (Ezekiel 34:25).

Moreover I will make *a covenant of peace* with them, and it shall be an ever-lasting covenant with them; I will establish them and multiply them, and I will set My sanctuary in their midst forevermore (Ezekiel 37:26).

♦ It is unalterable

My covenant I will not break, nor alter the word that has gone out of My lips (Psalm 89:34).

"As for Me," says the Lord, "this is My covenant with them: My Spirit who is upon you, and My words which I have put in your mouth, shall not depart from your mouth, nor from the mouth of your descendants, nor from the mouth of your descendants' descendants," says the Lord, "from this time and forevermore" (Isaiah 59:21).

And this I say, that the law, which was four hundred and thirty years later, cannot annul the covenant that was confirmed before by God in Christ, that it should make the promise of no effect (Galatians 3:17).

Refer also to Isaiah 54:10 (quoted earlier).

♦ It is everlasting

He has sent redemption to His people; He has commanded *His covenant for-ever*: Holy and awesome is His name (Psalm 111:9).

Incline your ear, and come to Me. Hear, and your soul shall live; and I will make *an everlasting covenant* with you—the sure mercies of David (Isaiah 55:3).

For I, the Lord, love justice; I hate robbery for burnt offering; I will direct their work in truth, and will make with them *an everlasting covenant* (Isaiah 61:8).

"Yet I will remember my covenant with you in the days of your youth, and *I will establish for you an everlasting covenant.* Then you will remember your ways and be ashamed when you take your sisters, both your elder and your younger, and I give them to you as daughters, but not on account of the cov-enant with you. I will establish my covenant with you, and you shall know that I am the Lord, that you may remember and be confounded, and never open your mouth again because of your shame, when I atone for you for all that you have done, declares the Lord God (Ezekiel 16:60–63, ESV).

Now may the God of peace who brought up our Lord Jesus from the dead, that great Shepherd of the sheep, through the blood of the *everlasting covenant* ... (Hebrews 13:20).

♦ All the saints (God's holy people) are interested in the covenant

The secret of the Lord is with those who fear Him, and He will show them His covenant (Psalm 25:14).

"I will establish his offspring forever and his throne as the days of the heavens. If his children forsake my law and do not walk according to my rules, if they violate my statutes and do not keep my commandments, then I will punish their transgression with the rod and their iniquity with stripes, but I will not remove from him my steadfast love or be false to my faithfulness. I will not violate my covenant or alter the word that went forth from my lips. Once for all I have sworn by my holiness; I will not lie to David. His offspring shall endure forever, his throne as long as the sun before me. Like the moon it shall be established forever, a faithful witness in the skies" (Psalm 89:29–37, ESV).

For this is the covenant that I will make with the house of Israel after those days, says the Lord: I will put My laws in their mind and write them on their hearts; and I will be their God, and they shall be My people (Hebrews 8:10).

◆ The wicked have no interest in the covenant

Remember that you were at that time separated from Christ, alienated from the commonwealth of Israel and strangers to the covenants of promise, having no hope and without God in the world (Ephesians 2:12, ESV).

◆ Blessings are connected with the covenant

For thus says the Lord: "To the eunuchs who keep my Sabbaths, who choose the things that please me and hold fast my covenant, I will give in my house and within my walls a monument and a name better than sons and daughters; I will give them an everlasting name that shall not be cut off. "And the foreigners who join themselves to the Lord, to minister to him, to love the name of the Lord, and to be his servants, everyone who keeps the Sabbath and does not profane it, and holds fast my covenant—these I will bring to my holy mountain, and make them joyful in my house of prayer; their burnt offerings and their sacrifices will be accepted on my altar for my house shall be called a house of prayer for all peoples" (Isaiah 56:4–7, ESV).

For this is the covenant that I will make with the house of Israel after those days, says the Lord: I will put My laws in their mind and write them on their hearts; and I will be their God, and they shall be My people. None of them shall teach his neighbour, and none his brother, saying, 'Know the Lord,' for all shall know Me, from the least of them to the greatest of them. For I will be merciful to their unrighteousness, and their sins and their lawless deeds I will remember no more (Hebrews 8:10–12).

◆ God is faithful to the covenant

Therefore know that the Lord your God, He is God, the faithful God who keeps covenant and mercy for a thousand generations with those who love Him and keep His commandments (Deuteronomy 7:9).

And he said: "Lord God of Israel, there is no God in heaven above or on earth below like You, who keep Your covenant and mercy with Your servants who walk before You with all their hearts" (1 Kings 8:23).

And I said: "I pray, Lord God of heaven, O great and awesome God, You who keep Your covenant and mercy with those who love You and observe Your commandments ..." (Nehemiah 1:5).

And I prayed to the Lord my God, and made confession, and said, "O Lord, great and awesome God, who keeps His covenant and mercy with those who love Him, and with those who keep His commandments ..." (Daniel 9:4).

♦ God is ever mindful of the covenant

He remembers His covenant forever, the word which He commanded, for a thousand generations (Psalm 105:8).

He has given food to those who fear Him; *He will ever be mindful of His covenant* (Psalm 111:5).

To perform the mercy promised to our fathers and *to remember His holy covenant* (Luke 1:72).

♦ The people of God should be mindful of the covenant

Remember His covenant forever, the word which He commanded, for a thousand generations (1 Chronicles 16:15).

♦ Caution against forgetting the covenant

Take heed to yourselves, lest you forget the covenant of the Lord your God which He made with you, and make for yourselves a carved image in the form of anything which the Lord your God has forbidden you (Deuteronomy 4:23).

♦ Plead in prayer regarding the covenant

Have respect to the covenant; for the dark places of the earth are full of the haunts of cruelty (Psalm 74:20).

Do not abhor us, for Your name's sake; do not disgrace the throne of Your glory. Remember, do not break Your covenant with us (Jeremiah 14:21).

◆ There is punishment for despising the covenant

How much worse punishment, do you think, will be deserved by the one who has trampled underfoot the Son of God, and has profaned the blood of the covenant by which he was sanctified, and has outraged the Spirit of grace? For we know him who said, "Vengeance is mine; I will repay." And again, "The Lord will judge his people" (Hebrews 10:29, 30, ESV).

B. The Main Eight Covenants in the Bible

A covenant—*berith* in Hebrew (Old Testament) and *diatheke* in Greek (New Testament)—is a promise or an agreement between God and Man. A covenant may be conditional or unconditional.

There are eight important covenants in the Bible.

1. The covenant with all repenting sinners to save them through Christ

Paul, a bondservant of God and an apostle of Jesus Christ, according to the faith of God's elect and the acknowledgment of the truth which accords with godliness, in hope of eternal life which God, who cannot lie, promised before time began (Titus 1:1, 2).

Now may the God of peace who brought up our Lord Jesus from the dead, that great Shepherd of the sheep, through the blood of the *everlasting covenant*, make you complete in every good work to do His will, working in you what is well pleasing in His sight, through Jesus Christ, to whom be glory forever and ever (Hebrews 13:20, 21).

This covenant is unconditional.

2. The covenant with Adam

Although the Bible does not explicitly mention a covenant until Genesis 6:18 (when God announces that he intends to establish a covenant with Noah), many theologians hold the view that God made a covenant with Adam, and there is some good evidence that supports this view.

The prophet Hosea sheds some light on this matter when he says that the people of his generation had transgressed a covenant like Adam: *'But like Adam they transgressed the covenant; there they dealt faithlessly with Me'* (Hosea 6:7, ESV). This verse strongly suggests that Adam was in a formal covenant relationship with God.

Further evidence for God making a covenant with Adam is the very language used by God in relation to Noah, when He says, *'Behold, I establish My covenant with you and with your descendants after you'* (Genesis 9:9). Every single time that this Hebrew phrase for *establish a covenant* is used in the Old Testament, it speaks of making good on or upholding a previously existing covenant, as opposed to making a brand-new covenant.

Therefore, it is God's covenant with Adam and his descendants that God renewed with Noah after the Flood. Through this covenant, God promised dominion over the earth to mankind and life everlasting in return for obedience.

Adam was required to obey God in order to secure God's blessing. Therefore, although the word *covenant* is not mentioned in connection with Adam, the various covenantal elements are present. If Adam remained obedient, he would enter into an eternal state of blessedness. However, if he failed to conform to that stipulation, then he would die.

We read about this covenant in the following references:

> And God blessed them. And God said to them, "Be fruitful and multiply and fill the earth and subdue it, and have dominion over the fish of the sea and over the birds of the heavens and over every living thing that moves on the earth" (Genesis 1:28, ESV).

> The Lord God took the man and put him in the garden of Eden to work it and keep it. And the Lord God commanded the man, saying, "You may surely eat of every tree of the garden, but of the tree of the knowledge of good and evil you shall not eat, for in the day that you eat of it you shall surely die" (Genesis 2:15–17, ESV).

"I will put enmity between you and the woman, and between your offspring and her offspring; he shall bruise your head, and you shall bruise his heel." To the woman he said, "I will surely multiply your pain in childbearing; in pain you shall bring forth children. Your desire shall be contrary to your husband, but he shall rule over you." And to Adam he said, "Because you have listened to the voice of your wife and have eaten of the tree of which I commanded you, 'You shall not eat of it,' cursed is the ground because of you; in pain you shall eat of it all the days of your life; thorns and thistles it shall bring forth for you; and you shall eat the plants of the field. By the sweat of your face you shall eat bread, till you return to the ground, for out of it you were taken; for you are dust, and to dust you shall return" (Genesis 3:15–19, ESV).

- God's covenant with Adam *before the fall*, that Adam could remain in Eden as long as he obeyed, was conditional.

- God's covenant with Adam *after the fall*, that God would someday send a Saviour, was unconditional.

3. The covenant with Noah

And when the Lord smelled the pleasing aroma, the Lord said in his heart, "I will never again curse the ground because of man, for the intention of man's heart is evil from his youth. Neither will I ever again strike down every living creature as I have done. While the earth remains, seedtime and harvest, cold and heat, summer and winter, day and night, shall not cease" (Genesis 8:21, 22, ESV).

"I establish my covenant with you, that never again shall all flesh be cut off by the waters of the flood, and never again shall there be a flood to destroy the earth." And God said, "This is the sign of the covenant that I make between me and you and every living creature that is with you, for all future generations … When the bow is in the clouds, I will see it and remember the everlasting covenant between God and every living creature of all flesh that is on the earth" (Genesis 9:11, 12, 16, ESV).

- The covenant with Noah was that the earth would not be destroyed by water again.

- The covenant was also that the seasons would continue until the end. This was unconditional.

4. The covenant with Abraham

"I will make you a great nation; I will bless you and make your name great; and you shall be a blessing. I will bless those who bless you, and I will curse him who curses you; and in you all the families of the earth shall be blessed." … Then the Lord appeared to Abram and said, "To your descendants I will give this land." And there he built an altar to the Lord, who had appeared to him (Genesis 12:2, 3, 7).

And the Lord said to Abram, after Lot had separated from him: "Lift your eyes now and look from the place where you are—northward, southward, eastward, and westward; for all the land which you see I give to you and your descendants forever. And I will make your descendants as the dust of the earth; so that if a man could number the dust of the earth, then your descendants also could be numbered. Arise, walk in the land through its length and its width, for I give it to you" (Genesis 13:14–17).

Then He brought him outside and said, "Look now toward heaven, and count the stars if you are able to number them." And He said to him, "So shall your descendants be." … On the same day the Lord made a covenant with Abram, saying: "To your descendants I have given this land, from the river of Egypt to the great river, the River Euphrates" (Genesis 15:5, 18).

And I will establish My covenant between Me and you and your descendants after you in their generations, for an everlasting covenant, to be God to you and your descendants after you. Also I give to you and your descendants after you the land in which you are a stranger, all the land of Canaan, as an everlasting possession; and I will be their God (Genesis 17:7, 8).

- The covenant that God made with Abraham was that God would make Abraham the founder of a great nation.

- The covenant also was that God would someday give Abraham and his descendants the land of Canaan forever. This was unconditional.

5. The covenant with Moses and the children of Israel

Moses went up to God. The Lord called to him out of the mountain, saying, "Thus you shall say to the house of Jacob, and tell the people of Israel: 'You yourselves have seen what I did to the Egyptians, and how I bore you on eagles' wings and brought you to myself. Now therefore, if you will indeed obey my voice and keep my covenant, you shall be my treasured possession among all peoples, for all the earth is mine; and you shall be to me a kingdom of priests and a holy nation.' These are the words that you shall speak to the people of Israel." So Moses came and called the elders of the people and set before them all these words that the Lord had commanded him. All the people answered together and said, "All that the Lord has spoken we will do." And Moses reported the words of the people to the Lord (Exodus 19:3-8, ESV).

Refer also to Leviticus 26 and Deuteronomy 28.

- God's covenant was that the children of Israel could have the land at that time to enjoy it if they obeyed Him.

- The covenant also meant that the children of Israel would be deprived of all God's blessings if they disobeyed. This was conditional.

6. The covenant with David

Should you not know that the Lord God of Israel gave the dominion over Israel to David forever, to him and his sons, by a covenant of salt? (2 Chronicles 13:5).

When your days are fulfilled and you lie down with your fathers, I will raise up your offspring after you, who shall come from your body, and I will establish his kingdom. He shall build a house for my name, and I will establish the throne of his kingdom forever. I will be to him a father, and he shall be to me a son. When he commits iniquity, I will discipline him with the rod of men, with the stripes of the sons of men, but my steadfast love will not depart from him, as I took it from Saul, whom I put away from before you. And your house and your kingdom shall be made sure forever before me. Your throne shall be established forever (2 Samuel 7:12–16, ESV).

Although my house is not so with God, yet He has made with me an everlasting covenant, ordered in all things and secure. For this is all my salvation and all my desire; will He not make it increase? (2 Samuel 23:5).

God's covenant with David was that:

- From David would come an everlasting throne.

- From David would come an everlasting kingdom.

- From David would come an everlasting King—this was unconditional.

7. The covenant with the Church

And I also say to you that you are Peter, and on this rock I will build My church, and the gates of Hades shall not prevail against it (Matthew 16:18).

For this is My blood of the new covenant, which is shed for many for the remission of sins (Matthew 26:28).

Likewise He also took the cup after supper, saying, "This cup is the new covenant in My blood, which is shed for you" (Luke 22:20).

Now may the God of peace who brought up our Lord Jesus from the dead, that great Shepherd of the sheep, through the blood of the everlasting covenant, make you complete in every good work to do His will, working in you what is well pleasing in His sight, through Jesus Christ, to whom be glory forever and ever. Amen (Hebrews 13:20–21).

This covenant included that:

- Christ would build His Church with His own blood.

- All the fury of hell would not destroy her.

- He would perfect all the members of His Church—this was unconditional.

8. The new covenant with the people of Israel

Refer to Jeremiah 31:31–34 (quoted earlier).

> I, the Lord, have called You in righteousness, and will hold Your hand; I will keep You and give You as a covenant to the people, as a light to the Gentiles (Isaiah 42:6).

> But now thus says the Lord, He who created you, O Jacob, He who formed you, O Israel: "Fear not, for I have redeemed you; I have called you by name, you are Mine. When you pass through the waters, I will be with you; and through the rivers, they shall not overwhelm you; when you walk through fire you shall not be burned, and the flame shall not consume you. For I am the Lord your God, the Holy One of Israel, your Saviour. I give Egypt as your ransom, Cush and Seba in exchange for you. Because you are precious in My eyes, and honoured, and I love you, I give men in return for you, peoples in exchange for your life. Fear not, for I am with you; I will bring your offspring from the east, and from the west I will gather you I will say to the north, give up, and to the south, do not withhold; bring My sons from afar and My daughters from the end of the earth" (Isaiah 43:1–6, ESV).

> These are the words that Moses spoke to all Israel beyond the Jordan in the wilderness, in the Arabah opposite Suph, between Paran and Tophel, Laban, Hazeroth, and Dizahab. It is eleven days' journey from Horeb by the way of Mount Seir to Kadesh-barnea. In the fortieth year, on the first day of the eleventh month, Moses spoke to the people of Israel according to all that the Lord had given him in commandment to them, after he had defeated Sihon the king of the Amorites, who lived in Heshbon, and Og the king of Bashan, who lived in Ashtaroth and in Edrei. Beyond the Jordan, in the land of Moab, Moses undertook to explain this law, saying, "The Lord our God said to us in Horeb, 'You have stayed long enough at this mountain. Turn and take your journey, and go to the hill country of the Amorites and to all their neighbours in the Arabah, in the hill country and in the lowland and in the Negeb and by the seacoast, the land of the Canaanites, and Lebanon, as far as the great river, the river Euphrates. See, I have set the land before you. Go in and take possession of the land that the Lord swore to your fathers, to Abraham, to Isaac, and to Jacob, to give to them and to their offspring after them.' "At that time I said to you, 'I am not able to bear you by myself'" (Deuteronomy 1:1–9, ESV).

For if that first covenant had been faultless, there would have been no occasion to look for a second. For he finds fault with them when he says: "Behold, the days are coming, declares the Lord, when I will establish a new covenant with the house of Israel and with the house of Judah, not like the covenant that I made with their fathers on the day when I took them by the hand to bring them out of the land of Egypt. For they did not continue in my covenant, and so I showed no concern for them, declares the Lord. For this is the covenant that I will make with the house of Israel after those days, declares the Lord: I will put my laws into their minds, and write them on their hearts, and I will be their God, and they shall be my people. And they shall not teach, each one his neighbour and each one his brother, saying, 'Know the Lord,' for they shall all know me, from the least of them to the greatest. For I will be merciful toward their iniquities, and I will remember their sins no more" (Hebrews 8:7–12, ESV).

For I do not desire, brethren, that you should be ignorant of this mystery, lest you should be wise in your own opinion, that blindness in part has happened to Israel until the fullness of the Gentiles has come in. And so all Israel will be saved, as it is written: "The Deliverer will come out of Zion, and He will turn away ungodliness from Jacob; for this is My covenant with them, when I take away their sins" (Romans 11:25–27).

This covenant included the following:

- God would bring the people of Israel back to Himself.

- He would forgive their iniquity and forget their sins.

- He would use them to reach the Gentiles.

- He would establish them in the land of Canaan forever—this was unconditional.

Now, we come to the highest point in the covenant, which is Christ and the covenant. This will be followed by the spiritual significance of the covenant and some practical points for our lives.

C. Christ and the Covenant

We have five main points about Christ and the covenant:

- **Christ first announced the covenant and made it with His disciples in the upper room on Great Thursday**

And as they were eating, Jesus took bread, blessed and broke it, and gave it to the disciples and said, "Take, eat; this is My body." Then He took the cup, and gave thanks, and gave it to them, saying, "Drink from it, all of you. *For this is My blood of the new covenant,* which is shed for many for the remission of sins" (Matthew 26:26–28).

- **Christ established the covenant through His death and resurrection**

And for this reason He is the Mediator of the new covenant, by means of death, for the redemption of the transgressions under the first covenant, that those who are called may receive the promise of the eternal inheritance. For where there is a testament, there must also of necessity be the death of the testator. For a testament is in force after men are dead, since it has no power at all while the testator lives (Hebrews 9:15–17).

Thus, the Old Testament came to an end, and the New Testament began and continued.

- **Christ is the *Substance* of the covenant**

I, the Lord, have called You in righteousness, and will hold Your hand; I will keep You and *give You as a covenant to the people,* as a light to the Gentiles (Isaiah 42:6).

Thus says the Lord: "In an acceptable time I have heard You, and in the day of salvation I have helped You; I will preserve You and *give You as a covenant to the people,* to restore the earth, to cause them to inherit the desolate heritages" (Isaiah 49:8).

- **Christ is the *Mediator* of the covenant**

But now He has obtained a more excellent ministry, inasmuch as He is also *Mediator* of a better covenant, which was established on better promises' (Hebrews 8:6).

And for this reason He is the *Mediator* of *the new covenant*, by means of death, for the redemption of the transgressions under the first covenant, that those who are called may receive the promise of the eternal inheritance (Hebrews 9:15).

To Jesus the Mediator of the new covenant, and to the blood of sprinkling that speaks better things than that of Abel (Hebrews 12:24).

- **Christ is the *Messenger* of the covenant**

"Behold, I send My messenger, and he will prepare the way before Me. And the Lord, whom you seek, will suddenly come to His temple, even *the Messenger of the covenant*, in whom you delight. Behold, He is coming," says the Lord of hosts (Malachi 3:1).

To sum up, we said that Christ announced the covenant in the upper room, established the covenant through His death and resurrection, is the Substance of the covenant, is the Mediator of the covenant, and is the Messenger of the covenant.

Now, we want to understand the spiritual significance of having a covenant relationship with God.

Spiritual Significance

1. The Covenant God

Therefore know that the Lord your God, He is God, the faithful God who keeps covenant and mercy for a thousand generations with those who love Him and keep His commandments (Deuteronomy 7:9).

God has bound Himself with a covenant with man because He knows our weakness and disbelief. In his disbelief, man behaves as if God cannot be trusted! Therefore, God offers Himself as the *Covenant God*. We need to remember that we are dealing with a Covenant God and we are in a relationship with a *Covenant God*. My God is a *Covenant God*. We need to put this phrase in our hearts and experience its implications.

Blessed is the man who truly knows God as his Covenant God, who knows what the covenant promises him, what unwavering confidence of expectations it secures, and what a claim and hold it gives him on the covenant-keeping God.

The full knowledge of what God wants to do for man and the assurance that it will be done by the almighty God, in addition to surrendering completely to God, can transform one's whole life.

God created man in His image so that man could receive God's life. When sin entered, it deformed the relationship between man and God. Hence, the flow of the stream of the divine life from God to man ceased. However, God's complete salvation restores the flow of His life to us.

Yet, man's problem was and still is his disbelief. This lack of belief saddens God's heart immensely. God was so vigilant over the people of Israel of old for many centuries to teach them faith and trust. It is written:

> But *without faith it is impossible to please Him,* for he who comes to God must believe that He is, and that He is a rewarder of those who diligently seek Him (Hebrews 11:6).

One of the most important things that God did to help man attain this mutual trust was *the covenant.* It is an assured divine treatment for man's recurring illness, which is his lack of faith.

In entering into a covenant with us, God's main objective is to draw us to Him and render us entirely dependent on Him. In this position, He can fill us with Himself and fill us with His love and His blessings.

> "For the mountains shall depart and the hills be removed, but My kindness shall not depart from you, nor shall My covenant of peace be removed," says the Lord, who has mercy on you (Isaiah 54:10).

2. The relation between the covenant of the Old Testament and the covenant of the New Testament

The divine school teaches man to differentiate between working out his salvation with his own efforts versus man's great need for God's grace that works in him and requires practising continuous trust in God day after day and allowing the stream of the divine life to work in us this salvation.

> This city has aroused my anger and wrath, from the day it was built to this day, so that I will remove it from my sight because of all the evil of the children of Israel and the children of Judah that they did to provoke me to anger—their kings and their officials, their priests and their prophets, the men of Judah and the inhabitants of Jerusalem. They have turned to me their back and not their face. *And though I have taught them persistently*, they have not listened to receive instruction. They set up their abominations in the house that is called by my name, to defile it (Jeremiah 32:31–34, ESV).

God was vigilant over the children of Israel to teach them, but they did not respond.

> For this is the covenant that I will make with the house of Israel after those days, says the Lord: I will put My laws in their mind and write them on their hearts; and I will be their God, and they shall be My people (Hebrews 8:10).

> This is the covenant that I will make with them after those days, says the Lord: I will put My laws into their hearts, and in their minds I will write them (Hebrews 10:16).

Refer also to Hebrews 8:7–12 (quoted earlier).

Galatians 4:21–31 reveals the difference between the two covenants:

> Tell me, you who desire to be under the law, do you not hear the law? For it is written that Abraham had two sons: the one by a bondwoman, the other by a freewoman. But he who was of the bondwoman was born according to the flesh, and he of the freewoman through promise, which things are symbolic. *For these are the two covenants*: the one from Mount Sinai which gives birth to bondage, which is Hagar—for this Hagar is Mount Sinai in Arabia, and corresponds to Jerusalem which now is, and is in bondage with her

children—but the Jerusalem above is free, which is the mother of us all. For it is written: "Rejoice, O barren, you who do not bear! Break forth and shout, you who are not in labour! For the desolate has many more children than she who has a husband." Now we, brethren, as Isaac was, are children of promise. But, as he who was born according to the flesh then persecuted him who was born according to the Spirit, even so it is now. Nevertheless what does the Scripture say? "Cast out the bondwoman and her son, for the son of the bondwoman shall not be heir with the son of the freewoman." So then, brethren, we are not children of the bondwoman but of the free.

There is the son of the flesh and the son of promise. Ishmael is the son of the flesh who symbolises man's fleshly wisdom and will in solving problems. This was manifested in Sarah's suggestion that Abraham marry her servant Hagar, who symbolises the power of the flesh. In fact, when Sarah brought up this suggestion, she herself was troubled a great deal by this idea. God said that Ishmael must be sent away as he cannot inherit with the son of promise.

Isaac, on the other hand, is the son of promise who symbolises the power of God. Faith is required so that God's power would flow despite the death of the flesh. Consequently, there would be life, and the son of promise would come. The son of promise alone should inherit, and God's purposes should continue through him.

Therefore, there is a great need for a true fellowship with God in which man continually realises his inability and weakness and thus submits completely to God so that God's life may flow continuously to him.

The Word of God is essential in illuminating this path for us and allowing God's life to flow continually to our fellowship with Him.

But, in the Old Testament, the purpose was to help man discover his weakness to be ready to receive the grace of the New Testament. Let us follow this revelation step by step:

The Old Testament, meaning the law, revealed sin:

> Moreover *the law entered that the offence might abound.* But where sin abounded, grace abounded much more (Romans 5:20).

What shall we say then? Is the law sin? Certainly not! On the contrary, *I would not have known sin except through the law*. For I would not have known covetousness unless the law had said, "You shall not covet" (Romans 7:7).

What purpose then does the law serve? It was added because of transgressions, till the Seed should come to whom the promise was made; and it was appointed through angels by the hand of a mediator (Galatians 3:19).

However, revealing and uncovering sin is not negative because the purpose is not merely to reveal something, but to teach man and draw his attention to the extent of the corruption hidden within him as a result of the fall:

For we know that the law is spiritual, but I am of the flesh, sold under sin. For I do not understand my own actions. For I do not do what I want, but I do the very thing I hate. Now if I do what I do not want, I agree with the law, that it is good. So now it is no longer I who do it, but sin that dwells within me. For I know that nothing good dwells in me, that is, in my flesh. For I have the desire to do what is right, but not the ability to carry it out. For I do not do the good I want, but the evil I do not want is what I keep on doing. Now if I do what I do not want, *it is no longer I who do it, but sin that dwells within me*. So I find it to be a law that when I want to do right, evil lies close at hand. For I delight in the law of God, in my inner being, but I see in my members another law waging war against the law of my mind and making me captive to the law of sin that dwells in my members. Wretched man that I am! Who will deliver me from this body of death? (Romans 7:14–24, ESV).

Man's sense of inability to obey God's commandments is due to the hidden corruption within him. This corruption has to be dealt with so that man may be prepared for the coming of Christ as the Saviour who grants the grace of complete salvation. Salvation does not only lift the condemnation of sin, but it also annuls the corruption caused by sin:

There is therefore now no condemnation to those who are in Christ Jesus, who do not walk according to the flesh, but according to the Spirit (Romans 8:1).

He then would have had to suffer often since the foundation of the world; but now, once at the end of the ages, *He has appeared to put away sin* by the sacrifice of Himself (Hebrews 9:26).

The next day John saw Jesus coming toward him, and said, "Behold! the Lamb of God who *takes away the sin* of the world!" (John 1:29).

Therefore, Apostle Paul was so inspired when he said:

Therefore the law was *our tutor* to bring us to Christ, that we might be justified by faith (Galatians 3:24).

This means that humanity, represented by the people of Israel, entered the school of the law to be prepared for the coming of Christ and the release of full salvation.

What is the practical implication for our lives?

Most likely, every believer goes through the following spiritually painful experience for a certain period in his life:

After receiving Christ and His saving grace, the person, in his initial spiritual enthusiasm, thinks that he can obey God and His commandments. However, after some time, he starts to sense his failure and inability. He already has the realisation that his condemnation had been lifted after he received Christ, yet he may not realise that corruption is still hidden inside him and needs to be dealt with.

Unfortunately, we usually think of the grace of God only as lifting the condemnation and death. This is true; however, the fall has caused two main problems that need dealing with:

- Man was condemned and cut off from life

- Inner corruption happened in his inner soul/being

As believers, we are justified in Christ and this means the condemnation is lifted. The judgement of death is lifted. We are reconciled with God the Father. But what about the inner corruption? This inner corruption is the main problem of our lives as believers. When we understand how to deal with it, everything in our lives will change.

The rich grace of the New Testament does not only deal with lifting the condemnation of sin, but it also deals with the inner corruption through the new life granted to man by God, the author of our salvation:

> Therefore, if anyone is in Christ, he is a new creation; old things have passed away; behold, all things have become new (2 Corinthians 5:17).

This new life bears within it *a new heart*. God's commandments are written and inscribed on this heart. Thus, this new heart creates within us a desire and longing to obey God and His commandments with joy and holy zeal, often combined with simple faith that trusts God and His promises and submits to His will.

But sometimes this inner heart gets buried and thus needs to be revived. We receive this new heart when we accept Christ, but it can easily be buried through the activity of the soul and the mind. We need to learn how to reactivate this new heart and push away the activity of the soul and the mind. In biblical terms, we have to put to death the activity of the mind and soul and release the power of the resurrection so that we can live with this new heart. Apostle Paul clarified this matter in Hebrews 8:10–12 in four points:

> For this is the covenant that I will make with the house of Israel after those days, says the Lord: *I will put My laws in their mind and write them on their hearts*; and *I will be their God, and they shall be My people. None of them shall teach his neighbour*, and none his brother, saying, 'Know the Lord,' for all shall know Me, from the least of them to the greatest of them. *For I will be merciful to their unrighteousness*, and their sins and their lawless deeds I will remember no more.

There are four main points in this passage that we need to pay attention to in order to better understand our covenant relationship with God.

- *I will put My laws in their mind and write them on their hearts*

This means that God's commandments will be written and kept in the new heart. Thus, the person will desire them and long for them. As a result, the commandments will no longer be a burden as they were in the Old Testament. There will no longer be a conflict between our fleshly desires and the commandment of God. We will no longer forget the commandments.

However, we need to pause and reflect on this point. Though we live in the New Testament, we still sometimes feel that God's commandments are a burden and we want to avoid them one way or another. Sometimes we experience a conflict between our desires and the commandments. When this happens, it indicates that our new heart is inactive and needs to be reactivated. We will explain this point shortly.

- *I will be their God, and they shall be My people*

This statement is the core of the *covenant relationship*. It sums up God's mind about the kind of covenant relationship that should be between Him and His people.

It is a description that is characteristic of the covenant relationship between God and man. Whenever we come across this statement in any part of the Scriptures, we ought to understand that it refers to the covenant relationship.

- *None of them shall teach his neighbour*

Who will teach us, then?

Doesn't the Epistle to the Ephesians say that there are teachers in the Church of God?

Yes, this is true, but this phrase indicates that the Spirit of God will teach us, whether directly or through the teachers whom He anoints for this role. As a result of the teaching of the Holy Spirit, the commandments will not be a mere set of rules to abide by, but they will be revealed by the Holy Spirit. Consequently, we will see the commandments in a new way, with new eyes. We will see them as protective measures that keep us from being defiled by the world or being lost.

More than this, when the Holy Spirit reveals the commandment, He releases from the commandment divine energy that will enable us to obey it with love and joy. In other words, He releases the grace inside the commandment. By this, the Holy Spirit will be our teacher, as we read in the following verses:

But you have an anointing from the Holy One, and you know all things (1 John 2:20).

But the anointing which you have received from Him abides in you, and you do not need that anyone teach you; but as *the same anointing teaches you* concerning all things, and is true, and is not a lie, and just as it has taught you, you will abide in Him (1 John 2:27).

Thus, the anointing will teach us.

- *For I will be merciful to their unrighteousness*

Because of the continuous presence of the power of His blood for forgiveness and purification, anything that hinders the new covenant relationship and its fruits is lifted:

If we confess our sins, He is faithful and just to forgive us our sins and to cleanse us from all unrighteousness (1 John 1:9).

3. Spiritual implications related to the covenant relationship with God in the New Testament

We will examine some biblical passages to know the spiritual implications related to the covenant relationship with God in the New Testament.

- Galatians 4:21–31

Tell me, you who desire to be under the law, do you not hear the law? For it is written that Abraham had two sons: the one by a bondwoman, the other by a freewoman. But he who was of the bondwoman was born according to the flesh, and he of the freewoman through promise, which things are symbolic. *For these are the two covenants*: the one from Mount Sinai which gives birth to bondage, which is Hagar—for this Hagar is Mount Sinai in Arabia, and corresponds to Jerusalem which now is, and is in bondage with her children—but the Jerusalem above is free, which is the mother of us all. For it is written: "Rejoice, O barren, you who do not bear! Break forth and shout, you who are not in labour! For the desolate has many more children than she who has a husband." Now we, brethren, as Isaac was, are children of promise. But, as he who was born according to the flesh then persecuted him who was born according to the Spirit, even so it is now. Nevertheless what does the Scripture say? "Cast out the bondwoman and her son, for the son of the bondwoman shall not be heir with the son of the freewoman." So then, brethren, we are not children of the bondwoman but of the free.

The passage describes Abraham's house. Abraham lived in a house with two wives and had two sons.

- Abraham's house is representative of the Church in Abraham's days.

- In this house, we see two categories. One is according to the flesh and is represented by Hagar and Ishmael, and the other is according to the spirit and is represented by Sarah and Isaac. There is also an apparent struggle between the two categories, where one rejects and mocks the other:

And Sarah saw the son of Hagar the Egyptian, whom she had borne to Abraham, *scoffing* (Genesis 21:9).

According to the original Hebrew language, the word *scoffing* here means *mocking*.

This situation reflects the state of God's people at all times; therefore, we need to take heed and know which category we belong to and according to which of them we live our Christian life today.

- Galatians 4:4–6

But when the fullness of the time had come, *God sent forth His Son*, born of a woman, born under the law, to redeem those who were under the law, that we might *receive the adoption* as sons. And because you are sons, *God has sent forth the Spirit of His Son* into your hearts, *crying out, "Abba, Father!"*

At the beginning of this passage, we read:

- *God sent forth His Son ... that we might receive the adoption*

Then, at the end of the passage, we read:

- *God has sent forth the Spirit of His Son ... crying out, "Abba, Father!"*

This means that when we receive the Son of God by faith, He grants us to become children of God, while His Spirit (*'the Spirit of His Son'*) enables us to live as children of God practically.

Thus, we can put it as follows:

God sent His Son ... we became children of God.

God sent His Spirit ... to help us to practically live as children of God.

Therefore, being God's children is not a theological fact, but it has become a practical fact. This highlights our continuous need for fellowship with the Holy Spirit, for He alone can make Christ's life flow continuously in us as the sap that flows in the vine. In John 15, Jesus said:

> I am the true vine, and My Father is the vinedresser. Every branch in Me that does not bear fruit He takes away; and every branch that bears fruit He prunes, that it may bear more fruit. You are already clean because of the word which I have spoken to you. Abide in Me, and I in you. As the branch cannot bear fruit of itself, unless it abides in the vine, neither can you, unless you abide in Me. I am the vine, you are the branches. He who abides in Me, and I in him, bears much fruit; for without Me you can do nothing. If anyone does not abide in Me, he is cast out as a branch and is withered; and they gather them and throw them into the fire, and they are burned (John 15:1–6).

This sap transfers to us the power of eternal life—the life of the Son of God—because we are branches in the vine.

When we receive the life of Christ continuously, it performs two divine works within us. The life of Christ has two aspects: the cross and the resurrection, and we need both acts continuously. The power of the cross puts to death the old man in us; while the power of resurrection releases the new man, the new heart, in us.

The problem is that we often live the opposite of this state, where the new man is weakened, the new heart is inactive, and the old man is strong. Deep within, we desire to walk in the spirit, but practically, in different situations, we find ourselves acting according to the flesh because the stronger part of the inner man comes forth rapidly, while the weaker part is inactive.

This situation occurs because despite being branches in the vine, we may not be receiving the sap continuously. If you look at a vine in any field, some branches will be alive while others are withered. The difference in the state of the branches is due to the difference in the flow of the sap to the branch. Therefore, if we want to live as children of God, we need the continuous flow of the life of Christ. The Holy Spirit is the Person of the Trinity who can bring this life of Christ into us. Therefore, God sent forth His Spirit so that we may practically live as children of God.

This is the privilege of the new covenant. Jesus is ready to continuously release His life to the branches. But, we need to have a close fellowship with the Holy Spirit who brings to us this life of Christ.

The Holy Spirit is a Person, not just a power. We cannot say, we receive the Holy Spirit by faith, and now we are filled with the Holy Spirit, and that is all. If I am truly relating to Him as a Person, I must admit that I am in a continuous process of knowing Him. If, for instance, you have been getting to know a person for three years, you will begin to be familiar with some of that person's characteristics; however, you would still need to know the person more to be able to communicate with him closely. The same happens in our relationship with the Holy Spirit. Therefore, we need to have quiet times to review our lives daily and find out to what degree we relate to the Holy Spirit as a Person. In the quietness, He will come near to teach me and to reveal Himself as a Person. He is keen on doing this if I am interested in receiving it!

We also ought to be aware of the biblical warning regarding the relationship with the Spirit:

- Do not grieve (Ephesians 4:30)

- Do not quench (1 Thessalonians 5:19)

- Do not resist (Acts 7:51)

- 2 Corinthians 3

In this chapter, Apostle Paul draws a comparison between the two testaments or covenants:

> Clearly you are an epistle of Christ, ministered by us, written not with ink but by the Spirit of the living God, not on tablets of stone but on tablets of flesh, that is, of the heart (2 Corinthians 3:3).

> Who also made us sufficient as ministers of *the new covenant*, not of the letter but of the Spirit; for the letter kills, but the Spirit gives life (2 Corinthians 3:6).

> Unlike Moses, who put a veil over his face so that the children of Israel could not look steadily at the end of what was passing away. But their minds were blinded. For until this day the same veil remains unlifted in the reading of the Old Testament, because the veil is taken away in Christ. But even to this day, when Moses is read, a veil lies on their heart. Nevertheless when one turns to the Lord, the veil is taken away. Now the Lord is the Spirit; and *where the Spirit of the Lord is, there is liberty*. But we all, with unveiled face, beholding as in a mirror the glory of the Lord, are being transformed into the same image from glory to glory, just as by the Spirit of the Lord (2 Corinthians 3:13–18).

These passages highlight the following:

- The Old Covenant or Testament was written on tablets of stone, whereas the New Testament is written on tablets of flesh, that is, the heart. Therefore, this New Testament is rooted in us, and hence, it is possible to obey it (verse 3).

- The Old Testament depended mainly on the *letter*, meaning obedience without complete understanding (the lack of understanding was caused by the darkness that entered into the human mind by the fall), whereas, in the New Testament, obedience is *of the spirit not of the letter* (verse 6) because of the light of God that comes to our minds.

- In the Old Testament, man was unable to behold the glory of God (because if he saw God's glory, he would die), whereas, in the New Testament, he is granted the ability to behold this glory and experience it (verses 13–15). Jesus even prayed that we may become partakers of His glory: *'And the glory which You gave Me I have given them, that they may be one just as We are one'* (John 17:22).

- All these matters depend on our obedience to the Holy Spirit, who grants us liberty (verses 17, 18).

Final Comments to Sum Up

- The Spirit of God is the great gift of the covenant, and, at the same time, He is the tutor who teaches us what the covenant means.

- The Spirit of God is:

  - The Spirit of Faith

  And since we have the same *spirit of faith*, according to what is written, "I believed and therefore I spoke," we also believe and therefore speak (2 Corinthians 4:13).

  - The Spirit of Power

  For God *has not given us a spirit of fear, but of power* and of love and of a sound mind (2 Timothy 1:7).

  - The Spirit of Grace

  And I will pour on the house of David and on the inhabitants of Jerusalem *the Spirit of grace* and supplication (Zechariah 12:10).

Through the Holy Spirit, obeying the covenant and having fellowship with God can be maintained without interruption.

- The Spirit of God is the Activator,[12] the Bearer,[13] and the Communicator of all the covenant promises. He reveals and glorifies Jesus.

- Remember that the Holy Spirit works only inasmuch as we give Him space and allow Him to work in us. Therefore, He works to a lesser degree if we neglect or grieve Him, whereas He works to a greater degree if we yield to Him and trust Him.

---

[12] Activator means He performs a role with us that is similar to how we process lectures or any material, by discussing them to become clear.

[13] Bearer means that He continuously brings new gifts, new enabling, and new understanding; the light comes and the grace comes.

III. Practical Considerations

In this section, we will discuss seven practical points:

1. Self-Denial

2. The Surety of Jesus

3. The Book of the Covenant

4. Obedience

5. The Grace of God

6. The Ministry of the New Testament

7. Kingly Priesthood

1. Self-Denial

- Hebrews 9:15, 16

And for this reason He is the Mediator of the new covenant, by means of death, for the redemption of the transgressions under the first covenant, that those who are called may receive the promise of the eternal inheritance. For where there is a testament, there must also of necessity be the death of the testator.

The Old Testament ended with the death of Christ, and the New Testament began with the resurrection of Christ.

These verses highlight that the death of Jesus was necessary so that the covenant would be active.

Similarly, in our practical life, it is necessary that the death of our ego may be completed. This death of the ego can occur in one experience, or it may happen gradually over a stage of receiving God's revelations through which one's mind is opened to understand the divine truths and live them out.

- Hebrews 13:20, 21

Now may the God of peace who brought up our Lord Jesus from the dead, that great Shepherd of the sheep, through the blood of the everlasting covenant, make you complete in every good work to do His will, working in you what is well pleasing in His sight, through Jesus Christ, to whom be glory forever and ever. Amen.

As God worked in Jesus and brought Him up from the dead, He also works in us the same work by the blood of the everlasting covenant, resurrecting us—bringing us from death to life.

Therefore, we must ask for an increased spiritual understanding of *the work of the blood* in terms of *the everlasting covenant.*

- Christ in the Gospel of John

It is interesting to read about Christ's absolute submission to God the Father more than 12 times in the Gospel of John. Jesus always said, *not My will, not My words, not My glory,* etcetera. Jesus always denied Himself and relied on the Father:

Then Jesus answered and said to them, "Most assuredly, I say to you, *the Son can do nothing of Himself,* but what He sees the Father do; for whatever He does, the Son also does in like manner" (John 5:19).

I can of Myself do nothing. As I hear, I judge; and My judgement is righteous, because *I do not seek My own will* but the will of the Father who sent Me (John 5:30).

Jesus said to them, "If God were your Father, you would love Me, for I proceeded forth and came from God; *nor have I come of Myself,* but He sent Me" (John 8:42).

For *I have not spoken on My own authority;* but the Father who sent Me gave Me a command, what I should say and what I should speak (John 12:49).

Do we do this in our ministry, or do we quite often live by the power of the ego and are so sensitive about our ego?

If the ego is put to death, Christ's life will be manifested with its glory and everybody will know that the glory of God rests upon this person. However, this requires death first, but resurrection comes after death.

We need to realise the truth about the authority of sin and our inability to live a victorious life in Christ, and hence cry unto God to grant us the desire and hunger for Him and open our eyes to comprehend the divine truths we discussed. The more we do so, the more our ego will be crucified. Thus, we will be in total surrender and obedience to God and will be ready for any cost we might face, relying on Him and His grace alone.

2. The Surety of Jesus

So when God desired to show more convincingly to the heirs of the promise the unchangeable character of his purpose, he guaranteed it with *an oath*, so that by *two unchangeable things*, in which it is impossible for God to lie, we who have fled for refuge might have strong encouragement to hold fast to the hope set before us. We have this as a sure and steadfast anchor of the soul, a hope that enters into the inner place behind the curtain, where Jesus has gone as a forerunner on our behalf, having become a high priest forever after the order of Melchizedek (Hebrews 6:17–20, ESV).

In this passage, the Scripture mentions two important things: *the promise* and *the oath*—the two unchangeable things—to assure us.

Christ has, thus, become a surety of a better and a greater covenant:

By so much more Jesus has become *a surety of a better covenant* (Hebrews 7:22).

But now He has obtained a more excellent ministry, inasmuch as He is also *Mediator of a better covenant*, which was established on better promises (Hebrews 8:6).

More than this, in Hebrews 6:19, we read:

This hope we have as *an anchor of the soul, both sure and steadfast*, and which enters the Presence behind the veil.

Jesus held the anchor of hope from one end and entered with it into the Holies, and He gave us the other end of the anchor so that we may hold on to it as we sail in the sea of the world. Whenever we face the waves or become weak and unable to sail, Jesus aligns and sets right our journey (because He is holding the anchor), preserves it, and completes it until we reach heaven. What a surety and what an assurance!

Jesus also intercedes on our behalf to save us to the uttermost:

> *Therefore He is also able to save to the uttermost* those who come to God through Him, since He always lives to make intercession for them (Hebrews 7:25).

> For if when we were enemies we were reconciled to God through the death of His Son, much more, having been reconciled, we shall be saved by His life (Romans 5:10).

We ought to believe these divine truths, fix our eyes on Jesus continuously, and call upon His name. Hence, His life will continuously be transferred to us to work despite our weaknesses and fears.

3. The Book of the Covenant

> Therefore not even the first covenant was inaugurated without blood. For when every commandment of the law had been declared by Moses to all the people, he took the blood of calves and goats, with water and scarlet wool and hyssop, and sprinkled both the book itself and all the people, saying, "This is the blood of the covenant that God commanded for you" (Hebrews 9:18–20, ESV).

> Then he took the Book of the Covenant and read it in the hearing of the people. And they said, "All that the Lord has spoken we will do, and we will be obedient." And Moses took the blood and threw it on the people and said, "Behold the blood of the covenant that the Lord has made with you in accordance with all these words" (Exodus 24:7–8, ESV).

Every covenant has a book. The book of the old covenant is the book of the Old Testament and the same applies to the new covenant. We ought to read the Old Testament with the eyes and spirit of the New Testament.

The people of Israel of old promised to obey God, yet they failed to do so:

> You go near and hear all that the Lord our God may say, and tell us all that the Lord our God says to you, and *we will hear and do it* (Deuteronomy 5:27).

However, in the New Testament, the Spirit of the New Testament—the Holy Spirit—teaches us the book of the new covenant and explains it to us, giving us the ability to obey it with joy.

4. Obedience

> And the Lord your God will circumcise your heart and the heart of your descendants, to love the Lord your God with all your heart and with all your soul, that you may live (Deuteronomy 30:6).

> In Him you were also circumcised with the circumcision made without hands, by putting off the body of the sins of the flesh, by the circumcision of Christ (Colossians 2:11).

It would be a mistake to think that the New Testament does not require any obedience, believing that grace does everything without any conditions or obligations on our part. In fact, the condition of obeying God's commandments is an essential condition in God's mind for both testaments, as highlighted throughout the entire Bible.

We need to perceive that though we have received a new life in Christ, there is corruption in the old man that needs to be dealt with. Therefore, we ought to ask for the circumcision of our hearts and allow the Holy Spirit to do this inner work in us. When our hearts are circumcised, we will have the ability to obey continuously.

Let us also remember that obedience does not only lead to blessing, but it is in itself the subject of blessing because it delights God's heart.

5. The Grace of God

We are not under the law but under the work of grace. This does not only happen at the start of our life in Christ, but it continues throughout our walk of faith in Christ:

For sin shall not have dominion over you, for you are *not under law but under grace* (Romans 6:14).

Moreover the law entered that the offence might abound. But where sin abounded, grace abounded much more, so that as sin reigned in death, even so grace might reign through righteousness to eternal life through Jesus Christ our Lord (Romans 5:20, 21).

Apostle Paul taught about grace and understood the dynamics of grace. He testified of the grace of God in his life, saying:

And the grace of our Lord was exceedingly abundant, with faith and love which are in Christ Jesus (1 Timothy 1:14).

But by the grace of God I am what I am, and His grace toward me was not in vain; but I laboured more abundantly than they all, yet not I, but the grace of God which was with me (1 Corinthians 15:10).

For the administration of this service not only supplies the needs of the saints, but also is abounding through many thanksgivings to God (2 Corinthians 9:12).

Apostle Paul also strengthened his disciple Timothy, saying:

You therefore, my son, *be strong in the grace* that is in Christ Jesus (2 Timothy 2:1).

Therefore, Apostle Paul draws our attention that we ought to ask for the support of grace and we will find it ready to help us at all times:

Let us therefore *come boldly to the throne of grace*, that we may obtain mercy and *find grace to help in time of need* (Hebrews 4:16).

6. The Ministry of the New Testament

You are our epistle written in our hearts, known and read by all men; clearly you are an epistle of Christ, ministered by us, written not with ink but by the Spirit of the living God, not on tablets of stone but on tablets of flesh, that is, of the heart. And we have such trust through Christ toward God. Not that we are sufficient of ourselves to think of anything as being from ourselves, but our sufficiency is from God, who also made us sufficient as ministers of the new covenant, not of the letter but of the Spirit; for the letter kills, but the Spirit gives life. But if the ministry of death, written and engraved on stones, was glorious, so that the children of Israel could not look steadily at the face of Moses because of the glory of his countenance, which glory was passing away, how will the ministry of the Spirit not be more glorious? (2 Corinthians 3:2–8).

The Holy Spirit works in us to sanctify us first, and then He works through us so that we may minister the ministry of the New Testament. We thus become ministers of spirit, life, and glory, as clear in verses 3, 6, and 8.

Are we truly ministers of the New Testament? Are we truly able to minister in spirit, life, and glory? We need to examine ourselves in this matter.

If we yield to the Holy Spirit in this process of sanctification, He will complete His work in us. Then, we will be entrusted with receiving the release of His stream in us, releasing life and glory.

This does not mean that we will always experience power and strength. On the contrary, as we acknowledge our weaknesses and limitations, the Holy Spirit works through us with power and assurance, as clear in the writing of Apostle Paul:

> And I, when I came to you, brothers, did not come proclaiming to you the testimony of God with lofty speech or wisdom. For I decided to know nothing among you except Jesus Christ and him crucified. And *I was with you in weakness and in fear and much trembling,* and my speech and my message were not in plausible words of wisdom, but in demonstration of the Spirit and of power, so that your faith might not rest in the wisdom of men but in the power of God (1 Corinthians 2:1–5, ESV).

The Apostle is saying here that he was with them in weakness, in fear, and in trembling. Because of this, he was entrusted with the power of the Spirit:

> For our gospel did not come to you in word only, but also *in power, and in the Holy Spirit and in much assurance,* as you know what kind of men we were among you for your sake (1 Thessalonians 1:5).

We ought to perceive our responsibility to lead people to enter into true fellowship with the Holy Spirit so that the Holy Spirit Himself would teach them and they would not be dependent on us alone for receiving teaching and guidance:

> But the anointing which you have received from Him abides in you, and you do not need that anyone teach you; but as the same anointing teaches you concerning all things, and is true, and is not a lie, and just as it has taught you, you will abide in Him (1 John 2:27).

7. Kingly Priesthood

> You also, as living stones, are being built up a spiritual house, a *holy priesthood*, to offer up spiritual sacrifices acceptable to God through Jesus Christ (1 Peter 2:5).

> But you are a chosen generation, *a royal priesthood*, a holy nation, His own special people, that you may proclaim the praises of Him who called you out of darkness into His marvellous light (1 Peter 2:9).

> And has *made us kings and priests* to His God and Father, to Him be glory and dominion forever and ever. Amen (Revelation 1:6).

It is easy to sing and pray, saying we are priests in Christ. But we ought to understand what the Bible says about this matter. It is a privilege and, at the same time, a responsibility.

One of the privileges of the New Testament is that we are granted to be priests and to act as channels between God and people to transfer to them God's blessings and will. This happens through the ministry of prophetic intercession with our High Priest, Jesus, in the Holies to transfer God's life, mind, and blessing to other people.

However, this privilege entails a responsibility as it requires complete consecration to the Lord, as we understand from the following references:

Then Moses stood in the entrance of the camp, and said, "Whoever is on the Lord's side—come to me!" And all the sons of Levi gathered themselves together to him. And he said to them, "Thus says the Lord God of Israel: 'Let every man put his sword on his side, and go in and out from entrance to entrance throughout the camp, and let every man kill his brother, every man his companion, and every man his neighbour.'" So the sons of Levi did according to the word of Moses. And about three thousand men of the people fell that day. Then Moses said, "*Consecrate yourselves today to the Lord, that He may bestow on you a blessing this day, for every man has opposed his son and his brother*" (Exodus 32:26–29).

And He was King in Jeshurun, when the leaders of the people were gathered, all the tribes of Israel together. "Let Reuben live, and not die, nor let his men be few." And this he said of Judah: "Hear, Lord, the voice of Judah, and bring him to his people; let his hands be sufficient for him, and may You be a help against his enemies" (Deuteronomy 33:5–7).

Then the Lord spoke to Moses, saying: "Phinehas the son of Eleazar, the son of Aaron the priest, has turned back My wrath from the children of Israel, because he was zealous with My zeal among them, so that I did not consume the children of Israel in My zeal. Therefore say, 'Behold, I give to him My covenant of peace; and it shall be to him and his descendants after him a covenant of an everlasting priesthood, because he was zealous for his God, and made atonement for the children of Israel'" (Numbers 25:10–13).

"Then you shall know that I have sent this commandment to you, that My covenant with Levi may continue," says the Lord of hosts. "My covenant was with him, one of life and peace, and I gave them to him that he might fear Me; so he feared Me and was reverent before My name. The law of truth was in his mouth, and injustice was not found on his lips. He walked with Me in peace and equity, and turned many away from iniquity" (Malachi 2:4–6).

The tribe of Levi—the priests of the Old Testament and who represent God's mind in general—were not given any earthly portions because the Lord was their portion. This refers to complete consecration to the Lord and being estranged from the world and from all that one can possess in the world.

Two Final Comments

There are two final comments on:

1. A Holy Covenant

2. Wholeheartedness

1. A Holy Covenant

We ought to understand that this covenant with all its privileges is a holy covenant:

> ... to perform the mercy promised to our fathers and to remember His holy covenant, the oath which He swore to our father Abraham: to grant us that we, being *delivered from the hand of our enemies*, might *serve Him* without fear, *in holiness and righteousness* before Him *all the days of our life* (Luke 1:72–75).

Holiness is a great mystery and an attribute of the Person of God. It links between His justice that condemns and His mercy that forgives. It is the main purpose of the covenant.

The main purpose of the covenant is to make us holy and set apart for our Holy God:

> Because it is written, "Be holy, for I am holy" (1 Peter 1:16).

> Speak to all the congregation of the children of Israel, and say to them: 'You shall be holy, for I the Lord your God am holy' (Leviticus 19:2).

> And you shall be holy to Me, for I the Lord am holy, and have separated you from the peoples, that you should be Mine (Leviticus 20:26).

God is the Holy One, who is far from man, because He is a consuming fire and, at the same time, He is the One who desires to come close to man because man is the subject of His delight: *'And my* [My] *delight was with the sons of men'* (Proverbs 8:31).

The covenant is described as the Holy Covenant to link us with God, the Holy. The two parties of the covenant are always God and man. Therefore, holiness is required from us. For this reason, Jesus prayed for us saying: *'Sanctify them by Your truth … that they also may be sanctified by the truth'* (John 17:17, 19).

The results of this are so great, as highlighted in Luke 1:68–75. It causes us to be delivered from the hand of our enemies and to serve Him in holiness and righteousness all the days of our life.

2. Wholeheartedness

Jesus said to him, "You shall love the Lord your God *with all your heart,* with all your soul, and with all your mind" (Matthew 22:37).

The first commandment that was and still is God's desire regarding man is that man would love the Lord with all his heart.

If man failed to do so in the Old Testament, in the New Testament, man is granted the grace and the work of the Holy Spirit that enable him to fulfil this commandment.

Wholeheartedness or *with all the heart* is always the key to entering into God's blessing in general and is the delight of the relationship with Him. Hence, it is also the key to the blessings of this new covenant:

And the Lord your God will circumcise your heart and the heart of your descendants, *to love the Lord your God with all your heart and with all your soul,* that you may live (Deuteronomy 30:6).

Then the king stood by a pillar and made a covenant before the Lord, to follow the Lord and to keep His commandments and His testimonies and His statutes, *with all his heart and all his soul,* to perform the words of this covenant that were written in this book. And all the people took a stand for the covenant (2 Kings 23:3).

Then they entered into a covenant to seek the Lord God of their fathers *with all their heart and with all their soul* (2 Chronicles 15:12).

Then the king stood in his place and made a covenant before the Lord, to follow the Lord, and to keep His commandments and His testimonies and His statutes *with all his heart and all his soul,* to perform the words of the covenant that were written in this book (2 Chronicles 34:31).

Then I will give them a heart to know Me, that I am the Lord; and they shall be My people, and I will be their God, for they shall return to Me *with their whole heart* (Jeremiah 24:7).

And you will seek Me and find Me, when you search for Me *with all your heart* (Jeremiah 29:13).

The amazing thing is that God Himself responds to us with all His heart and His soul:

And I will make an everlasting covenant with them, that I will not turn away from doing them good; but I will put My fear in their hearts so that they will not depart from Me. Yes, I will rejoice over them to do them good, and I will assuredly plant them in this land, *with all My heart and with all My soul* (Jeremiah 32:40–41).

CHAPTER 4

THE BLOOD OF JESUS
HAS RECONCILED ME TO AND
GRANTED ME PEACE WITH GOD THE FATHER,
ALL PEOPLE, AND ALL CREATION

Readings

There are four main references in the New Testament about reconciliation:

For if when we were enemies we were *reconciled to God* through the death of His Son, much more, having been reconciled, we shall be saved by His life (Romans 5:10).

Now all things are of God, who has *reconciled us to Himself* through Jesus Christ, and has given us the *ministry of reconciliation*, that is, that God was in Christ reconciling the world to Himself, not imputing their trespasses to them, and has committed to us the word of reconciliation (2 Corinthians 5:18, 19).

And that He might *reconcile them* both to God in one body through the cross, thereby putting to death the enmity (Ephesians 2:16).

And by Him to *reconcile all things to Himself,* by Him, whether things on earth or things in heaven, having made peace through the blood of His cross (Colossians 1:20).

Introduction

We will discuss this topic in three main sections:

I. The Meaning of the Word *Reconciliation*

II. Theological Considerations

III. A Mystical Revelation

I. The Meaning of the Word *Reconciliation*

A. The Linguistic Meaning

The word *reconcile* means:

1. To restore to friendship or harmony
    To settle and resolve; *reconcile* differences

2. To make consistent or harmonious; *reconcile* an ideal with reality

3. To cause to submit to or accept something unpleasant—*reconciled* to hardship

4. To check (a financial account) against another for accuracy
    To account for, to become *reconciled*

B. The Meaning According to the Hebrew Language of the Old Testament

It is interesting to know that there is no corresponding Hebrew word in the Old Testament. It is the only word in the economy of salvation that is exclusively a New Testament word. Other words in the economy of salvation, such as *redemption, atonement, forgiveness, righteousness,* and *sanctification,* have corresponding Hebrew words.

C. The Meaning According to the Greek Language of the New Testament

According to the Greek language of the New Testament, the word *reconcile* means the following:

*   To re-establish proper friendly interpersonal relations after they have been disrupted or broken; to reconcile; to make things right with one another; reconciliation

- All this is done by God who reconciled us to Himself through Christ:

Now all things are of God, *who has reconciled us to Himself through Jesus Christ,* and has given us the ministry of reconciliation (2 Corinthians 5:18).

- Through Christ, we were reconciled with God:

And not only that, but we also rejoice in God through *our Lord Jesus Christ, through whom we have now received the reconciliation* (Romans 5:11).

- Through Christ, God reconciled the whole world to Himself:

And *by Him to reconcile all things to Himself,* by Him, *whether things on earth or things in heaven,* having made peace through the blood of His cross (Colossians 1:20).

The verse says, *things on earth or things in heaven.* Saying *things on earth* is understandable because we ourselves need to be reconciled to God. But, what about *things in heaven?*

The creatures in heaven are the angels. Do angels need to be reconciled to God?! If God reveals this in His Word, it means He wants us to understand at least something about what is happening in the heavens. God revealed to some fathers and scholars from early centuries a valuable truth in this respect. We will understand it at the end of this topic because we need to move in this revelation step by step.

- To be reconciled to someone, meaning to make peace with that person:

Leave your gift there before the altar, and go your way. First *be reconciled to your brother,* and then come and offer your gift (Matthew 5:24).

- To settle or come to an agreement concerning a dispute or issue

When you go with your adversary to the magistrate, *make every effort along the way to settle with him,* lest he drag you to the judge, the judge deliver you to the officer, and the officer throw you into prison (Luke 12:58).

These words mean to make an effort to come to an agreement with your adversary or settle the issue with him.

- To cause a state of peace or reconciliation between persons; to make peace; to make things right

Making peace or re-establishing peace between persons is a distinctive feature of reconciliation, but the focus is on the resulting state rather than the process itself.

God made things right between Himself and mankind through the death of His Son on the cross (Colossians 1:20).

- A person who restores peace between people (a peacemaker) or someone who works for peace:

Blessed are the peacemakers, for they shall be called sons of God (Matthew 5:9).

Refer also to Colossians 1:20 (quoted above).

There are four important New Testament passages that focus on the reconciliatory work of Christ:

- Romans 5:10

  For if when we were enemies we were reconciled to God through the death of His Son, much more, having been reconciled, we shall be saved by His life.

- 2 Corinthians 5:18

  Now all things are of God, who has reconciled us to Himself through Jesus Christ, and has given us the ministry of reconciliation.

- Ephesians 2:16

  And that He might reconcile them both to God in one body through the cross, thereby putting to death the enmity.

- Colossians 1:19, 20

  For it pleased the Father that in Him all the fullness should dwell, and by Him to reconcile all things to Himself, by Him, whether things on earth or things in heaven, having made peace through the blood of His cross.

Other references in this context include Romans 11:15:

> For if their being cast away is the reconciling of the world, what will their acceptance be but life from the dead?

In all these references, a specific Greek word and its derivatives are used. When the Bible uses a word and its derivatives more than once, this means that there is an emphasis on a specific idea in God's mind that we ought to discover and understand. The Greek words used are the noun *katallagē* and the verbs *katallassō* and *apokatallassō*.

The use of these words means and indicates the following:

- There was an element of enmity; reconciliation puts an end to this enmity.

This indicates that the parties being reconciled were formerly hostile to one another.

Due to his open inner spiritual eyes, Apostle Paul was able to understand the work of the cross from different aspects and perceive that Christ has done something so valuable for us on the cross. Thus, he coined the word *reconciliation* and introduced it in the New Testament because he wanted to convey the idea that we were previously in conflict or enmity with God and that dealing with this enmity is an important element in the Christian life.

Do you know how this enmity is expressed or manifested?

For example, if we preach the gospel to someone and this person says he is not interested in things related to God, this reflects the inner enmity of the person towards God. Even we as believers may have some of this enmity remaining in us. When this enmity is dealt with, we will be able to read the Bible for hours without sensing any boredom, inability, or restriction.

- We were enemies of God (Romans 5:10).

We usually understand this matter in a general way and hence lose the treasures in the Word of God. We understand that we were enemies in the sense that we were sinners. But now we understand that even as believers we need to get rid of any remaining enmity within us in order to have a closer and more intimate fellowship with God. This is the work of reconciliation. Perceiving this truth and living it out can transform our lives.

Apostle Paul highlighted the same idea again in Colossians 1:21:

> And you, *who once were alienated and enemies* in your mind by wicked works, *yet now He has reconciled.*

Repeating the same idea in two different epistles indicates that he wanted to stress it.

Interestingly, it is not only Apostle Paul who mentions this idea of enmity, but also Apostle James refers to it:

> Adulterers and adulteresses! Do you not know that *friendship with the world is enmity with God*? Whoever therefore wants to be a friend of the world makes himself an enemy of God (James 4:4).

The love of the world is enmity with God. Even as believers, we sometimes find ourselves drawn to different things in the world because something within us needs dealing with.

- Christ died to put away our sin:

> He then would have had to suffer often since the foundation of the world; but now, once at the end of the ages, *He has appeared to put away sin* by the sacrifice of Himself (Hebrews 9:26).

Through His death, Christ dealt with the enmity between man and God. He took it out of the way and opened the way for humanity to come back to God. This act is described as *reconciliation*.

- It is interesting to notice that no New Testament passage speaks of Christ as reconciling God to man.

The focus is always on man being reconciled to God. This is important because it highlights that God has no enmity towards man, not even sinners. God is love; He cannot change His nature. It is man's sin that caused the enmity and brought the enmity into us. It is man's sin that must be dealt with. Man needed to be reconciled to God:

> Now then, we are ambassadors for Christ, as though God were pleading through us: we implore you on Christ's behalf, *be reconciled to God* (2 Corinthians 5:20).

- Paul highlighted that through Christ, we received reconciliation:

> And not only that, but we also rejoice in God through our Lord Jesus Christ, *through whom we have now received the reconciliation* (Romans 5:11).

II. Theological Considerations

We will discuss four points pertaining to the theological considerations:

A. Reconciliation With God as Revealed in the New Testament

B. The Two Aspects of Reconciliation

C. Reconciliation, Atonement, Redemption (The Difference Between Them)

D. Reconciliation and Peace

A. Reconciliation With God as Revealed in the New Testament

- **It was prophesied of**

But He was wounded for our transgressions, He was bruised for our iniquities; the chastisement for our peace was upon Him, and by His stripes we are healed (Isaiah 53:5).

- **It was proclaimed by angels at the birth of Christ**

Glory to God in the highest, and on earth peace, goodwill toward men! (Luke 2:14).

- **It was accomplished for man:**

  - By God in Christ

… that is, that *God was in Christ reconciling the world to Himself,* not imputing their trespasses to them, and has committed to us the word of reconciliation (2 Corinthians 5:19).

  - By the death of Christ (Romans 5:10; Ephesians 2:16)

And you, who once were alienated and enemies in your mind by wicked works, yet now *He has reconciled* in the body of His flesh *through death,* to present you holy, and blameless, and above reproach in His sight (Colossians 1:21, 22).

♦ By the blood of Christ

But now in Christ Jesus you who once were far off have been brought near *by the blood of Christ* (Ephesians 2:13).

Refer also to Colossians 1:20 (quoted earlier).

♦ While he was alienated from God (Colossians 1:21)

♦ While he was an enemy of God (Romans 5:10)

- **God gave us the ministry of reconciliation**

Now all things are of God, *who has reconciled us to Himself through Jesus Christ, and has given us the ministry of reconciliation,* that is, that God was in Christ reconciling the world to Himself, not imputing their trespasses to them, and has committed to us the word of reconciliation. Now then, we are ambassadors for Christ, as though God were pleading through us: we implore you on Christ's behalf, be reconciled to God (2 Corinthians 5:18–20).

- **The results/fruits of the reconciliation with God are:**

♦ Peace with God

Therefore, having been justified by faith, *we have peace with God* through our Lord Jesus Christ (Romans 5:1).

And that He might reconcile them both to God in one body through the cross, thereby putting to death the enmity. And *He came and preached peace to you* who were afar off and to those who were near (Ephesians 2:16, 17).

♦ Access to God

Through whom also we have access by faith into this grace in which we stand, and rejoice in hope of the glory of God (Romans 5:2).

For *through Him we both have access* by one Spirit to the Father (Ephesians 2:18).

♦ The joining together of Jews and Gentiles

For He Himself is our peace, who has made both one, and has broken down the middle wall of separation (Ephesians 2:14).

♦ The joining together of things in heaven and on earth

And by Him to reconcile all things to Himself, by Him, *whether things on earth or things in heaven,* having made peace through the blood of His cross (Colossians 1:20).

That in the dispensation of the fullness of the times He might gather together in one all things in Christ, *both which are in heaven and which are on earth—* in Him (Ephesians 1:10).

Thus, the message of the Scripture is that we are reconciled to God by the death of His Son, His cross, and the blood of Jesus.

B. The Two Aspects of Reconciliation

Reconciliation has two aspects:

• The first aspect is related to God

Christ's death removed the enmity that existed between God and man and that had caused a barrier in their fellowship. Thus, the way was opened for reconciliation:

Having *abolished in His flesh the enmity,* that is, the law of commandments contained in ordinances, so as to create in Himself one new man from the two, thus making peace (Ephesians 2:15).

This is only one aspect of reconciliation. But for this reconciliation to happen, man needs to receive it. He needs to understand this truth and exercise his faith. Therefore,

• The second aspect is related to man

This aspect is reflected in the change of man's attitude toward God. This change occurs in man's heart through a vision of the cross of Christ. Thus, a change from enmity to friendship takes place:

Now then, we are ambassadors for Christ, as though God were pleading through us: we implore you on Christ's behalf, be reconciled to God (2 Corinthians 5:20).

Through these two aspects, reconciliation is completed.

C. Reconciliation, Atonement, Redemption

Redemption indicates that the cross of Christ has dealt with our condition of slavery to sin, while *reconciliation* indicates that our hostility towards God has been changed.

Romans 5:6–11 describes our alienation from God and that we were enemies of God (verse 10):

For while we were still weak, at the right time Christ died for the ungodly. For one will scarcely die for a righteous person—though perhaps for a good person one would dare even to die—but God shows his love for us in that while we were still sinners, Christ died for us. Since, therefore, we have now been justified by his blood, much more shall we be saved by him from the wrath of God. *For if while we were enemies we were reconciled to God by the death of his Son,* much more, now that we are reconciled, shall we be saved by his life. More than that, we also rejoice in God through our Lord Jesus Christ, through whom we have now received reconciliation (Romans 5:6–11, ESV).

Though we were enemies of God due to sin, He was the One who sought us and took the initiative towards us so that we may receive reconciliation.

In 2 Corinthians 5:20, Apostle Paul highlights that it is as though God pleads through him to implore them to *'be reconciled to God'*.

Christ's death on the cross granted us redemption, atonement, and reconciliation. However, these salvific acts become activated in our lives when we practise our faith.

A brief word about the connection of these three salvific acts to our lives before we come to Christ and receive the faith:

- *Redemption* highlights the aspects of the work of the cross that deliver us from our misery resulting from sin, our slavery, and our hopelessness.

- *Atonement* indicates that outside Christ, we face judgement and destruction.

- *Reconciliation* indicates that we were in a state of hostility towards God, meaning we hated God and the divine matters.

Grace operates through these salvific acts to deal with these problems of the fallen humanity.

D. Reconciliation and Peace

The emphasis of *reconciliation* is on making peace with God. Through reconciliation, man, who was estranged from God, is brought into communion with God.

Sin created a barrier between man and God and rendered man hostile towards God:

> Behold, the Lord's hand is not shortened, that it cannot save; nor His ear heavy, that it cannot hear. But your iniquities have separated you from your God; and your sins have hidden His face from you, so that He will not hear (Isaiah 59:1, 2).

Refer also to Colossians 1:21, 22; James 4:4 (quoted earlier).

Through Christ, this enmity with God was removed (Romans 5:10).

Reconciliation may thus be defined as *God removing the barrier of sin, producing peace, and enabling man to be saved.*

There is an objective and a subjective aspect to reconciliation:

The objective aspect of reconciliation is that in which man is reconciled to God before receiving the faith and man is rendered savable. This is *provided reconciliation*, meaning it has already been granted to us, yet we need to receive it by faith (2 Corinthians 5:18, 19).

The subjective aspect of reconciliation is that in which man is reconciled to God when he believes (2 Corinthians 5:18b, 19b). This is *experiential reconciliation*.

The word *reconciliation* comes from the Greek word *katallassō* which means *to effect a change; to reconcile.*

God is the one who initiated this change or reconciliation; He took the initiative to reconcile sinful man to Himself (2 Corinthians 5:18, 19). On the other hand, man is the object of reconciliation. It was man who had moved out of fellowship with God; therefore, man needed to be restored. This reconciliation has been provided for the whole world, but it is effective only when it is received through personal faith.

Reconciliation is *manward*, meaning directed to humanity. Man was the one who had moved out of fellowship with God because of sin, and man needed to be reconciled to renew this fellowship.

III. A Mystical Revelation

Now we come to the mystical revelation related to what happened in the heavens and how we can be reconciled to creation, not only to God and to each other.

In Colossians 1:15–20, we read:

> He is the image of the invisible God, *the firstborn over all creation*. For by Him all things were created that are in heaven and that are on earth, visible and invisible, whether thrones or dominions or principalities or powers. All things were created through Him and for Him. And He is before all things, and in Him all things consist. And He is *the head of the body, the church*, who is the beginning, the firstborn from the dead, that in all things He may have the preeminence. For it pleased the Father that in Him all the fullness should dwell, and by Him to reconcile all things to Himself, by Him, *whether things on earth or things in heaven*, having made peace through the blood of His cross (Colossians 1:15–20).

Apostle Paul is saying here that Christ is the firstborn of creation; He is above creation. At the same time, He is the head of the Church, the believers. Therefore, He did not only accomplish reconciliation between us and God, but also between us and creation.

In the original Greek language, the word *creation* means *the whole universe*, and it includes even the non-rational creation.

The passage in Romans 8:19–21 helps us see the link in this respect:

> For the earnest expectation of the creation eagerly waits for the revealing of the sons of God. For the creation was subjected to futility, not willingly, but because of Him who subjected it in hope; because the creation itself also will be delivered from the bondage of corruption into the glorious liberty of the children of God.

These verses highlight that the land submits to the redeemed who live their full calling in Christ, hence the land becomes no longer bound by the old curse and bears manifold fruits. This has happened and is still happening in many generations and there are historical proofs for this.

Also, due to the manifestation of redemption, wild beasts are rid of their beastly nature and befriend man. Remember that Jesus Himself was with wild beasts in the wilderness and they did not harm Him:

> And He was there in the wilderness forty days, tempted by Satan, and *was with the wild beasts*; and the angels ministered to Him (Mark 1:13).

When the redeemed people of God live their calling in its fullness, God's blessing does not only extend to human beings but also to the non-rational creation (animals, lands, etc.).

Not only did reconciliation take place between heaven and earth, as highlighted in Colossians 1:20, but according to some scholars, verse 20 implies that reconciliation also took place in heaven between heaven dwellers as a fruit of the crucifixion and redemption.

What could this reconciliation look like, and how did it happen?

We may not be able to have a complete understanding of this matter, but, some scholars and fathers of the Church who were given revelations and saw visions, said:

When the angels saw the astounding humility of God in His incarnation, they completely got rid of the effects of the fall of Satan and his angels. This matter had shaken the heavenly hosts, mainly because of the pride of the fallen devil.

The Bible highlights that the fall of Satan was due to pride. In the books of Isaiah and Ezekiel, we read the following about the fall of the cherub, who became Satan:

> How you are fallen from heaven, O Lucifer, son of the morning! How you are cut down to the ground, you who weakened the nations! For you have said in your heart: 'I will ascend into heaven, I will exalt my throne above the stars

of God; I will also sit on the mount of the congregation on the farthest sides of the north; I will ascend above the heights of the clouds, I will be like the Most High.' Yet you shall be brought down to Sheol, to the lowest depths of the Pit (Isaiah 14:12–15).

You were the anointed cherub who covers; I established you; you were on the holy mountain of God; you walked back and forth in the midst of fiery stones … Your heart was lifted up because of your beauty; you corrupted your wisdom for the sake of your splendour; I cast you to the ground, I laid you before kings, that they might gaze at you (Ezekiel 28:14, 17).

Satan and his angels who fell constituted one-third of the heavenly hosts. This was not an easy situation. It created a bad atmosphere in heaven at that time. But when the angels saw the astounding humility of the Son in His incarnation, His self-denial, and His self-emptying, the angels became settled and stood firm in their places and ministry.

St. Ephrem the Syrian (4ᵗʰ century) wrote the following poetic verses in this context:

Today is your day[14]

The day when all the powers of heaven

Were protected from that illness

That the ugly one Lucifer, who loved God's power,

Introduced pride to heavenly ranks

It came from his love

But it was love without wisdom

It was the love of power

Love to be like God without God

Refrain: Blessed be the One who took off His glory to reveal His love

---

[14] The reference here is to the Day of Incarnation.

One-third of the powers followed him

They all fell into darkness

That darkness where there is light

But only for those who love the light

'In God,' says that apostle, 'there is no darkness'

But with pride comes blindness

And Light cannot be received

Refrain: Blessed be the One who took off His glory to reveal His love

What is light? It is love

What is love? It is life

What is life? It is God

Do not ask what is God

This was a question that Lucifer tried to answer

He saw power before love

He loved what he saw

He did not share his vision

For if he did, God would have told him

That he does not covet anything because He is good

Refrain: Blessed be the One who took off His glory to reveal His love

Today, Lord, you established those who chose light

You made your abode in the womb of Mary

What confusion has taken place in heaven

When all looked at Your throne and saw it empty

There was the Father and the Holy Spirit

Where is the Logos, the Choir-Master

Of the heavenly powers?

He is not on His throne

He cannot be seen on earth

Yet, His light still fills all

Becoming unknown seems strange

When He nods the hymns and melody come

Where is He now?

Refrain: Blessed be the One who took off His glory to reveal His love

The Father and the Holy Spirit pointed to the earth

There, no one could see

The glory was hidden

Love had put it aside

The angels saw Him not before in that form

They worshipped Him before that wonderful day

Now they asked "Who is this Son of Man;

How can we worship Him?"

We see in Him what we have not seen before

Love and humility which are alien to humans

The Holy Spirit inspired them

They fell down and worshipped Him

The Father pointed not with His hand but by His pleasure

They all sang to Jesus' love

Today is the day on which all forms of separation came to an end.[15]

Amen

---

[15] Ephrem the Syrian. *The First Day of the Incarnation of the Son of God: Ephrem the Syrian* (G. H. Bebawi, Trans.).

CHAPTER 5

THE BLOOD OF JESUS
HAS GRANTED ME
FORGIVENESS OF ALL MY SINS

Readings

In Him we have redemption through His blood, *the forgiveness of sins, according to the riches of His grace* (Ephesians 1:7).

In whom we have redemption through His blood, *the forgiveness of sins* (Colossians 1:14).

Introduction

What is forgiveness?

It is the kiss on the traitor's brow.

It is the tender look across the courtyard at erring Peter.

It is the strong promise spoken to the dying thief.

It is the healing touch.

It is the cancelling of debt—remission or releasing an obligation.

In order to fully understand this great biblical revelation, we need to study the biblical topic of forgiveness.

We will discuss this topic in five main sections:

   I.　The Meaning of the Word *Forgiveness*

  II.　Theological and Biblical Deductions Related to Forgiveness

 III.　Comments on Biblical Passages Related to the Theme of Forgiveness

 IV.　The Christian Experience of Forgiveness

  V.　Forgiving One Another

I. The Meaning of the Word *Forgiveness*

A. The Linguistic Meaning

Forgiveness as a noun refers to the act of forgiving.

Forgiving as an adjective means:

1. Willing or able to forgive
2. Allowing room for error or weakness

B. The Meaning According to the Hebrew Language of the Old Testament

1. In the Old Testament, the idea of forgiveness is mainly conveyed by words from *three roots:*

- kāp̄ar/kaw-far/

This word is close to the English word *cover* and it means putting a cover on sins. It usually carries the idea of atonement and is frequently used in connection with sacrifices. Its use for *forgive* implies that atonement is made.

- The verb *nś* (nasa)

It basically means *lift* and *carry*. It presents a vivid picture of sin being lifted from the sinner and carried away.

- The root *slḥ* (salach)

It occurs about 45 times in the Old Testament. It is of unknown derivation, but it corresponds in use pretty closely to the word *forgive* that we know.

The first and the last are always used to refer to *God's forgiveness*, but *nś* is used to refer to *human forgiveness* as well.

When forgiveness is granted, it ought to be received with gratitude and regarded with awe and wonder. Sin deserves punishment. Pardon is an astounding grace. Forgiveness, then, is possible only because God is a God of grace, and a God ready to pardon, as Nehemiah says:

> They refused to obey, and they were not mindful of Your wonders that You did among them. But they hardened their necks, and in their rebellion they appointed a leader to return to their bondage. But *You are God, ready to pardon, gracious and merciful*, slow to anger, abundant in kindness, and did not forsake them (Nehemiah 9:17).

Also, in Daniel 9:9, we read:

> *To the Lord our God belong mercy and forgiveness*, though we have rebelled against Him.

The passage in Exodus 34 reveals the whole Old Testament's understanding of forgiveness:

> The Lord, the Lord God, merciful and gracious, longsuffering, and abounding in goodness and truth, keeping mercy for thousands, *forgiving iniquity and transgression and sin*, by no means clearing the guilty (Exodus 34:6, 7).

God said these words to Moses when he was on the mountain the second time.

Moses was first with God on the mountain for forty days, receiving the law. The law was very strict—if one sins, he dies. Moses was in tune with God; thus, he was able to perceive that God is just, and he perceived the value of justice. He agreed with every word he received from God in the law. Then, he went down the mountain, saw the people of Israel worshipping the calf, and he broke the tablets of the law. After that, he went up the mountain again for another forty days, during which God came to him saying these words.

He expected God to say a word of judgement on the people because he had understood from the law that sin meant death. However, to his surprise, the Lord said, *'The Lord, the Lord God, merciful and gracious, longsuffering ...'*

This was the first time for God to speak about Himself as merciful. Moses was shaken because he knew God as the just God, so how could He be merciful even in such a situation?! Thus, a new measure of understanding about God came to him—new width, new depth, and new light came into his spirit. The light that was received and perceived in his spirit reflected on his face; thus, his face was shining when he came down from the mountain. This can happen to us as well. When we receive a new light in our spirits, it ought to be reflected on our faces.

Forgiveness is rooted in the nature of God as gracious. But it requires repentance from the sinner. Penitent sinners are forgiven. Impenitent men, who continue in their wicked way, are not forgiven.

2. The concept of pardon and forgiveness is conveyed through other imagery (not only through the use of the three basic words for forgiveness):

The Psalmist tells us that *'as far as the east is from the west, so far has He removed our transgressions from us'* (Psalm 103:12).

This description indicates that our transgressions will never be seen again.

Isaiah speaks of God as casting all the prophet's sins behind His back and as *blotting out* the people's transgressions:

Indeed it was for my own peace that I had great bitterness; but You have lovingly delivered my soul from the pit of corruption, for *You have cast all my sins behind Your back* (Isaiah 38:17).

I, even I, *am He who blots out your transgressions* for My own sake; and I will not remember your sins (Isaiah 43:25).

The Psalmist also asks God to blot out his transgressions:

Have mercy upon me, O God, according to Your lovingkindness; according to the multitude of Your tender mercies, *blot out my transgressions* ... Hide Your face from my sins, and blot out all my iniquities (Psalm 51:1, 9).

In Jeremiah 31, the Lord says, *I will remember their sin no more*:

> No more shall every man teach his neighbour, and every man his brother, saying, 'Know the Lord,' for they all shall know Me, from the least of them to the greatest of them, says the Lord. For I will forgive their iniquity, *and their sin I will remember no more* (Jeremiah 31:34).

Sometimes, we remember the sins and wounds caused to us by others, but God does not remember our sins.

Micah speaks of God as casting all our sins *into the depths of the sea*:

> Who is a God like You, pardoning iniquity and passing over the transgression of the remnant of His heritage? He does not retain His anger forever, because He delights in mercy. He will again have compassion on us, and will subdue our iniquities. *You will cast all our sins into the depths of the sea* (Micah 7:18, 19).

Such vivid language emphasises the completeness of God's forgiveness. When He forgives, men's sins are dealt with thoroughly. God sees them no more.

C. The Meaning According to the Greek Language of the New Testament

In the New Testament there are two main verbs to consider:

- *Charizomai*

It means *to deal graciously with*.

- *Aphiēi*

It means *to send away; to loose*. The noun *aphesis*, which means *remission*, is also frequently used.

There are also two other words:

- *Apolyō*

It means *to release* and is used in Luke 6:37:

> Forgive, and you will be forgiven.

- *Paresis*

It means *letting go* and is used in Romans 3:25 of God's passing over of sins committed in earlier days:

> Whom God set forth as a propitiation by His blood, through faith, to demonstrate His righteousness, because *in His forbearance God had passed over the sins that were previously committed.*

Based on these meanings, several important points are revealed in the New Testament regarding forgiveness:

- The forgiven sinner must forgive others.

A readiness to forgive others is part of the indication that we have truly repented. Forgiving others ought to be wholehearted. It springs from Christ's forgiveness towards us; thus, it ought to be like Christ's forgiveness, as we read in Colossians 3:13: *'As the Lord has forgiven you, so you also must forgive'* (ESV).

Christ emphasised this principle several times. For example, He highlighted this idea in His parable of the unmerciful servant mentioned in Matthew 18:23–35.

- Forgiveness is not often linked directly with the cross, though sometimes it is, as in Ephesians 1:7:

> In Him we have *redemption through His blood, the forgiveness of sins*, according to the riches of His grace.

Similarly, in Matthew 26, we read that Christ's blood was shed *for many for the forgiveness of sins:*

For this is My blood of the covenant, which is poured out for many *for the forgiveness of sins* (Matthew 26:28, ESV).

- It is more usual to find forgiveness directly linked with Christ Himself:

And be kind to one another, tenderhearted, *forgiving one another, even as God in Christ forgave you* (Ephesians 4:32).

Him God has exalted to His right hand to be Prince and Saviour, to give repentance to Israel and forgiveness of sins (Acts 5:31).

Therefore let it be known to you, brethren, that through this Man *is preached to you the forgiveness of sins* (Acts 13:38).

- We should add to these passages the other passages where Jesus, during the days of His incarnation, declared that men were forgiven.

In the incident of the healing of the paralysed man lowered through the roof, Jesus performed the miracle and then said: *'that you may know that the Son of Man has power on earth to forgive sins'* (Mark 2:10).

However, we should not separate the Person of Christ from His work. Forgiveness, by or through Jesus Christ, means *forgiveness arising from all that He is and all that He does.*

Therefore, Jesus sometimes proclaimed forgiveness in His ministry—a matter that may cause some to wonder if forgiveness was separate from the cross since Christ had not yet been crucified when He proclaimed forgiveness in His ministry. However, as we mentioned here, the Person of Christ should not be separated from His work. Therefore, what He said was related to what He was to complete on the cross.

- Forgiveness is based on the atoning work of Christ, meaning it is an act of sheer grace:

He is faithful and just to forgive us our sins (1 John 1:9).

- On man's side, repentance is insisted upon again and again.

John the Baptist preached *'a baptism of repentance for the forgiveness of sins'* (Mark 1:4, ESV).

Apostle Peter highlights the same theme of repentance when referring to Christian baptism:

> Then Peter said to them, "Repent, and let every one of you be baptised in the name of Jesus Christ for the remission of sins; and you shall receive the gift of the Holy Spirit" (Acts 2:38).

Christ Himself directed that *'repentance and forgiveness of sins should be preached in His name'* (Luke 24:47, RSV).

- Forgiveness is similarly linked with faith.[16]

> To Him all the prophets witness that, through His name, *whoever believes in Him will receive remission of sins* (Acts 10:43).

> And *the prayer of faith* will save the sick, and the Lord will raise him up. And if he has committed sins, he will be forgiven (James 5:15).

We should not think that *faith* and *repentance* are merits by which we deserve forgiveness, but they are only means by which we receive the grace of God.

- Two difficulties must be mentioned here:

  - One of these difficulties is regarding the sin against the Holy Spirit, which can never be forgiven, as we read in the following references:

> Therefore I say to you, every sin and blasphemy will be forgiven men, *but the blasphemy against the Spirit will not be forgiven men* (Matthew 12:31).

> Assuredly, I say to you, all sins will be forgiven the sons of men, and whatever blasphemies they may utter; *but he who blasphemes against the Holy Spirit never has forgiveness*, but is subject to eternal condemnation (Mark 3:28–29).

---

[16] Forgiveness is linked with both repentance and faith.

And anyone who speaks a word against the Son of Man, it will be forgiven him; *but to him who blasphemes against the Holy Spirit, it will not be forgiven* (Luke 12:10).

If anyone sees his brother sinning a sin which does not lead to death, he will ask, and He will give him life for those who commit sin not leading to death. There is sin leading to death. I do not say that he should pray about that (1 John 5:16).

This sin is never defined or specified. But in the light of the New Testament teaching, it is impossible to think of it as any specific act of sin. The reference is rather to the continual blasphemy against the Spirit of God by one who consistently rejects God's gracious call. This is blasphemy indeed.

- The other difficulty is regarding the words written in John 20:23:

If you forgive the sins of *any*, they are forgiven.

It is difficult to think that Christ left in men's hands the determination of whether the sins of other men are to be forgiven or not. However, noting the following points will help us better understand the meaning of this verse:

♦ The plural form: the word *any* is plural in the Greek origin; it points to categories, not to individuals.

♦ The perfect tense: The phrase *are forgiven* means *have been forgiven*, not *will be forgiven*.

Thus, according to the original Greek language, the verse means: you can proclaim the forgiveness of those whose sins have already been forgiven. In other words, this verse is related to discernment. Sometimes new believers cannot discern and need to be assured that their sins are forgiven. Therefore, the servant of God ought to be sensitive in the spirit and discern that this person has repented and has been forgiven, and then reassure that person that he has been forgiven.

Accordingly, the meaning of the verse is:

Since the followers of Jesus are inspired by the Holy Spirit (as highlighted in the previous verse, verse 22), they will be able to say with accuracy which categories of men have sins forgiven and which do not.[17]

Important notes regarding New Testament Greek which will help us understand God's mind regarding forgiveness:

- The event of wrongdoing is not undone, but the guilt resulting from such an event is pardoned.

To forgive, therefore, means essentially *to remove the guilt* resulting from wrongdoing.

And forgive us our debts, as we forgive our debtors (Matthew 6:12).

Judge not, and you shall not be judged. Condemn not, and you shall not be condemned. Forgive, and you will be forgiven (Luke 6:37).

Therefore, *to forgive sins* is literally *to forgive guilt and penalty*.

Though terms used to refer to *forgiveness* often literally mean *to wipe away*, *to blot out*, or *to do away with*, it is obviously not possible to blot out or to wipe away an event, but it is possible to remove or erase the associated guilt and penalty, meaning setting the person free in his relationship with God. Despite this, the person may sometimes have to be judged by the law of his country in the case of crimes of stealing, murder, and the like.

- The focus is sometimes on the means by which forgiveness is accomplished:

Therefore, in all things He had to be made like His brethren, that He might be a merciful and faithful High Priest in things pertaining to God, to make propitiation for the sins of the people (Hebrews 2:17).

---

[17] Marshall, I. Howard; Millard, A.R.; Packer, J. I.; & Wiseman, D.J. (editors). *New Bible Dictionary*. (3rd ed.). 1996.

- Sometimes the focus is on *the basis of one's gracious attitude* toward an individual:

  For what is it in which you were inferior to other churches, except that I myself was not burdensome to you? Forgive me this wrong! (2 Corinthians 12:13).

The point is that after I ask forgiveness, the other person needs to release forgiveness, saying, "I forgive you" or "I release forgiveness to you." This is what this verse says.

- At other times the focus is upon *the means by which sins are forgiven*. Christ Himself is the means by which our sins are forgiven:

  And He Himself is the propitiation for our sins, and not for ours only but also for the whole world (1 John 2:2).

- Sometimes the focus is on *the location or place where sins are forgiven* (the term *mercy seat* is sometimes used):

  And above it were the cherubim of glory *overshadowing the mercy seat*. Of these things we cannot now speak in detail (Hebrews 9:5).

II. Theological and Biblical Deductions Related to Forgiveness

- **Forgiveness in the Scriptures is not cheap:**

And according to the law almost all things are purified with blood, and *without shedding of blood there is no remission* (Hebrews 9:22).

This verse reveals an eternal and unchanging law of the universe:

Without the shedding of blood there is no remission, meaning there is no forgiveness.

Therefore, forgiveness is not cheap as it involves the shedding of blood.

- **Christ shed His blood for the remission of sins:**

For this is My blood of the new covenant, which is *shed for many for the remission of sins* (Matthew 26:28).

- **All who trust in Him as the Lamb of God are forgiven all trespasses— past, present, and future:**

And you, being dead in your trespasses and the uncircumcision of your flesh, He has made alive together with Him, having forgiven you all trespasses (Colossians 2:13).

I write to you, little children, because your sins are forgiven you for His name's sake (1 John 2:12).

- **Everyone who trusts in Him is delivered from all condemnation forever:**

Most assuredly, I say to you, he who hears My word and believes in Him who sent Me has everlasting life, and shall not come into judgement, but has passed from death into life (John 5:24).

- Thus, *forgiveness solves the problem of sin in the believer's life* (this includes all sins past, present, and future):

Having forgiven you *all trespasses* (Colossians 2:13).

This is different from the daily cleansing from sin that is necessary to maintain fellowship with God:

If we confess our sins, He is faithful and just to forgive us our sins and to cleanse us from all unrighteousness (1 John 1:9).

- The principles of forgiveness in the New Testament insist not only on penitence as a condition for forgiveness (2 Corinthians 7:10) but also on *the need to forgive others* (Matthew 6:14, 15).

If the person who receives forgiveness does not forgive others, this is a clear sign that his repentance is not complete.

Several times in His parables the Lord insists that the readiness to forgive others is a sign of true repentance (Luke 6:37; Matthew 18:23–35).

Christ taught that to forgive is a duty, and no limits can be set on it. It must be granted without reservation, even to 70 times 7:

Then Peter came to Him and said, "Lord, how often shall my brother sin against me, and I forgive him? Up to seven times?" Jesus said to him, "I do not say to you, up to seven times, but up to seventy times seven" (Matthew 18:21, 22).

Forgiveness is part of the mutual relationship of believers. Since all are dependent upon God's forgiveness, all are required to forgive one another (Colossians 3:13).

- In every act of forgiveness, there is *a commissioning to new tasks.*

Biblical examples include:

- David: His new commissioning was to teach transgressors (Psalm 51:13)

- Isaiah: He received a new mission (Isaiah 6:8)

- Peter: He was commissioned to feed His sheep (John 21:17)

- Paul: He was called a chosen vessel for the Gentiles (Acts 9:15)

- **Repentance releases forgiveness, but regret is of no value.**

Peter repented, while Judas regretted.

- Judas:

Then Judas, His betrayer, seeing that He had been condemned, was remorseful and brought back the thirty pieces of silver to the chief priests and elders, saying, "I have sinned by betraying innocent blood." And they said, "What is that to us? You see to it!" (Matthew 27:3, 4).

- Esau regretted but did not repent:

Lest there be any fornicator or profane person like Esau, who for one morsel of food sold his birthright. For you know that afterward, when he wanted to inherit the blessing, he was rejected, for he found no place for repentance, though he sought it diligently with tears (Hebrews 12:16, 17).

III. Comments on Biblical Passages Related to the Theme of Forgiveness

- **Ephesians 1:7 and Colossians 1:14**

    In Him we have redemption through His blood, the forgiveness of sins, *according to the riches of His grace* (Ephesians 1:7).

    In whom we have redemption through His blood, the forgiveness of sins (Colossians 1:14).

Forgiveness is *according to the riches of His grace.*

The phrase *according* to is the translation of *kata* in Greek, which is a preposition that has the idea of *down*. The word *down* indicates *domination*. The word *domination* indicates *control*. Therefore, the degree of this forgiveness is controlled and dominated by the riches. In other words, the forgiveness that is released is controlled and dominated by the riches of grace.

Riches is the translation of the Greek word *ploutos*, which means *wealth, abundance, and plenitude of God's grace.*

God wants to give us abundant grace to deal with every sin and to ensure complete forgiveness.

Therefore, forgiveness is complete, unqualified, and unchanging, for it is controlled by the plenitude of God's grace, and that plenitude is infinite in proportion.

From the comments of expositors in this context, we quote the following:[18]

'The freeness of this divine favour in the form of grace, the unmerited nature of the divine goodness, is what Paul most frequently magnifies with praise and wonder.

---

[18] Wuest, K. S. (1973). *Wuest's Word Studies from the Greek New Testament: For the English Reader* (Vol. 1). Wm. B. Eerdmans Publishing. (Comments on Ephesians 1:7).

Here, it is the mighty measure of the largesse, the grace in its quality of riches, which is introduced.

This magnificent conception of the wealth of the grace that is bestowed on us by God and that which is in Christ for us, is a peculiarly Pauline idea.'

- **Matthew 18:18**

  Assuredly, I say to you, whatever you bind on earth will be bound in heaven, and whatever you loose on earth will be loosed in heaven.

Believers often apply this verse incorrectly. Some pray, saying, "Lord, You said that whatever we bind on earth will be bound in heaven; therefore, in Your name, we bind this and that."

In fact, some scholars suggest another understanding of this verse based on the old languages. Accordingly, the verse reads:

I say to you, what is already bound in heaven, you can bind on earth, and then it will be bound in heaven.

In other words, it means:

You can bind on earth the things that are already bound in heaven. Then, if you bind them on earth, they will be bound in heaven.

Some may ask: If these things are already bound in heaven, why do we need to bind them on earth?

In fact, these are the dynamics of heaven and earth. When something is bound in heaven, this means it is bound in God's mind; it is bound according to His will but not yet in action. God still needs a person living on earth to actualise it on earth, meaning to proclaim it by faith based on perceiving and discerning that it is God's mind. Then, heaven will turn it into action. As a result, it will no longer only be an idea in God's mind and a will in His heart, but it will also be an action.

It happens in this way because as clear in the Bible, God gave earth to man. In Genesis 2, God said to Adam to tend the land and God gave him authority over the land. In Psalm 115:16, it is written: *'The heaven, even the heavens, are the Lord's; but the earth He has given to the children of men.'* When God says something, He does not take it back. He said to man that earth belongs to him and He sticks to His word. Therefore, when He wants to do something on earth, He goes through man. Of course, He still can do what He wants at any time, but doing it this way pleases Him. He wants His Church to exercise by faith what is in His mind. Therefore, His Church ought first to discern what is in His mind.

The use of the words *binding* and *loosing* in the New Testament:

- Binding and loosing (Aramaic: *'ᵃsar* and *šᵉrā'*; Greek: *deō* and *lyō*)

These are rabbinic terms used in Matthew 16:19 to refer to Peter's authority to declare things forbidden or permitted and used in Matthew 18:18 to refer to the disciples' disciplinary authority to condemn or absolve. The disciplinary authority differs from personal rabbinic power in being inseparable from the gospel proclaimed.

  - *Deō*, meaning *to bind*, when used alone, is used symbolically:

    ♦ To refer to the bond of marriage

But this I say, brethren, the time is short, so that from now on even those who have wives should be as though they had none (1 Corinthians 7:29).

    ♦ To refer to legal ties

For the woman who has a husband *is bound* by the law to her husband as long as he lives. But if the husband dies, she is released from the law of her husband (Romans 7:2).

    ♦ To refer to Paul's service

And see, now I go *bound* in the spirit to Jerusalem, not knowing the things that will happen to me there (Acts 20:22).

- *Lyō*, meaning *to loosen and unbind*, when used alone, is used:

  ◆ To refer to laws being relaxed

  Whoever therefore breaks one of the least of these commandments, and teaches men so, shall be called least in the kingdom of heaven; but whoever does and teaches them, he shall be called great in the kingdom of heaven (Matthew 5:19).

  ◆ To refer to sins being forgiven

  And from Jesus Christ, the faithful witness, the firstborn from the dead, and the ruler over the kings of the earth. To Him who loved us and washed us from our sins in His own blood (Revelation 1:5).

  ◆ To refer to deliverance[19]

  So ought not this woman, being a daughter of Abraham, whom Satan has bound—think of it—for eighteen years, *be loosed from* this bond on the Sabbath? (Luke 13:16).

• Jesus referred to binding and loosing on two different occasions:

  - After Peter's confession that Jesus was the Messiah, Jesus said to him:

    And I will give you the keys of the kingdom of heaven, and whatever you bind on earth will be bound in heaven, and whatever you loose on earth will be loosed in heaven (Matthew 16:19).

  - Later, Jesus gave the same authority to bind and loose to all of the disciples (Matthew 18:18).

Matthew is the only Gospel writer to record those specific words of Jesus.

According to the Gospel of John, Jesus addressed similar but not identical words to the disciples after the resurrection:

If you forgive the sins of any, they are forgiven them; if you retain the sins of any, they are retained (John 20:23).

---

[19] Marshall, I. Howard; Millard, A.R.; Packer, J. I.; & Wiseman, D.J. (editors). *New Bible Dictionary.* (3rd ed.). 1996.

- A problem arises in identifying both the nature and the extent of the authority Jesus gave in binding and loosing.

Bind and *loose* are the translations of two Greek words which are themselves translations of words in Aramaic, the language spoken by Jesus.

In the days of Jesus, the Jews used the two Aramaic words as technical rabbinic terms. They referred to the verdict of a teacher of the Law who, on the basis of his authority as an expert in the interpretation of the Mosaic Law, could declare some action *bound* (meaning forbidden) or *loosed* (meaning permitted).

Compare with Matthew 23:2–3, where Jesus said:

> The scribes and the Pharisees sit in Moses' seat. Therefore whatever they tell you to observe, that observe and do, but do not do according to their works; for they say, and do not do.

In addition to that, the two terms were also used in judicial contexts. They referred to the imposition or the removal of a ban or judgement. In that context, the words meant *to condemn or imprison* and *to absolve or set free*. Both sets of meanings have been used to interpret the two texts in Matthew.

The precise meaning of the words in Matthew must be understood on the basis of their use in specific situations and in the light of the general New Testament understanding of apostolic authority.

In Matthew 16:19, Peter's authority to bind and loose is connected with his receiving *the keys of the Kingdom of heaven.*

In the Gospels, the Kingdom of heaven or the Kingdom of God is the sphere of God's rule—the community of people whom He rules as Lord. In a figurative sense, Peter was entrusted with the keys to that kingdom— that *building* which belongs to God. (See 1 Corinthians 3:9, 16–17; Ephesians 2:20–22; and 1 Peter 2:4–5 for the idea of the people of God being His building.)

The keys symbolise the authority entrusted to Peter as the one who confesses Jesus as Lord (Matthew 16:16), and as the one who represents all those disciples who utter the same confession.

According to Matthew 23:13 and Luke 11:52, the scribes were understood to be guardians of the Kingdom, since the knowledge of God had been entrusted to them:

> But woe to you, scribes and Pharisees, hypocrites! For you shut up the Kingdom of heaven against men; for you neither go in yourselves, nor do you allow those who are entering to go in (Matthew 23:13).

> Woe to you lawyers! For you have taken away the key of knowledge. You did not enter in yourselves, and those who were entering in you hindered (Luke 11:52).

But they did not fulfil the commission entrusted to them; they shut the doors of the Kingdom. Therefore, their task was transferred to Peter, the spokesman for the 12 disciples, who were representatives of a new Israel:

> Therefore I say to you, the Kingdom of God will be taken from you and given to a nation bearing the fruits of it (Matthew 21:43).

- **Luke 7:36–50**

> Then one of the Pharisees asked Him to eat with him. And He went to the Pharisee's house, and sat down to eat. And behold, a woman in the city who was a sinner, when she knew that Jesus sat at the table in the Pharisee's house, brought an alabaster flask of fragrant oil, and stood at His feet behind Him weeping; and she began to wash His feet with her tears, and wiped them with the hair of her head; and she kissed His feet and anointed them with the fragrant oil. Now when the Pharisee who had invited Him saw this, he spoke to himself, saying, "This Man, if He were a prophet, would know who and what manner of woman this is who is touching Him, for she is a sinner." And Jesus answered and said to him, "Simon, I have something to say to you." So he said, "Teacher, say it." "There was a certain creditor who had two debtors. One owed five hundred denarii, and the other fifty. And when they had nothing with which to repay, he freely forgave them both. Tell Me, therefore,

which of them will love him more?" Simon answered and said, "I suppose the one whom he forgave more." And He said to him, "You have rightly judged." Then He turned to the woman and said to Simon, "Do you see this woman? I entered your house; you gave Me no water for My feet, but she has washed My feet with her tears and wiped them with the hair of her head. You gave Me no kiss, but this woman has not ceased to kiss My feet since the time I came in. You did not anoint My head with oil, but this woman has anointed My feet with fragrant oil. Therefore I say to you, her sins, which are many, are forgiven, for she loved much. But to whom little is forgiven, the same loves little." Then He said to her, "Your sins are forgiven." And those who sat at the table with Him began to say to themselves, "Who is this who even forgives sins?" Then He said to the woman, "Your faith has saved you. Go in peace."

Some comments on this great story of deep repentance:

- The way of sitting at the table at that time was such that people's feet were partly behind them. This woman did not look Christ in the face but came behind him and performed the task of a *maidservant*, whose role was to *wash the feet* of the guests, as we read in 1 Samuel 25:41:

  Then she arose, bowed her face to the earth, and said, "Here is your maidservant, a servant to wash the feet of the servants of my lord."

This helps us understand the attitude of this repentant woman.

- It is an attitude of deep repentance with a contrite heart.

She stood behind Jesus weeping. *Her eyes* had been the inlets and outlets of sin, and now she makes them fountains of tears. *Her face* is now foul with weeping, which perhaps used to be covered with paints. *Her hair* is now made a towel, which before had been plaited and adorned. We have reason to think that she had before sorrowed for sin; but, now that she had an opportunity of coming into the presence of Christ, the wound bled afresh and her sorrow was renewed.

- Her strong affection for the Lord Jesus was what our Lord Jesus took special notice of.

In verses 42 and 47, Jesus pointed out that she *loved much*.

According to the Greek language, this is the fruit and proof of forgiveness and not the reason for it.[20]

• Repentance leads to forgiveness from God, resulting in affection for Christ, as the woman had shown.

On the other hand, the lack of repentance leads to no forgiveness, resulting in no affection for Christ, as shown by Simon.

• Thanks to you, most blessed sinner! You have shown the world a safe enough place for sinners—the feet of Jesus, which despises none, rejects none, repels none, and receives and admits all.

---

[20] The perfect passive form of the verb is used. She washed his feet; she kissed his feet; she wiped them with her hair; she anointed his feet with the ointment, owing Him hereby to be the Messiah, the Anointed.

IV. The Christian Experience of Forgiveness

The Christian understanding of forgiveness has broad implications:

- **It reflects the character of God as One who pardons and enters into a meaningful relationship with man, causing a change in man's relationship with Him.**

This has been done through the costly anguish of the cross of Christ.

- **It expresses the effectiveness of divine atonement in the reconciliation of man with God.**

Those who truly realise their condition as sinners know that God can remove sin and redeem sinners. This must be experienced, not just comprehended intellectually.

In Christ's death, sin is condemned and absolutely judged, and yet Christ bears the penalty on our behalf by His sacrifice.

- **For Apostle Paul, the bare concept of forgiveness does not convey deeply enough the full results of this forgiveness. Instead, he speaks of** *being justified.*

To be *treated as righteous* is:

- A rich consequence of forgiveness

But to him who does not work but believes on Him who justifies the ungodly, his faith is accounted for righteousness (Romans 4:5).

- A gift of God's grace

Being justified freely by His grace through the redemption that is in Christ Jesus (Romans 3:24).

- A present experience for those who have a faith relationship with Christ

For I know of nothing against myself, yet I am not justified by this; but He who judges me is the Lord (1 Corinthians 4:4).

To demonstrate at the present time His righteousness, that He might be just and the justifier of the one who has faith in Jesus (Romans 3:26).

Thus, *justification* is the positive relationship that forgiveness provides.

- **Forgiveness implies that God has reconciled man to Himself:**

For He Himself is our peace, who has made both one, and has broken down the middle wall of separation, having abolished in His flesh the enmity, that is, the law of commandments contained in ordinances, so as to create in Himself one new man from the two, thus making peace, and that He might reconcile them both to God in one body through the cross, thereby putting to death the enmity. And He came and preached peace to you who were afar off and to those who were near (Ephesians 2:14–17).

The outcome is:

- Peace with God

Therefore, having been justified by faith, we have peace with God through our Lord Jesus Christ (Romans 5:1).

And the peace of God, which surpasses all understanding, will guard your hearts and minds through Christ Jesus (Philippians 4:7).

And let the peace of God rule in your hearts, to which also you were called in one body; and be thankful (Colossians 3:15).

- A reconciliation accomplished by the cross

And by Him to reconcile all things to Himself, by Him, whether things on earth or things in heaven, having made peace through the blood of His cross (Colossians 1:20).

- **Forgiveness includes the theme of fellowship with:**

  - God the Father

  Remembering without ceasing your work of faith, labour of love, and patience of hope in our Lord Jesus Christ in the sight of our God and Father (1 Thessalonians 1:3).

  - The Son

  God is faithful, by whom you were called into the fellowship of His Son, Jesus Christ our Lord (1 Corinthians 1:9).

  - The Holy Spirit

  The grace of the Lord Jesus Christ, and the love of God, and the communion of the Holy Spirit be with you all. Amen (2 Corinthians 13:14).

This kind of fellowship is expressed in the Pauline phrase *in Christ* or *in the Lord* (used around 164 times), indicating a profound relationship of communion and union with God.

Forgiveness as reconciliation and restoration to fellowship with God comprises the whole nature of the Christian life. Sanctification is its fruit, and glorification is its objective.

In forgiveness, God ultimately remains God, and the erring sinner is brought home to the Father who has eternally loved him.

V. Forgiving One Another

- **Christ set an example of this:**

  Then Jesus said, "Father, forgive them, for they do not know what they do" (Luke 23:34).

- **Christ commanded us to forgive one another:**

  And whenever you stand praying, if you have anything against anyone, forgive him, that your Father in heaven may also forgive you your trespasses (Mark 11:25).

  Beloved, do not avenge yourselves, but rather give place to wrath; for it is written, "Vengeance is Mine, I will repay," says the Lord (Romans 12:19).

- **Forgiving one another ought to be unlimited:**

  Jesus said to him, "I do not say to you, up to seven times, but up to seventy times seven" (Matthew 18:22).

  And if he sins against you seven times in a day, and seven times in a day returns to you, saying, 'I repent,' you shall forgive him (Luke 17:4).

- **Forgiving one another is a characteristic of saints:**

  And they stoned Stephen as he was calling on God and saying, "Lord Jesus, receive my spirit." Then he knelt down and cried out with a loud voice, "Lord, do not charge them with this sin." And when he had said this, he fell asleep (Acts 7:59, 60).

- **Forgiving one another is motivated by:**

  - The mercy of God (Luke 6:36)

  - Our need for forgiveness (Mark 11:25)

  - God's forgiveness of us (Ephesians 4:32)

  - Christ's forgiveness of us (Colossians 3:13)

- **Forgiving one another is a glory to saints:**

  The discretion of a man makes him slow to anger, and his glory is to overlook a transgression (Proverbs 19:11)

- **Forgiving one another should be accompanied by:**

  - Forbearance (Colossians 3:13)

  - Kindness (Genesis 45:5–11; Romans 12:20)

  - Blessing and prayer (Matthew 5:44).

- **Promises to those who forgive one another:**

  For if you forgive men their trespasses, your heavenly Father will also forgive you (Matthew 6:14).

  Judge not, and you shall not be judged. Condemn not, and you shall not be condemned. Forgive, and you will be forgiven (Luke 6:37).

- **There is no forgiveness without forgiving one another:**

  But if you do not forgive men their trespasses, neither will your Father forgive your trespasses (Matthew 6:15).

  For judgement is without mercy to the one who has shown no mercy. Mercy triumphs over judgement (James 2:13).

- **The necessity of forgiving one another was illustrated through the parable of the unforgiving servant (Matthew 18:23–35)**

- **Forgiving one another was exemplified in:**

  - Joseph (Genesis 50:20, 21)

  - David (1 Samuel 24:7; 2 Samuel 18:5; 19:23)

  - Solomon (1 Kings 1:53)

  - Stephen (Acts 7:60)

  - Paul (2 Timothy 4:16)

In conclusion, we can quote the saying:

To err is human, to forgive, divine! [21]

---

[21] Alexander Pope, *An Essay On Criticism*

CHAPTER 6

THE BLOOD OF JESUS,
THE SON OF GOD,
CLEANSES ME FROM ALL SIN

Readings

But if we walk in the light as He is in the light, we have fellowship with one another, and *the blood of Jesus Christ His Son cleanses us from all sin.* If we say that we have no sin, we deceive ourselves, and the truth is not in us. If we *confess* our sins, He is *faithful and just* to *forgive* us our sins and to *cleanse us from all unrighteousness* (1 John 1:7–9).

Introduction

To understand the full truth revealed in these verses, we need to examine the meaning of the keywords:

- *Cleanse*

- *Confess*

- *Sin* (and the possible deception related to it)

- *Unrighteousness*

- *Faithful and just*

- *Forgive*[22]

Therefore, we will discuss this topic in three main sections:

I. The Meaning of the Keywords in This Topic

II. Biblical and Theological Considerations

III. Practical Considerations

There are multiple ways of examining a biblical passage to understand it better. One way is to go back to the original language to better understand the meaning. Alternatively, we can understand a biblical passage by focusing on the meaning of its keywords, as we will do with the words listed here. Another way is to connect biblical verses and passages together because, as the early fathers say, the best way to interpret a verse or biblical passage is through another verse or another biblical passage. This method helps us see the complete truth, not a partial truth as we often do when we take separate bits from here and there.

---

[22] Refer to the previous statement for the detailed explanation of *forgiveness*.

We need to learn to love the Word of God more, to the extent that we desire to go deeper in studying it and are ready to spend time and effort. Due to our fallen nature, we often don't want to put in the effort; we want to receive the thing we desire but without the effort involved.

Therefore, we ought not only to love the Word of God more, but out of our love for the Word of God be ready to spend time and effort to go deeper into it. We should also continue to pray with the teaching we receive from this study so that it may turn into revelation—light, life, and love for Jesus. All that is received ought to help in transforming us into Christlikeness.

Therefore, one digs hard into the Bible verses not to receive knowledge, meditate on the verses, and have some ideas to share and preach. This is a dangerous temptation. But one digs hard in order to encounter Jesus and be transformed into His likeness. The fathers of the Church say that when one opens the Bible, one ought to be careful because Jesus is in the Bible—one ought to be ready to meet Him. Isn't it worth the effort?

I. The Meaning of the Keywords in This Topic

Cleanse

A. The Linguistic Meaning

Cleanse (verb); cleansed; cleansing (meaning to purify); clean means *especially* to rid of impurities by or as if by washing

B. The Meaning According to the Original Greek Language

- *katharós* (meaning clean, pure)
- *katharízō* (meaning to cleanse, purify)
- *kathaírō* (meaning to make clean)
- *katharótēs* (meaning purity)
- *akáthartos* (meaning unclean, impure)
- *akatharsía* (meaning impurity)
- *katharismós* (meaning cleansing or purification)
- *ekkathaírō* (meaning to cleanse)

Confess

A. The Linguistic Meaning

- To tell or make known (something wrong or damaging to oneself—admit (he *confessed* his guilt)
- To acknowledge (sin) to God or to a priest
- To receive the confession of (a penitent)
- To declare faith in or adherence to—profess
- To give evidence of

B. The Meaning According to the Original Greek Language

The Greek word for *confess* is *homologeo*, which means *speak the same thing*, meaning *acknowledge*. Therefore, confessing sins does not mean saying that you're sorry, but it means agreeing with God that a particular act is sin—thus taking sides with Him and against yourself and what you have done.

In simpler words, *confess* means to agree with God and say the same thing as God says. When I confess, I know that God is saying to me, "Son, you have sinned"; thus, I say, "Yes, Lord I have sinned, I confess."

Sin

What is sin?

- It is lawlessness in relation to God as the Lawgiver
- It is rebellion in relation to God as the Lawful Ruler
- It is missing the mark in relation to God as our Creator
- It is guilt in relation to God as the Judge
- It is uncleanness in relation to God as the Holy One

Sin is a perversity touching each one of us at every point in our lives. Apart from Jesus Christ, no human being has ever been free of its infection. It appears in desires as well as deeds, and motives as well as actions.

The good news, however, is that sins can be forgiven. In Psalm 130:3, 4, we read:

> If You, Lord, should mark iniquities, O Lord, who could stand? *But* there is forgiveness with You, that You may be feared.

Notice here the use of the word *but*, which is central to the message of the gospel.

Note also the plural, as compared with the singular, *sin*, in 1 John 1:8, 9 (quoted above). The plural indicates that the confession is to be *specific* as well as *general*.

Unrighteousness

Sin is *the transgression of the law*, and the law is the expression of God's *righteousness*. Therefore, sin is *unrighteousness*, and it is offensive to God, who is just and righteous.

But again the good news is that the Righteous One, who calls us into fellowship with Himself, purges away the *unrighteousness* which is contrary to His nature, and which makes fellowship impossible.

The word *unrighteousness* occurs in Apostle John's writings:

> He who speaks from himself seeks his own glory; but He who seeks the glory of the One who sent Him is true, and no *unrighteousness* is in Him (John 7:18).

> All *unrighteousness* is sin, and there is sin not leading to death (1 John 5:17).

Faithful and Just (Just means Righteous)

• *Faithful*

The word *faithful* is *pistos* in the original Greek language.

According to Vincent[23] (Vincent's Word Studies), the word *faithful* indicates that God is true to His own nature and promises, and He keeps faith with Himself and with man.

- The word *faithful* is applied to God:

♦ As fulfilling His own promises:

Let us hold fast the confession of our hope without wavering, for He who promised is *faithful* (Hebrews 10:23).

---

[23] Vincent's Word Studies, by Marvin R. Vincent, [1886], at sacred-texts.com

By faith Sarah herself also received strength to conceive seed, and she bore a child when she was past the age, because she judged Him *faithful* who had promised (Hebrews 11:11).

♦ As fulfilling the purpose for which He has called men:

He who calls you is faithful, who also will do it (1 Thessalonians 5:24).

God is faithful, by whom you were called into the fellowship of His Son, Jesus Christ our Lord (1 Corinthians 1:9).

♦ As responding with guardianship to the trust put in Him by men:

No temptation has overtaken you except such as is common to man; *but God is faithful*, who will not allow you to be tempted beyond what you are able, but with the temptation will also make the way of escape, that you may be able to bear it (1 Corinthians 10:13).

Therefore let those who suffer according to the will of God commit their souls to Him in doing good, *as to a faithful Creator* (1 Peter 4:19).

He remains faithful; He cannot deny Himself (2 Timothy 2:13).

- The same term is applied to Christ:

But *the Lord is faithful*, who will establish you and guard you from the evil one (2 Thessalonians 3:3).

Therefore, in all things He had to be made like His brethren, that He might be a merciful and *faithful High Priest* in things pertaining to God, to make propitiation for the sins of the people (Hebrews 2:17).

Who was *faithful to Him who appointed Him*, as Moses also was faithful in all His house (Hebrews 3:2).

Here God's faithfulness refers not only to His faithfulness as essential to His own being, but also to His faithfulness towards us. Thus, He is faithful to His own nature and essence, which is truth and light, and at the same time, He is faithful towards us.

- *Just or Righteous*

The term is applied both to God and to Christ:

> And I heard the angel of the waters saying: *"You are righteous, O Lord,* the One who is and who was and who is to be, because You have judged these things" (Revelation 16:5).

> *O righteous Father!* The world has not known You, but I have known You; and these have known that You sent Me (John 17:25).

> My little children, these things I write to you, so that you may not sin. And if anyone sins, we have an Advocate with the Father, *Jesus Christ the righteous* (1 John 2:1).

> Little children, let no one deceive you. He who practises righteousness is righteous, just as *He is righteous* (1 John 3:7).

> For Christ also suffered once for sins, *the just* for the unjust, that He might bring us to God, being put to death in the flesh but made alive by the Spirit (1 Peter 3:18).

The two words, *faithful* and *righteous/just,* imply each other.

They unite in a true conception of God's character. God, who is *absolute righteousness,* must be *faithful* to His own nature.

- God is faithful to His covenant and word by which He has promised forgiveness to penitent believing confessors.

- He is just to Himself and His glory and has provided such a sacrifice, by which His righteousness is declared in the justification of sinners.

- He is just to His Son. Not only has He sent His Son for such service, but also promised Him that those who come through Him shall be forgiven on His account.

- He is gracious. Therefore, He forgives the contrite confessor all his sins, cleanses him from the guilt of all unrighteousness, and in due time delivers him from the power and practice of it.

Forgive [24]

St. Augustine (5th century) said in Latin:

"Vis ut ille ignoscat? Tu agnosce." It means: *Do you wish Him to forgive? Do you confess.*

His words are exactly to the point, but his play on the words *pardon* and *confess* cannot be reproduced in English.

---

[24] Refer to statement five of the Blood of Jesus for a detailed explanation of *forgiveness.*

II. Biblical and Theological Considerations

Two types of confession are mentioned in the Bible:

1. Individuals confess that they have sinned and are therefore guilty before God, often confessing a particular sin.

And it shall be, when he is guilty in any of these matters, that he shall confess that he has sinned in that thing (Leviticus 5:5).

David said to Nathan, "I have sinned against the Lord" (2 Samuel 12:13).

If we confess our sins, He is faithful and just to forgive us our sins and to cleanse us from all unrighteousness (1 John 1:9).

In such confession one agrees or acknowledges:

- That he or she has broken God's law

It is time for You to act, O Lord, for they have regarded Your law as void (Psalm 119:126).

- That the penalty for the sin is justly deserved

For the wages of sin is death, but the gift of God is eternal life in Christ Jesus our Lord (Romans 6:23).

- That in some specific way God's standard of holiness has not been met

Speak to all the congregation of the children of Israel, and say to them: 'You shall be holy, for I the Lord your God am holy' (Leviticus 19:2).

Therefore you shall be perfect, just as your Father in heaven is perfect (Matthew 5:48).

The men of God were quick to confess. Daniel, Ezra, and Nehemiah confessed their nation's sins, agreeing with God that His punishment of the people (including themselves) was just, yet praying for God's mercy and deliverance.

Now while I was speaking, praying, and *confessing my sin and the sin of my people Israel,* and presenting my supplication before the Lord my God for the holy mountain of my God (Daniel 9:20).

Now while Ezra was praying, and *while he was confessing,* weeping, and bowing down before the house of God, a very large assembly of men, women, and children gathered to him from Israel; for the people wept very bitterly (Ezra 10:1).

Please let Your ear be attentive and Your eyes open, that You may hear the prayer of Your servant which I pray before You now, day and night, for the children of Israel Your servants, *and confess the sins of the children of Israel which we have sinned against You.* Both my father's house and I have sinned (Nehemiah 1:6).

2. **Individuals confess that God is God and that He rules the world (1 Chronicles 29:10–13), that He is faithful in showing His love and kindness (Psalm 118:2–4), and that He has helped His people (Psalm 105:1–6).**

Such confession or agreement, expressed publicly in worship or song (Psalm 100:4), is referred to in the Old Testament as *blessing the Lord:*

Enter into His gates with thanksgiving, and into His courts with praise. Be thankful to Him, and bless His name (Psalm 100:4).

The two types of confession are often combined in the Bible, producing many psalms of thanksgiving.

The same Hebrew word means both *praise* and *confession of sin;* the two meanings were part of a single concept. The Psalmist began by admitting sin and proclaiming God's justice, and he ended by confessing God's forgiveness and His delivering power.

Both those meanings also occur in the New Testament. When Christians confess, this means that they declare as a matter of conviction that Jesus is the Christ and that they belong to Him:

Whoever confesses Me before men, him I will also confess before My Father who is in heaven (Matthew 10:32).

Not to confess Christ is the same as denying Him (Matthew 10:33; Luke 12:8; cf. 2 Timothy 2:11–13; Revelation 3:5).

The Christian life therefore begins with a confession of faith, which is a public declaration before witnesses:

> If you confess with your mouth the Lord Jesus and believe in your heart that God has raised Him from the dead, you will be saved. For with the heart one believes unto righteousness, and with the mouth confession is made unto salvation (Romans 10:9, 10).

> Fight the good fight of faith, lay hold on eternal life, to which you were also called and *have confessed the good confession in the presence of many witnesses* (1 Timothy 6:12).

- An additional dimension of the Christian's confession is provided in 1 John 4:2:

> By this you know the Spirit of God: Every spirit that confesses that Jesus Christ has come in the flesh is of God.

One must confess that *Jesus Christ has come in the flesh,* meaning to acknowledge Christ's divinity and His pre-existence as the Son of God (that He *has come*)[25] as well as Christ's humanity and incarnation (that He has come *in the flesh*).

The Greek word *confession* literally means *saying the same thing.* The Christian's *good confession* is modelled after the pattern of Christ's confession:

> Fight the good fight of faith, lay hold on eternal life, to which you were also called and have confessed the good confession in the presence of many witnesses. I urge you in the sight of God who gives life to all things, and before *Christ Jesus who witnessed the good confession before Pontius Pilate* (1 Timothy 6:12, 13).

---

[25] Refer also to 1 John 4:15.

The New Testament discusses the confession of sin in a few yet important passages:

- Those being baptised by John the Baptist publicly admitted their sins and repented (Matthew 3:6; Mark 1:4, 5).

- In Paul's ministry: '*And many who had believed came confessing and telling their deeds*' (Acts 19:18).

- According to Apostle John, all Christians must agree with God that they are sinners (1 John 1:8–10).

- Apostle James presented a fuller picture, highlighting that when a Christian is ill, the elders should visit and give the person an opportunity to confess any sins.[26]

- As in the Psalms, forgiveness and healing (both the emotional/mental and the physical) are linked to confession.

- Recalling that principle, Apostle James urged Christians to confess their sins to one another.[27]

---

[26] James 5:14, 16

[27] James 5:16

III. Practical Considerations

We have four practical points in this section:

- Father and son, not Judge and lawbreaker

- Jesus as an Advocate and Propitiation

- Deception or truth?

- The sinner is to believe ... The saint is to confess!

1. Father and son, not Judge and lawbreaker

The relationship of Christians with God is that of a Father and His children, not a relationship between a Judge and a lawbreaker!

This understanding is taken directly from the First Epistle of John. When one continues to be in this kind of relationship with God, God continues to cleanse him and lead him to righteousness.

Christians ought to be ready at all times to acknowledge any sin which God's light may expose to them. Therefore, John the Evangelist wrote:

> If we confess our sins, He is faithful and just to forgive us our sins and to cleanse us from all unrighteousness (1 John 1:9).

John's thought might be paraphrased according to the Greek origin as follows:

If we confess our sins, He ... will forgive the sins we confess and moreover will even cleanse us from all unrighteousness.

Naturally, only God knows at any moment the full extent of a person's unrighteousness. Each Christian, however, is responsible to acknowledge whatever the light of God makes him aware of. When he does so, a complete and perfect cleansing is granted him.

It is comforting to learn that the forgiveness which is promised here is absolutely assured (because God *is faithful*) and also is in no way contrary to His holiness (for He is *just*); this is due to the full atonement of Jesus.

In modern times, some have occasionally denied that a Christian needs to confess his sins and ask forgiveness. It is claimed that a believer already has forgiveness in Christ.

But this point of view confuses the perfect position which a Christian has in Christ as being seated with Him in the heavenly places (Ephesians 2:6) with his natural conduct and spiritual needs as a failing individual on earth. We are sinners or failing individuals, but we are forgiven because of God's mercy and love.

It is perfectly understandable how a son may need to ask his father to forgive him for his faults while at the same time his position within the family is not hindered or negatively affected.

A Christian who never asks his heavenly Father for forgiveness for his sins has no sensitivity to the ways in which he grieves his Father. The Lord Jesus Himself taught His followers to seek forgiveness of their sins in a prayer that was obviously intended for daily use: *'Give us this day our daily bread. And forgive us our debts, as we forgive our debtors'* (Matthew 6:11–12).

Apostle John never connected the confession of sin with the acquisition of eternal life, which is always conditioned on faith. 1 John 1:9 is not said or written to the unsaved but to the believers.

If the idea of walking in the light or in darkness is correctly understood on an experiential level, these concepts offer no difficulty. When a believer loses personal touch with the God of light, he begins to live in darkness. But confession of sin is the way back into the light.

2. Jesus as an Advocate and Propitiation

Apostle John gives two interesting titles to Jesus Christ:

- *Advocate* (He intercedes for us)

- *Propitiation* (He covers our sins)

> My little children, these things I write to you, so that you may not sin. And if anyone sins, we have *an Advocate* with the Father, Jesus Christ the righteous. And He Himself is *the propitiation* for our sins, and not for ours only but also for the whole world (1 John 2:1–2).

It's important that we understand these two titles because they refer to two ministries that only the Lord Himself performs. They are two acts that the Lord Jesus performs for our sake.

• *Propitiation*

This word was used in the Greek world to refer to offerings and sacrifices to the gods in order to appease them and avoid their anger. This was common in heathen religions.

Though this is not the biblical meaning at all, Apostles John and Paul chose this word and introduced it in the Bible. They said Jesus was a sacrifice. But the word refers to a sacrifice to appease someone and avoid his anger. How then could this apply to Jesus?!

Of course, we cannot say that Jesus will appease His Father or avoid His anger because He is one with His Father. However, Jesus knows that there is anger or wrath in God's heart against the sin of the fallen humanity. The sadness that needs to be appeased is due to breaking the heavenly laws of holiness. God said to Adam that if he broke the law, he would die. These are heavenly laws related to holiness and these laws cannot be changed. Thus, the situation had to be corrected. Jesus offered Himself as a sacrifice to deal with this problem of breaking God's law. The practical implication is that whenever we sin, we ought to remember that this is what happens.

Because we don't know this matter, we sin, and then go to God so easily and simply, saying, "Forgive me", and we receive forgiveness. Everything seems to be easy and simple for us. Thus, we thank God and leave. This is fine, there is no problem with this. But if we want to be more sensitive and come closer to the Holy God, we ought to develop in our inner man the sense of what happens when we sin. Every time we sin, God's law of holiness is affected. Therefore, when we receive forgiveness, we must feel indebted to God because all along the sacrifice of Jesus continues to correct this situation for everyone who believes.

Therefore, the word *propitiation* does not mean appeasing an angry God as the linguistic meaning suggests. Rather, it means *to satisfy God's holy law.*

'God is light' (1 John 1:5) and, therefore, He cannot close His eyes to sin. But *'God is love'* (1 John 4:8) too and wants to save sinners.

How, then, can a holy God uphold His own justice and still forgive sinners?

The answer is in the sacrifice of Christ. At the cross, God, in His holiness, judged sin. God, in His love, offers Jesus Christ to the world as Saviour. God was *just* in that He punished sin, but He is also *loving* in that He offers free forgiveness through what Jesus did at Calvary.

> In this is love, not that we loved God, but that He loved us and sent His Son to be the propitiation for our sins (1 John 4:10).

Refer also to Romans 3:23–26.

Christ is the Sacrifice for the sins of the whole world, but He is *Advocate* only *for believers*:

> We [Christians] have *an Advocate* with the Father (1 John 2:1).

• *Advocate*

The word *advocate* was used to refer to lawyers at that time. In this verse (1 John 2:1), Apostle John used the very same word that Jesus used when He was speaking in John 14 and 15 about the Holy Spirit (the Parakletos) whom the Father would send:

And I will pray the Father, and He will give you another *Helper*, that He may abide with you forever ... But *the Helper*, the Holy Spirit, whom the Father will send in My name, He will teach you all things, and bring to your remembrance all things that I said to you (John 14:16, 26).

But when *the Helper* comes, whom I shall send to you from the Father, the Spirit of truth who proceeds from the Father, He will testify of Me (John 15:26).

The word literally means *someone who is called alongside*. When a person was summoned to court, he took an advocate (or a lawyer) with him to stand at his side and plead his case.

In 1 John 2:1, the apostle says that after all that Jesus has done for us, Jesus still wants to say, "My son, whenever you sin, not only is forgiveness ready for you, but I Myself, I, your Saviour, will be at your side, defending your case."

This is because there is an accuser—Satan.

When Jesus shows up in this scene of Satan's accusation, Satan can no longer accuse and he flees.

Jesus finished His work on earth (John 17:4)—the work of giving His life as a sacrifice for sin. Today, He is doing another work for our sake in heaven. *He represents us before God's throne.* As our High Priest, He sympathises with our weaknesses and temptations and gives us grace:

> For we do not have a High Priest who cannot sympathise with our weaknesses, but was in all points tempted as we are, yet without sin. Let us therefore come boldly to the throne of grace, that we may obtain mercy and find grace to help in time of need (Hebrews 4:15–16).

Also there were many priests, because they were prevented by death from continuing. But He, because He continues forever, has an unchangeable priesthood. *Therefore He is also able to save to the uttermost those who come to God through Him, since He always lives to make intercession for them.* For such a High Priest was fitting for us, who is holy, harmless, undefiled, separate from sinners, and has become higher than the heavens; who does not need daily, as those high priests, to offer up sacrifices, first for His own sins and then for the people's, for this He did once for all when He offered up Himself.

For the law appoints as high priests men who have weakness, but the word of the oath, which came after the law, appoints the Son who has been perfected forever (Hebrews 7:23–28).

As our Advocate, He helps us *when we sin*. When we confess our sins to God, God forgives us because of Christ's advocacy.

- The Old Testament presents a beautiful picture of this matter:

In Zechariah 3, we read the following story about Joshua, the high priest:

> Then he showed me Joshua the high priest standing before the Angel of the Lord, and Satan standing at his right hand to oppose him. And the Lord said to Satan, "The Lord rebuke you, Satan! The Lord who has chosen Jerusalem rebuke you! Is this not a brand plucked from the fire?" Now Joshua was clothed with filthy garments, and was standing before the Angel. Then He answered and spoke to those who stood before Him, saying, "Take away the filthy garments from him." And to him He said, "See, I have removed your iniquity from you, and I will clothe you with rich robes." And I said, "Let them put a clean turban on his head." So they put a clean turban on his head, and they put the clothes on him. And the Angel of the Lord stood by. Then the Angel of the Lord admonished Joshua, saying, "Thus says the Lord of hosts: 'If you will walk in My ways, and if you will keep My command, then you shall also judge My house, and likewise have charge of My courts; I will give you places to walk among these who stand here'" (Zechariah 3:1–7).

Joshua was the high priest when the children of Israel returned to their land following their captivity in Babylon.[28] The nation had sinned. To symbolise this, Joshua stood before God in filthy garments and Satan stood at Joshua's right hand to accuse him. God the Father was the Judge. Joshua, representing the people of Israel, was the accused. Satan was the accuser. The Bible calls Satan *the accuser of our brethren* (Revelation 12:10). But Joshua had an Advocate who stood at God's right hand, and this changed the whole situation. Christ gave Joshua a change of garments and silenced the accusations of Satan.

---

[28] Joshua the high priest is not to be confused with Joshua who entered the promised land with the people of Israel.

This story presents a picture or an illustration of what is meant by saying Jesus is our *Advocate*. Because He sits at the right hand of the Father, He can apply His sacrifice to our needs day by day. All He asks is that when we err, we confess our sins, meaning *to say the same thing*, that is, to agree with God about it.

- Cleansing has two sides: the judicial and the personal.

The blood of Jesus Christ, shed on the cross, delivers us from the guilt of sin and gives us right standing before God. God is able to forgive because Christ's death has satisfied His holy Law.

But God is also interested in cleansing a sinner inwardly. David prayed, *'Create in me a clean heart, O God'* (Psalm 51:10). When our confession is sincere, God performs an inner cleansing work in our hearts [*'If we confess our sins, He is faithful and just to forgive us our sins and to cleanse us from all unrighteousness'* (1 John 1:9)] by His Spirit and through His Word [*'You are already clean because of the word which I have spoken to you'* (John 15:3)].

When should we confess our sin?

We should do so immediately when we realise it. It is written:

> He who covers his sins will not prosper, but whoever confesses and forsakes them will have mercy (Proverbs 28:13).

By walking in the light, we are able to see the dirt in our lives and deal with it immediately.

3. Deception or truth?

The apostle shows us the dreadful consequences of denying sin. He highlights two points in this respect:

- **1 John 1:8**

If we say that we have no sin, we deceive ourselves, and the truth is not in us.

The more we see our sins, the more we will value the remedy. If we deny our sins, the truth is not in us.

- The Christian life is a life of continued repentance.

- It is a life of continual faith in, thankfulness for, and love of the Redeemer.

- It is a life of hopeful and joyful expectation of a day of glorious redemption in which the believer shall be fully and finally acquitted, and sin abolished forever.

- **1 John 1:10**

If we say that we have not sinned, we make Him a liar, and His word is not in us.

Not only do we deceive ourselves if we deny our sin, but this denial also reflects dishonour towards God. God has given His testimony to the continued sin and sinfulness of the world by providing a sufficient and effective sacrifice for sin that will be needed in all ages. He has also given His testimony to the continued sinfulness of believers themselves by requiring them continually to confess their sins and commit themselves by faith to the blood of Jesus.

Therefore, when believers confess sin, they admit their continual need of Christ's cleansing blood. Though occasional sin will not place them in darkness, they must always affirm and confess their need for Christ's sacrifice. Also, believers must always affirm their fellowship with the *light* by actions of righteousness that include practice of truth and dependence upon ongoing forgiveness.

The phrase *to cleanse us from every wrong* (1 John 1:9) highlights that sin should not be denied in Christian lives but that its effects have been and will be completely dealt with by the blood of Christ.

4. The sinner is to believe ... the saint is to confess!

Apostle John instructs the saints on what to do about sins in their lives. The pronoun *we* mentioned in 1 John 1:9 includes Apostle John as well, and it seems that he is speaking here of believers, for in other places he gives directions to the unsaved as to what they must do in relation to their sinful state and their sins.

The sinner is to *believe* (John 3:16). The saint is to *confess.*

This teaches that the constant attitude of the saint toward sin should be one of a contrite heart, always eager to discover any sin in his life through the conviction of the Holy Spirit, and always eager to confess it and put it out of his life by the power of the Holy Spirit as well.

David wrote concerning that kind of heart when he said, *'The sacrifices of God are a broken spirit,* **a broken and a contrite heart**—*these, O God, You will not despise'* (Psalm 51:17).

Conclusion

In conclusion, we can sum up with the following two points:

A. Confession of Sin and the Cleansing of Sin According to the Bible

B. A Related Subject: Repentance

A. Confession of Sin and the Cleansing of Sin According to the Bible: An Overview

1. God requires the confession of sin:

I will return again to My place *till they acknowledge their offence.* Then they will seek My face; in their affliction they will earnestly seek Me (Hosea 5:15).

2. God considers and values the confession of sin:

Then he looks at men and says, 'I have sinned, and perverted what was right, and it did not profit me.' He will redeem his soul from going down to the Pit, and his life shall see the light (Job 33:27, 28).

Now while I was speaking, praying, and *confessing my sin* and the sin of my people Israel, and presenting my supplication before the Lord my God for the holy mountain of my God, yes, while I was speaking in prayer, the man Gabriel, whom I had seen in the vision at the beginning, being caused to fly swiftly, reached me about the time of the evening offering. And he informed me, and talked with me, and said, "O Daniel, I have now come forth to give you skill to understand. At the beginning of your supplications the command went out, and I have come to tell you, for you are greatly beloved; therefore consider the matter, and understand the vision" (Daniel 9:20–23).

3. Confession of sin should be accompanied with:

- Prayer for forgiveness

And David's heart condemned him after he had numbered the people. So David said to the Lord, "I have sinned greatly in what I have done; but now, I pray, O Lord, take away the iniquity of Your servant, for I have done very foolishly" (2 Samuel 24:10).

For Your name's sake, O Lord, pardon my iniquity, for it is great (Psalm 25:11).

Have mercy upon me, O God, according to Your lovingkindness; according to the multitude of Your tender mercies, blot out my transgressions (Psalm 51:1).

O Lord, though our iniquities testify against us, do it for Your name's sake; for our backslidings are many, we have sinned against You. O the Hope of Israel, his Saviour in time of trouble, why should You be like a stranger in the land, and like a traveller who turns aside to tarry for a night? Why should You be like a man astonished, like a mighty one who cannot save? Yet You, O Lord, are in our midst, and we are called by Your name; do not leave us! ... We acknowledge, O Lord, our wickedness and the iniquity of our fathers, for we have sinned against You (Jeremiah 14:7–9, 20).

- Godly sorrow

For I will declare my iniquity; I will be in anguish over my sin (Psalm 38:18).

See, O Lord, that I am in distress; my soul is troubled; my heart is overturned within me, for I have been very rebellious. Outside the sword bereaves, at home it is like death (Lamentations 1:20).

- Forsaking sin

He who covers his sins will not prosper, but whoever confesses and forsakes them will have mercy (Proverbs 28:13).

- Restitution if needed

Speak to the children of Israel: 'When a man or woman commits any sin that men commit in unfaithfulness against the Lord, and that person is guilty, then he shall confess the sin which he has committed. *He shall make restitution for his trespass in full*, plus one-fifth of it, and give it to the one he has wronged' (Numbers 5:6, 7).

4. Confession of sin should be full and unreserved

I acknowledged my sin to You, and my iniquity I have not hidden. I said, "I will confess my transgressions to the Lord," and You forgave the iniquity of my sin (Psalm 32:5).

For I acknowledge my transgressions, and my sin is always before me (Psalm 51:3).

We have sinned with our fathers, we have committed iniquity, we have done wickedly (Psalm 106:6).

5. Confession of sin should be followed by pardon

I acknowledged my sin to You, and my iniquity I have not hidden. I said, "I will confess my transgressions to the Lord," and You forgave the iniquity of my sin (Psalm 32:5).

If we confess our sins, He is faithful and just to forgive us our sins and to cleanse us from all unrighteousness (1 John 1:9).

6. Confession of sin should be demonstrated

And the son said to him, 'Father, I have sinned against heaven and in your sight, and am no longer worthy to be called your son' (Luke 15:21).

And the tax collector, standing afar off, would not so much as raise his eyes to heaven, but beat his breast, saying, 'God, be merciful to me a sinner!' (Luke 18:13).

7. Confession of sin was exemplified by:

- The children of Israel

So they gathered together at Mizpah, drew water, and poured it out before the Lord. And they fasted that day, and said there, "We have sinned against the Lord" (1 Samuel 7:6).

And all the people said to Samuel, "Pray for your servants to the Lord your God, that we may not die; for we have added to all our sins the evil of asking a king for ourselves" (1 Samuel 12:19).

- David

And David's heart condemned him after he had numbered the people. So David said to the Lord, "I have sinned greatly in what I have done; but now, I pray, O Lord, take away the iniquity of Your servant, for I have done very foolishly" (2 Samuel 24:10).

- Ezra

And I said: "O my God, I am too ashamed and humiliated to lift up my face to You, my God; for our iniquities have risen higher than our heads, and our guilt has grown up to the heavens" (Ezra 9:6).

- Nehemiah

Please let Your ear be attentive and Your eyes open, that You may hear the prayer of Your servant which I pray before You now, day and night, for the children of Israel Your servants, and confess the sins of the children of Israel which we have sinned against You. Both my father's house and I have sinned. We have acted very corruptly against You, and have not kept the commandments, the statutes, nor the ordinances which You commanded Your servant Moses (Nehemiah 1:6, 7).

- Job

Have I sinned? What have I done to You, O watcher of men? Why have You set me as Your target, so that I am a burden to myself? (Job 7:20).

- Daniel

And I prayed to the Lord my God, and made confession, and said, "O Lord, great and awesome God, who keeps His covenant and mercy with those who love Him, and with those who keep His commandments" (Daniel 9:4).

- Peter

When Simon Peter saw it, he fell down at Jesus' knees, saying, "Depart from me, for I am a sinful man, O Lord!" (Luke 5:8).

- The penitent thief on the cross

And we indeed justly, for we receive the due reward of our deeds; but this Man has done nothing wrong (Luke 23:41).

B. A Related Subject: Repentance

Repentance is closely related to the theme of confession of sins and cleansing of sins.

1. Repentance in the Old and the New Testaments

The most important aspect of repentance in the Old Testament is contained in the Hebrew word *shub*, which expresses the idea of *turning back*, retracing one's steps in order to return to the right way.

In the early stages of the history of the children of Israel, the nation was more conscious of its collective guilt than of its individual guilt. Therefore, in times of national catastrophes, it celebrated liturgies of repentance that included an assembly of the people, fasting, lamentation, and the confession of sin.

However, the prophets of the eighth century B.C., and those who followed, directed a strong criticism against merely liturgical repentance (meaning the mere outer rituals). Amos complains that the people did not turn to the Lord (4:6, 8, 9, 10, and 11). Hosea, after describing a liturgy of repentance

(6:1–3), says that Israel's love *'is like a morning cloud, and like the early dew it goes away'* (6:4). Isaiah pleads for social justice rather than empty ritual (1:10–17; cf. 58:5–7; Amos 5:21–24). The prophets, therefore, insist upon an interior conversion manifested in justice, kindness, and humility (Micah 6:6–8). Jeremiah calls upon the people of Israel to acknowledge their guilt (3:11–14) and Ezekiel brings the notion of individual responsibility to a climax (3:16–21; 18; 33:10–20).

For all of their harshness, however, the prophets also hold out hope to the people of Israel. Jeremiah and Ezekiel look to a day when God will place a new heart within his people (Jeremiah 24:7; Ezekiel 36:26–31) and Isaiah promises forgiveness to those who will repent (1:18, 19).

In the New Testament, the notion of repentance is to turn to the Lord. The Hebrew word *shub* is expressed in the Greek verb *metanoein*. However, the idea is slightly modified. The Greek word includes the concept of changing one's mind, coming to a new way of thinking.

John the Baptist is the immediate successor of the prophets. Like them he calls the people to repentance and demands proof of authentic conversion (Matthew 3:9, 10). His preaching leads to repentance and forgiveness of sins (Mark 1:4; Luke 3:3). Yet John's message also differs from that of the prophets in that his call for repentance is intimately connected to the imminent arrival of God's Kingdom and the coming of the Messiah (Matthew 3:2, 11–12; Luke 3:15–17). Moreover, John seals this repentance with a baptism of water.

Jesus' call to repentance is also closely linked to the arrival of the Kingdom (Mark 1:14, 15). Also, the summons to conversion is associated with His own Person so that a decision for or against Him signifies a choice for or against repentance (Matthew 11:20–24; 12:41, 42). In the eyes of Jesus, all are sinners and in need of repentance (Luke 13:1–5). He comes to call sinners and not the just (Luke 5:32), and He tells parables that promise God's forgiveness to those who recognise their sinfulness (Luke 15; 18:9–14).

Apostle Paul sometimes used the term *repentance* (Romans 2:4; 2 Corinthians 7:9, 10; Hebrews 6:4–6). Apostle John also used it in calling the seven churches to repentance (Revelation 2:5, 16; 3:3, 19). Both apostles assume repentance as a requirement in their concept of faith, which demands a turning away from sin. The general understanding of the New Testament is that repentance is an ongoing act.

2. An important passage in the New Testament that speaks about repentance

> Now I rejoice, not that you were made sorry, but that your sorrow led to repentance. For you were made sorry in a godly manner, that you might suffer loss from us in nothing. For godly sorrow produces repentance leading to salvation, not to be regretted; but the sorrow of the world produces death. For observe this very thing, that you sorrowed in a godly manner: What diligence it produced in you, what clearing of yourselves, what indignation, what fear, what vehement desire, what zeal, what vindication! In all things you proved yourselves to be clear in this matter (2 Corinthians 7:9–11).

This passage contains an interesting and full description of such corporate repentance involving the elements of sorrow for sin and a determined resolve to forsake old sinful ways and to behave properly.

Repentance is rooted in convictions about the sinner's own need before a holy God.

3. Can God repent?!

Occasionally, in some translations of the Old Testament (such as KJV), God is said to repent. A classic example is found in His treatment of Nineveh during Jonah's prophetic ministry there. In Jonah 3, we read:

> Then God saw their works, that they turned from their evil way; and *God relented* from the disaster that He had said He would bring upon them, and He did not do it (Jonah 3:10, NKJV).

And God saw their works, that they turned from their evil way; and *God repented* of the evil, that He had said that He would do unto them; and He did it not (Jonah 3:10, KJV).

God told Jonah to proclaim judgement to Nineveh, yet once they repented, God relented or repented (KJV), hence no judgement came.

Such an attitude should not be understood as denoting either personal sorrow on God's part or a change in His eternal purpose, but rather a change in, or an updating of, His announced purpose and His relations with people as they themselves change.

CHAPTER 7

THE BLOOD OF JESUS
JUSTIFIES ME FROM ALL CONDEMNATION
SO ALL THE ACCUSATIONS OF THE DEVIL
AGAINST ME ARE NULLIFIED;
HE MAKES ME RIGHTEOUS
AS THOUGH I HAVE NEVER SINNED

Readings

*B*eing *justified freely by His grace* through the redemption that is in Christ Jesus (Romans 3:24).

Much more then, *having now been justified by His blood,* we shall be saved from wrath through Him (Romans 5:9).

Introduction

We will study this topic in seven main points as follows:

   I. What is Justification?

  II. What is the Difference Between Justification and Righteousness?

 III. What is Righteousness?

 IV. Theological Considerations About Righteousness/Justification

  V. Important Implications

 VI. Practical Considerations

VII. Conclusion: Righteousness in the Bible in General

I. What is Justification?

A. The Linguistic Meaning

1. The act, process, or state of being justified by God

2. The act or an instance of justifying—vindication

B. The Biblical Meaning

Apostle Paul uses the Greek word *dikaios* which means *righteous* or *just*, and its derivatives, in its purely classical sense in Romans 5:7:

> For scarcely for a *righteous* man will one die; yet perhaps for a good man someone would even dare to die.

In the biblical sense, *dikaios* means *what is right and conforms to right.*

Justification, in the biblical sense, is the act of God removing from the believing sinner his guilt and the penalty incurred by that guilt, and bestowing a positive righteousness—Christ Jesus Himself in whom the believer stands, not only innocent and not condemned, but actually righteous in point of law for time and for eternity.

The words *justify, justification, righteous,* and *righteousness,* when used to refer to man's relationship with God, have a legal, judicial basis. God is the standard of all righteousness.

The white linen curtains of the court of the Tabernacle symbolised:

- The righteousness which God is

- The righteousness which God demands of any human being who desires to have fellowship with Him

- The righteousness which God provides on the basis of the acceptance on the sinner's part of the Lord Jesus, who perfectly satisfied the just demands of God's holy Law which we broke

A just person, therefore, is one who has been thus declared righteous:

For in it the righteousness of God is revealed from faith to faith; as it is written, "The just shall live by faith" (Romans 1:17).

II. What is the Difference Between Justification and Righteousness?

The noun *justification* and the verb *to justify* are not often used in the Scriptures. In the KJV, for example, the verb is found in the Old Testament less than 25 times. In the New Testament, both terms are used only 40 times.

The more frequent and more important terms that translate the same Hebrew and Greek original words are *righteousness* and *to declare (or make) righteous.* Any understanding of justification, therefore, directly involves a biblical understanding of righteousness.

III. What is Righteousness?

A. The Linguistic Meaning

Righteous as an adjective means:

1. Acting in accordance with divine or moral law—free from guilt or sin

2. Morally right or justifiable—a righteous decision

B. The Biblical Meaning

In the Hebrew language, the word is *sedeq*, translated in the Septuagint as *dikaiosynē* (Greek).

The Hebrew *sedeq* probably derives from an Arabic root meaning *straightness*, leading to the notion of an action which conforms to a norm. There is, however, a considerable richness in the biblical understanding of this term and it is difficult to render either the Hebrew or the Greek word by a simple English equivalent.

One basic component of the idea of righteousness in the Old Testament is *relationship*—between God and man and between man and man.

- Between God and man

Let the heavens declare His righteousness, for God Himself is Judge (Psalm 50:6)

"But let him who glories glory in this, that he understands and knows Me, that I am the Lord, exercising lovingkindness, judgement, and righteousness in the earth. For in these I delight," says the Lord (Jeremiah 9:24).

- Between man and man

You shall in any case return the pledge to him again when the sun goes down, that he may sleep in his own garment and bless you; and it shall be righteousness to you before the Lord your God (Deuteronomy 24:13).

Thus says the Lord: "Execute judgement and righteousness, and deliver the plundered out of the hand of the oppressor. Do no wrong and do no violence to the stranger, the fatherless, or the widow, nor shed innocent blood in this place" (Jeremiah 22:3).

Thus, we can say:

- Righteousness is the state of being in the right or being vindicated.

- Righteousness is truth passing into action.

- It is more than pardon; it makes the person right and in right standing with God.

IV. Theological Considerations About Righteousness/Justification

A. Occurrence of the Word in the New Testament

It occurs 39 times in the New Testament:

- 27 times in Paul's epistles, especially in Romans and Galatians

- 8 times in the Synoptic Gospels

- 3 times in the Book of Acts

- 2 times in the Book of Revelation

B. The Scriptural Meaning of the Term

- It is a change in a man's relationship with or standing before God. It has to do with relationships that have been disturbed by sin, and these relationships are personal. It is a change from guilt and condemnation to acquittal and acceptance.

We can thus see that there is a difference between *justification* and *regeneration*:[29]

- *Regeneration* has to do with the change of the believer's nature; *justification* with the change of his standing before God.

- *Regeneration* is subjective; *justification* is objective.

- *Regeneration* has to do with man's state; *justification* with man's standing.

---

[29] In the Bible, regeneration is a spiritual process that represents a radical change from a state of death and separation from God to a new life and receiving the new nature.

- According to Deuteronomy 25:1, the word means to declare or to cause to appear innocent or righteous; according to Romans 4:2–8, it means to reckon righteous; and according to Psalm 32:2, it means not to impute iniquity.

If there is a dispute between men, and they come to court, that the judges may judge them, *and they justify the righteous* and condemn the wicked (Deuteronomy 25:1).

For if Abraham was justified by works, he has something to boast about, but not before God. For what does the Scripture say? "Abraham believed God, and *it was accounted to him for righteousness.*" Now to him who works, the wages are not counted as grace but as debt. But to him who does not work but believes on Him who justifies the ungodly, *his faith is accounted for righteousness,* just as David also describes the blessedness of the man *to whom God imputes righteousness* apart from works: "Blessed are those whose lawless deeds are forgiven, and whose sins are covered; blessed is *the man to whom the Lord shall not impute sin*" (Romans 4:2–8).

Blessed is the man *to whom the Lord does not impute iniquity,* and in whose spirit there is no deceit (Psalm 32:2).

It is clear from these verses that *to justify* does not mean *to make one righteous.* Neither the Hebrew nor the Greek word bears such meaning.

To justify means *to declare righteous in a legal sense, to put a person in a right relation.* It does not deal directly with character or conduct; it is a matter of relationship. Of course, both character and conduct are conditioned and controlled by this relationship.

C. Two Main Elements in Righteousness/Justification According to the Bible

- **The forgiveness of sin and the removal of its guilt and punishment**

It is difficult for us to understand God's feelings towards sin. To us, forgiveness seems easy, mostly because we are indifferent towards sin. But to a holy God, it is different.

Who is a God like You, pardoning iniquity and passing over the transgression of the remnant of His heritage? He does not retain His anger forever, because He delights in mercy. He will again have compassion on us, and will subdue our iniquities. You will cast all our sins into the depths of the sea (Micah 7:18, 19).

But there is forgiveness with You, that You may be feared (Psalm 130:4).

What a wondrous forgiveness!

Forgiveness may be considered as:

- The cessation of the moral anger and resentment of God against sin[30]

- The release from the guilt of sin which oppresses the conscience

- The remission of the punishment of sin, which is eternal death

In justification, then, all our sins are forgiven, and the guilt and punishment are removed:

Therefore let it be known to you, brethren, that through this Man is preached to you the forgiveness of sins; and by Him *everyone who believes is justified* from all things from which you could not be justified by the law of Moses (Acts 13:38, 39).

There is therefore now *no condemnation to those who are in Christ Jesus*, who do not walk according to the flesh, but according to the Spirit (Romans 8:1).

God sees the believer as without sin and guilt in Christ:

He *has not observed iniquity in Jacob, nor has He seen wickedness in Israel.* The Lord his God is with him, and the shout of a King is among them (Numbers 23:21).

Who shall bring a charge against God's elect? It is God who justifies. Who is he who condemns? It is Christ who died, and furthermore is also risen, who is even at the right hand of God, who also makes intercession for us (Romans 8:33, 34).

---

[30] Note that His resentment is against sin, not against the sinner.

- **The imputation of Christ's righteousness and restoration to God's favour**

The forgiven sinner is not like the discharged prisoner who has served out his term and is discharged from further punishment but with no rights of citizenship. No, justification means much more than acquittal. The repentant sinner receives back in his pardon, the full rights of citizenship. The sinner is also granted the righteousness of Jesus Christ:

> Even the righteousness of God, through faith in Jesus Christ, to all and on all who believe (Romans 3:22).

> For if by the one man's offence death reigned through the one, much more those who receive abundance of grace and of the gift of righteousness will reign in life through the One, Jesus Christ. Therefore, as through one man's offence judgement came to all men, resulting in condemnation, even so through one Man's righteous act the free gift came to all men, resulting in justification of life. For as by one man's disobedience many were made sinners, so also by one Man's obedience many will be made righteous. Moreover the law entered that the offence might abound. But where sin abounded, grace abounded much more, so that as sin reigned in death, even so grace might reign through righteousness to eternal life through Jesus Christ our Lord (Romans 5:17–21).

> But of Him you are in Christ Jesus, who became for us wisdom from God— and righteousness and sanctification and redemption (1 Corinthians 1:30).

D. The Means of Justification/Righteousness

- **Not by works of the Law**

> Therefore by the deeds of the law no flesh will be justified in His sight, for by the law is the knowledge of sin (Romans 3:20).

The word *therefore* here implies that a judicial trial has taken place and a judgement has been pronounced.

The reason why the Law cannot justify is stated here: *'For by the law is the knowledge of sin'*. The Law can only open the sinner's eyes to his sin, but it cannot remove it.

- **It is by God's free grace—the origin or source of justification**

Being justified freely by His grace through the redemption that is in Christ Jesus (Romans 3:24).

The word *freely* indicates that justification is granted without anything done on our part to merit or deserve it.

- **By the blood of Jesus Christ—the basis of justification**

Being justified freely by His grace *through the redemption that is in Christ Jesus* (Romans 3:24).

Much more then, *having now been justified by His blood*, we shall be saved from wrath through Him (Romans 5:9).

For He made Him who knew no sin to be sin for us, that we might become the righteousness of God in Him (2 Corinthians 5:21).

The shedding of Christ's blood is connected here with justification:

Without shedding of blood there is no remission [of sin] (Hebrews 9:22).

- **By believing in Jesus Christ—the condition of justification**

Knowing that a man is not justified by the works of the law, but *by faith of Jesus Christ* (Galatians 2:16).

To demonstrate at the present time His righteousness, that He might be just and the justifier of *the one who has faith in Jesus* (Romans 3:26).

'The one who has faith in Jesus' (Romans 3:26) is contrasted with *'For as many as are of the works of the law'* (Galatians 3:10).

We should not take good works lightly or underestimate them for they have their place. However, they follow, not precede justification. The tree *shows* its life by its fruits, but it was alive before the fruit or even the leaves ever appeared.

To sum up, we may say that a person is justified:

- Judicially by God

Who shall bring a charge against God's elect? It is God who justifies (Romans 8:33).

- Meritoriously by Christ

He shall see the labour of His soul, and be satisfied. By His knowledge My righteous Servant shall justify many, for He shall bear their iniquities (Isaiah 53:11).

- Mediately by faith

Therefore, having been justified by faith, we have peace with God through our Lord Jesus Christ (Romans 5:1).

- Evidentially by works

What does it profit, my brethren, if someone says he has faith but does not have works? Can faith save him? ... But someone will say, "You have faith, and I have works." Show me your faith without your works, and I will show you my faith by my works. You believe that there is one God. You do well. Even the demons believe—and tremble! But do you want to know, O foolish man, that faith without works is dead? Was not Abraham our father justified by works when he offered Isaac his son on the altar? Do you see that faith was working together with his works, and by works faith was made perfect? And the Scripture was fulfilled which says, "Abraham believed God, and it was accounted to him for righteousness." And he was called the friend of God. You see then that a man is justified by works, and not by faith only (James 2:14, 18–24).

E. Results and Fruits of Righteousness/Justification

We find these fruits in Romans 5:1–11:

> Therefore, having been justified by faith, *we have peace with God* through our Lord Jesus Christ, through whom also we *have access by faith into this grace in which we stand,* and rejoice in hope of the glory of God. And not only that, but we also *glory in tribulations,* knowing that tribulation produces perseverance; and perseverance, character; and character, hope. Now hope does not disappoint, because the love of God has been poured out in our hearts by the Holy Spirit who was given to us. For when we were still without strength, in due time Christ died for the ungodly. For scarcely for a righteous man will one die; yet perhaps for a good man someone would even dare to die. But God demonstrates His own love toward us, in that while we were still sinners, Christ died for us. Much more then, having now been justified by His blood, we shall be saved from wrath through Him. For if when we were enemies we were reconciled to God through the death of His Son, much more, having been reconciled, we shall be saved by His life. And not only that, but we also rejoice in God through our Lord Jesus Christ, through whom we have now received the reconciliation.

1. Peace with God

2. Access to God

3. Examined by tribulation

4. Pleasure in hope

5. Power to love

6. Pathway to glory

V. Important Implications

How has Christ delivered us from the bondage of the Law?

The passage in Romans 7 provides insight into this matter.

> Or do you not know, brethren (for I speak to those who know the law), that the law has dominion over a man as long as he lives? For the woman who has a husband is bound by the law to her husband as long as he lives. But if the husband dies, she is released from the law of her husband. So then if, while her husband lives, she marries another man, she will be called an adulteress; but if her husband dies, she is free from that law, so that she is no adulteress, though she has married another man. Therefore, my brethren, you also have become dead to the law through the body of Christ, that you may be married to another—to Him who was raised from the dead, that we should bear fruit to God (Romans 7:1–4).

This passage helps us understand how Jesus released us from the bondage of the Law. It is actually a very revelatory and wonderful passage.

Here Paul compares the relationship between man and the Law with the relationship between a husband and a wife. *The Law is the husband* and *human beings are the wife.* It is a binding relationship. This woman (human beings) is married to a very harsh husband (the Law). This was the case throughout the Old Testament. Though the Law is the Word of God and it brought life, it also brought bondage at the same time, as we will shortly understand.

This husband is harsh because every Israelite has to strictly follow the Law and the Law is difficult due to the fallen human nature. The fallen nature cannot fulfil the Law/the commandments in the absence of grace.

This harsh husband, thus, keeps telling his wife about things that she has to do which she is unable to do, to the extent that she wishes that either she dies or he dies so that she would be free.

Yet, if she dies, she will not live free, and, at the same time, he cannot die because *he is the holy Word of God* that cannot die.

Jesus offered the solution to this dilemma. He united Himself with the woman, took her in Him to the cross, and died on the cross; hence, she died and was freed from the husband. She was free because she was no longer alive. She died with Christ and in Christ. Then, Christ arose from the dead, and the woman arose with Him. As a result, she lived in Him and was freed from the husband. Thus, she can thereafter live free and bear the fruits of life.

If we look at each of the above verses, we shall clearly see the following:

- Verse 1 shows that the Law completely dominates Man and binds him.

- Verse 2 reveals that the relationship between Man and the Law is similar to the relationship between a husband and a wife.

As long as the husband is alive, the woman is under his authority, but if he dies she will be freed from his authority. This means that the human being (the woman) needs the Law (the husband) to die so that she may be freed from slavery.

- Verse 3 states that as long as the husband is alive, the woman will be an adulteress if she marries someone else.

As long as the Law is alive, she is bound to him. Yet, if this husband (the Law) dies, she is free from the Law.

But how can he die, he is the Law!

- Verse 4 sums up the whole revelation in one verse.

Paul says that we have become dead to the Law through the body of Christ. This means that when we became united with Christ, it is as though we died with Him on the cross and hence were freed from the Law.

The purpose of this is to belong to another after being freed from the first bondage. This other one is the One who arose from the dead (Jesus); thus, we can bear fruits to God.

To sum up this story:

Paul says that Christ loved His Church (and every soul in her), therefore, He wanted to free her from the one that she was united with. Thus, He took her, became united with her, died with her, and hence she was freed. Then, He arose with her and made her free to bear fruits for the Kingdom of God!

The difference between Apostle Paul's and Apostle James' teachings about justification

The Epistle of James is often seen to be in conflict with Paul's teaching on justification because Paul says that justification is by faith not by works of the Law.

Yet, is there really a difference between the two teachings?

Speaking about this topic, Apostle James says:

> What good is it, my brothers, if someone says he has faith but does not have works? Can that faith save him? If a brother or sister is poorly clothed and lacking in daily food, and one of you says to them, "Go in peace, be warmed and filled," without giving them the things needed for the body, what good is that? So also faith by itself, if it does not have works, is dead. But someone will say, "You have faith and I have works." Show me your faith apart from your works, and I will show you my faith by my works. You believe that God is one; you do well. Even the demons believe—and shudder! Do you want to be shown, you foolish person, that faith apart from works is useless? Was not Abraham our father justified by works when he offered up his son Isaac on the altar? You see that faith was active along with his works, and faith was completed by his works; and the Scripture was fulfilled that says, "Abraham believed God, and it was counted to him as righteousness"—and he was called a friend of God. You see that a person is justified by works and not by faith alone. And in the same way was not also Rahab the prostitute justified by works when she received the messengers and sent them out by another way? For as the body apart from the spirit is dead, so also faith apart from works is dead (James 2:14–26, ESV).

The point is, when Paul and James speak of *works*, they actually speak of different concepts.

Paul is speaking of works of the Law, meaning works as an expression of the Law, or what might be called *Law-works* (Romans 3:20).

James, on the other hand, never speaks of works of the Law but rather of works that give expression to faith, or what might be called *faith-works*.

Paul speaks about Law-works, while James speaks about faith-works. Therefore, Paul says that Law-works have no place, while James says that faith-works are necessary.

James regards faith without works as dead—that is, as no faith at all (James 2:17). For him faith is expressed and perfected by works.

Both Apostle Paul and Apostle James affirm that a person comes into a living relationship with God and continues in this relationship through faith, which is accompanied by the love and obedience that are born of faith.

VI. Practical Considerations

How do the points we discussed affect our spiritual life and what is their practical value for us?

Salvation is by faith not by works; however, true faith has works and bears fruits that are not the works of the Law.

What are these works then?

The answer is in the following verses:

> For what the law could not do in that it was weak through the flesh, God did by sending His own Son in the likeness of sinful flesh, on account of sin: He condemned sin in the flesh, *that the righteous requirement of the law might be fulfilled* in us who do not walk according to the flesh but according to the Spirit (Romans 8:3, 4).

This passage highlights that the requirement of the Law is to live in righteousness. However, due to man's fallen nature, man was unable to live in righteousness. Therefore, Jesus came to solve this problem. How? The passage in Matthew 22:35–40 provides the answer:

> Then one of them, a lawyer, asked Him a question, testing Him, and saying, "Teacher, which is the great commandment in the law?" Jesus said to him, "'You shall love the Lord your God with all your heart, with all your soul, and with all your mind.' This is the first and great commandment. And the second is like it: 'You shall love your neighbour as yourself.' On these two commandments hang all the Law and the Prophets."

Man was struggling, not knowing how to obey the Law. He was actually lost in the multitude of commandments, not knowing what to do. Jesus came and summed up the whole Law in one principle, highlighting that the Law simply means love: to love God and love others. God is love; therefore, His Law is love. The same principle is highlighted in other verses in the New Testament to confirm it:

Now *the purpose of the commandment is love* from a pure heart, from a good conscience, and from sincere faith, from which some, having strayed, have turned aside to idle talk, desiring to be teachers of the law, understanding neither what they say nor the things which they affirm (1 Timothy 1:5–7).

The same principle is also reflected in Romans 13:8–10. Love is the fulfilment of the Law:

Owe no one anything except to love one another, *for he who loves another has fulfilled the law.* For the commandments, "You shall not commit adultery," "You shall not murder," "You shall not steal," "You shall not bear false witness," "You shall not covet," and if there is any other commandment, are all summed up in this saying, namely, "You shall love your neighbour as yourself." Love does no harm to a neighbour; therefore love is the fulfilment of the law (Romans 13:8–10).

A heart that is full of love is free in what it does. It acts according to the law of liberty. Thus, love leads to liberty:

But he who looks into *the perfect law of liberty* and continues in it, and is not a forgetful hearer but a doer of the work, this one will be blessed in what he does (James 1:25).

So speak and so do as those who will be judged by *the law of liberty* (James 2:12).

If you really fulfil the *royal law* according to the Scripture, "You shall love your neighbour as yourself," you do well (James 2:8).

The *royal law* here indicates that the person would act with liberty as a king would.

There is no difference in achieving righteousness in the Old Testament and in the New Testament because God's mind is unchangeable. But His plans and economy can change according to the people He is addressing. Therefore, achieving righteousness is the same in both the Old and New Testaments. However, in the Old Testament, it is achieved from the outside (externally) through the order of the Law, whereas, in the New Testament, it is achieved from the inside (internally) by the Holy Spirit. In the Old

Testament, everyone failed because of the weakness of human nature. Hence, failure in the Old Testament to keep the commandments was not due to a fault in the Law but due to the weakness in human nature, as we read in Romans 7:7–14 and Hebrews 8:7–13.

In the New Testament, everyone can succeed because of the enabling of the Holy Spirit. Not only this, but also in the New Testament, we have received a new heart. Thus, we have the Holy Spirit and we have a new heart. This principle is not only stated in the New Testament but it was prophetically proclaimed in the Old Testament.

In Ezekiel 36, the prophet speaks about the new heart:

> I will give you *a new heart and put a new spirit* within you; I will take the heart of stone out of your flesh and give you a heart of flesh (Ezekiel 36:26).

Also, in Jeremiah 31, we read:

> Behold, the days are coming, says the Lord, when I will make a new covenant with the house of Israel and with the house of Judah—not according to the covenant that I made with their fathers in the day that I took them by the hand to lead them out of the land of Egypt, My covenant which they broke, though I was a husband to them, says the Lord. But this is the covenant that I will make with the house of Israel after those days, says the Lord: *I will put My law in their minds, and write it on their hearts*; and I will be their God, and they shall be My people (Jeremiah 31:31–33).

Thus, we can see that the commandments are written by the Spirit on the new heart:

> Clearly you are an epistle of Christ, ministered by us, written not with ink but by the Spirit of the living God, not on tablets of stone but on tablets of flesh, that is, of the heart (2 Corinthians 3:3).

> For this is the covenant that I will make with the house of Israel after those days, says the Lord: I will put My laws in their mind and write them on their hearts; and I will be their God, and they shall be My people (Hebrews 8:10).

Note that what Apostle Paul states in Romans 8:3, 4 is that the Law depended on man's ability, thus, it failed (Galatians 3:10–13). However, grace works in man by the Holy Spirit, leading to success. It is thus written:

> Now hope does not disappoint, because the love of God has been poured out in our hearts by the Holy Spirit who was given to us (Romans 5:5).

> But the fruit of the Spirit is love, joy, peace, longsuffering, kindness, goodness, faithfulness, gentleness, self-control. Against such there is no law (Galatians 5:22–23).

When love reigns in the heart and its fruits start to appear, this heart no longer needs the judgement of the Law.

This leads us to an important principle:

Love, in the New Testament, is not without challenges, but it has its special law or rule. The law of love is obedience. If we truly love God, we will surely be obedient to Him whatever the cost:

> But this is what *I commanded them*, saying, '*Obey My voice*, and I will be your God, and you shall be My people. And walk in all the ways that I have commanded you, that it may be well with you' (Jeremiah 7:23).

> "If you love Me, keep My commandments" … "He who has My commandments and keeps them, it is he who loves Me. And he who loves Me will be loved by My Father, and I will love him and manifest Myself to him." … Jesus answered and said to him, "If anyone loves Me, he will keep My word; and My Father will love him, and We will come to him and make Our home with him. He who does not love Me does not keep My words; and the word which you hear is not Mine but the Father's who sent Me" (John 14:15, 21, 23, 24).

Therefore, our responsibility lies in:

• Our relationship with the Word of God and our obedience to it

> But whoever keeps His word, truly the love of God is perfected in him. By this we know that we are in Him (1 John 2:5).

- Acquiring a life of prayer to have a living fellowship with the Holy Spirit continuously

  And *do not grieve the Holy Spirit of God,* by whom you were sealed for the day of redemption' (Ephesians 4:30).

  Do *not quench the Spirit* (1 Thessalonians 5:19).

  You stiff-necked and uncircumcised in heart and ears! You always *resist* the Holy Spirit; as your fathers did, so do you (Acts 7:51).

VII. Conclusion: Righteousness in the Bible in General

1. Righteousness is obedience to God's Law (Deuteronomy 6:25; Romans 10:5; Luke 1:6; Psalm 1:2).

2. God loves righteousness (Psalm 11:7).

3. God looks for righteousness (Isaiah 5:7).

4. Christ:

   a. Christ is the Sun of Righteousness (Malachi 4:2).

   b. Christ loves righteousness (Psalm 45:7; Hebrews 1:9).

   c. Christ was girded with righteousness (Isaiah 11:5).

   d. Christ put on righteousness as a breastplate (Isaiah 59:17).

   e. Christ was sustained by righteousness (Isaiah 59:16).

   f. Christ preached righteousness (Psalm 40:9).

   g. Christ fulfilled all righteousness (Matthew 3:15).

   h. Christ is made righteousness to His people (1 Corinthians 1:30).

   i. Christ is the end of the Law for righteousness (Romans 10:4).

   j. Christ has brought in everlasting righteousness (Daniel 9:24).

   k. Christ shall judge with righteousness (Psalm 72:2; Isaiah 11:4; Acts 17:31; Revelation 19:11).

   l. Christ shall reign in righteousness (Psalm 45:6; Isaiah 32:1; Hebrews 1:8).

   m. Christ shall execute righteousness (Psalm 99:4; Jeremiah 23:6).

5. None, by nature, have righteousness (Job 15:14; Psalm 14:3; Romans 3:10).

6. Righteousness cannot come by the Law (Galatians 2:21; 3:21).

7. No justification by works of righteousness (Romans 3:20; 9:31, 32; Galatians 2:16).

8. No salvation by works of righteousness (Ephesians 2:8, 9; 2 Timothy 1:9; Titus 3:5).

9. The unrepentant man seeks to be justified by works of righteousness— like the Pharisee in the parable of the Pharisee and the tax collector (Luke 18:9–14; Romans 10:3).

10. The blessing of God is not to be attributed to our works of righteousness (Deuteronomy 9:5).

11. Saints:

   a. Saints have righteousness in Christ (Isaiah 45:24; 54:17; 2 Corinthians 5:21).

   b. Righteousness is attributed to the saints (Romans 4:11, 22).

   c. Saints are covered with the robe of righteousness (Isaiah 61:10).

   d. Saints receive righteousness from God (Psalm 24:5).

   e. Saints are renewed in righteousness (Ephesians 4:24).

   f. Saints are led in the paths of righteousness (Psalm 23:3).

   g. Saints are servants of righteousness (Romans 6:16,18).

   h. Saints are characterised by righteousness (Genesis 18:25; Psalm 1:5,6).

   i. Saints know righteousness (Isaiah 51:7).

   j. Saints do righteousness (1 John 2:29; 3:7).

   k. Saints work righteousness by faith (Hebrews 11:33).

   l. Saints follow after righteousness (Isaiah 51:1).

   m. Saints put on righteousness (Job 29:14).

   n. Saints wait for the hope of righteousness (Galatians 5:5).

   o. Saints pray for the spirit of righteousness (Psalm 51:10).

p. Saints hunger and thirst after righteousness (Matthew 5:6).

q. Saints walk before God in righteousness (1 Kings 3:6).

r. Saints offer the sacrifice of righteousness (Psalm 4:5; 51:19).

s. Saints put no trust in their own righteousness (Philippians 3:6–9).

t. Saints count their own righteousness as filthy rags (Isaiah 64:6).

u. Saints should seek righteousness (Zephaniah 2:3).

v. Saints should live in righteousness (Titus 2:12; 1 Peter 2:24).

w. Saints should serve God in righteousness (Luke 1:75).

x. Saints should present their members as instruments of righteousness (Romans 6:13).

y. Saints should present their members as slaves of righteousness (Romans 6:19).

z. Saints should put on the breastplate of righteousness (Ephesians 6:14).

aa. Saints shall receive a crown of righteousness (2 Timothy 4:8).

bb. Saints shall see God's face in righteousness (Psalm 17:15).

12. The righteousness of saints endures forever (Psalm 112:3, 9; 2 Corinthians 9:9).

13. Righteousness is evidence of the new birth (1 John 2:29).

14. The Kingdom of God is righteousness (Romans 14:17).

15. The fruit of the Spirit is in all righteousness (Ephesians 5:9).

16. The Scriptures instruct in righteousness (2 Timothy 3:16).

17. Judgements are designed to lead to righteousness (Isaiah 26:9).

18. Chastisements yield the fruit of righteousness (Hebrews 12:11).

19. Righteousness has no fellowship with unrighteousness (lawlessness) (2 Corinthians 6:14).

20. Ministers (the servants of the Lord) should:

    a. be preachers of righteousness (2 Peter 2:5).

    b. reason about righteousness (Acts 24:25).

    c. follow after righteousness (1 Timothy 6:11; 2 Timothy 2:22).

    d. be clothed with righteousness (Psalm 132:9).

    e. be armed with righteousness (2 Corinthians 6:7).

    f. pray for the fruit of righteousness in their people (2 Corinthians 9:10; Philippians 1:11).

21. Righteousness keeps saints in the right way (Proverbs 11:5; 13:6).

22. Judgement should be executed in righteousness (Leviticus 19:15).

23. Those who walk in righteousness and follow righteousness:

    a. are righteous (1 John 3:7).

    b. are the excellent of the earth (Psalm 16:3; Proverbs 12:26).

    c. are accepted by God (Acts 10:35).

    d. are loved by God (Psalm 146:8; Proverbs 15:9).

    e. are blessed by God (Psalm 5:12).

    f. are heard by God (Luke 18:7; James 5:16).

    g. are objects of God's watchful care (Job 36:7; Psalm 34:15; Proverbs 10:3; 1 Peter 3:12).

    h. are tried by God (Psalm 11:5).

    i. are exalted by God (Job 36:7).

    j. dwell in security (Isaiah 33:15,16).

k. are bold as a lion (Proverbs 28:1).

l. are delivered out of all troubles (Psalm 34:19; Proverbs 11:8).

m. are never forsaken by God (Psalm 37:25).

n. are abundantly provided for (Proverbs 13:25; Matthew 6:25-33).

o. are enriched (Psalm 112:3; Proverbs 15:6).

p. think and desire good (Proverbs 11:23; 12:5).

q. know the secret of the Lord (Psalm 25:14; Proverbs 3:32).

r. have their prayers heard (Psalm 34:17; Proverbs 15:29; 1 Peter 3:12).

s. have their desires granted (Proverbs 10:24).

t. are those who follow righteousness, find righteousness, life, and honour (Proverbs 21:21).

u. The righteous shall hold on to his way (Job 17:9).

v. He who walks uprightly shall never be moved (Psalm 15:2,5b; 55:22; Proverbs 10:30; 12:3).

w. The righteous shall always be remembered (Psalm 112:6).

x. The righteous shall flourish as a branch (Proverbs 11:28).

24. The righteous shall be glad in the Lord (Psalm 64:10).

25. Righteousness brings its own reward (Proverbs 11:18; Isaiah 3:10).

26. Righteousness leads to life (Proverbs 11:19; 12:28).

27. The work of righteousness will be peace (Isaiah 32:17).

28. The effect of righteousness will be quietness and assurance forever (Isaiah 32:17).

29. Righteousness is a crown of glory to the aged (Proverbs 16:31).

30. The wicked:

   a. are far from righteousness (Psalm 119:150; Isaiah 46:12).

   b. are free from righteousness (Romans 6:20).

   c. are enemies of righteousness (Acts 13:10).

   d. cast down righteousness to the earth/cease to do righteousness (Amos 5:7; Psalm 36:3).

   e. do not follow after righteousness (Romans 9:30).

   f. do not practise righteousness (1 John 3:10.

   g. do not obey righteousness (Romans 2:8; 2 Thessalonians 2:12).

   h. love lying rather than righteousness (Psalm 52:3).

   i. make mention of God, but not in righteousness (Isaiah 48:1).

   j. though favoured, will not learn righteousness (Isaiah 26:10; Psalm 106:43).

   k. speak contemptuously (meaning mockingly or scornfully) against those who follow righteousness (Psalm 31:18; Matthew 27:39-44).

   l. hate those who follow righteousness (Psalm 34:21).

   m. slay those who follow righteousness (Psalm 37:32; 1 John 3:12; Matthew 23:35).

   n. should break off their sins by righteousness (Daniel 4:27).

   o. should awake to righteousness (1 Corinthians 15:34).

   p. should sow to themselves in righteousness (Hosea 10:12).

   q. vainly wish to die the death of the righteous (Numbers 23:10).

31. The throne of kings is established by righteousness (Proverbs 16:12; 25:5).

32. Nations are exalted by righteousness (Proverbs 14:34).

33. Blessedness of:

   a. the man to whom God imputes righteousness without works (Romans 4:6).

   b. he who does righteousness (Psalm 106:3).

   c. those who hunger and thirst for righteousness (Matthew 5:6).

   d. those who suffer for righteousness' sake (1 Peter 3:14).

   e. those who are persecuted for righteousness' sake (Matthew 5:10).

   f. those who turn others to righteousness (Daniel 12:3).

34. Righteousness is promised to the Church (Isaiah 32:16; 45:8; 61:11; 62:1).

35. Righteousness is promised to saints (Isaiah 60:21; 61:3).

36. Righteousness was exemplified in:

   a. Jacob (Genesis 30:33).

   b. David (2 Samuel 22:21).

   c. Zacharias (Luke 1:6).

   d. Abel (Hebrews 11:4).

   e. Lot (2 Peter 2:8).

CHAPTER 8

THE BLOOD OF JESUS
SANCTIFIES ME AND CONSECRATES ME
SO I BECOME BELONGING TO MY LORD,
DEDICATED TO HIM,
AND SET APART FOR HIS MINISTRY

Readings

E lect according to the foreknowledge of God the Father, *in sanctification of the Spirit,* for obedience and sprinkling of the blood of Jesus Christ: Grace to you and peace be multiplied (1 Peter 1:2).

Therefore Jesus also, *that He might sanctify the people with His own blood,* suffered outside the gate (Hebrews 13:12–13).

Introduction

We will study the topic of sanctification in five main titles:

I. The Linguistic Meaning of the Word *Sanctification*, Including the Original Hebrew and Greek Languages

II. The Biblical Meaning of Sanctification

III. Theological Considerations

IV. Practical Considerations

V. Summary: Sanctification According to the Bible

I. The Meaning of the Word *Sanctification*

A. The Linguistic Meaning

Sanctification (noun)

1. An act of sanctifying

2. The state of being sanctified

3. The state of growing in divine grace as a result of Christian commitment after baptism or conversion

Sanctify (verb)

1. To set apart for a sacred purpose or religious use—*consecrate*

2. To free from sin—*purify*

3. To impart or attribute respect or sacredness that is never to be broken

4. To make holiness or piety fruitful—observe the Sabbath day, to *sanctify* it (Deuteronomy 5:12)

B. The Meaning According to the Hebrew Language of the Old Testament

The main Hebrew root denoting holiness or the holy is *qdŝ*,[31] meaning *separate from the ordinary or profane.*

It appears as a noun, verb, and adjective over 850 times in the Old Testament.

Sanctification in the Old Testament was a long journey of training that depended on various factors:

- The people consecrating themselves before they could approach the Lord (Exodus 19:22–24; Leviticus 20:7, 8, 26)

---

[31] In the Septuagint, the *qdŝ* group is translated primarily by the *hagios* group.

- Keeping the Sabbath as a sign of sanctification (Exodus 31:13; Ezekiel 20:12, 20)

- Clinging to the Lord (Exodus 29:43; Deuteronomy 4:4)

- God's covenant that kept the people of Israel in relation with the Holy God who sanctified them (Exodus 19:5, 6)

- Rituals such as sprinkling with blood sanctified places, objects, and persons (Exodus 24:8) OR, sometimes, using water for the same purpose (Numbers 19:9, 20; 31:21–23)

These were the main factors that helped the people of Israel in the Old Testament to be sanctified. These factors or means were suitable for their spiritual stature at that time. In the meantime, this was the training process that would bring them into the New Testament sanctification.

C. The Meaning According to the Greek Language of the New Testament

The Greek biblical term *hagiázō* or *hagiasmos* means *to consecrate* or *to sanctify*.

Important points that reflect God's mind regarding sanctification:

- We are requested to hallow and sanctify God's name (Matthew 6:9).

- Jesus sanctifies Himself (John 17:19) and His Church (Ephesians 5:26)—a divine work.

- The Father sanctifies Christ (John 10:36) so that Christ may sanctify His disciples (John 17:19). Christ sanctifies His disciples through His reconciling work (Hebrews 2:11; 10:10). Thus, according to Apostle Paul, we are *the sanctified* (1 Corinthians 1:2), and this is a state (1 Corinthians 6:11).

- The sanctified have an inheritance (Acts 20:32). They ought to sanctify Christ in their hearts (1 Peter 3:15) and be holy in conduct, for Christ makes them holy by dwelling in them (1 Peter 1:15, 16).

II. Biblical Meanings

Biblically, there are three main meanings for sanctification:

1. To make holy (Exodus 19:10; Joshua 3:5)

2. To set apart (2 Corinthians 7:1)

3. To be separate from sin (Romans 6:19)

III. Theological Considerations

The Definition of *Sanctification*

Sanctification is the process by which, according to the will of God, we are made partakers of His holiness.

It is a progressive work that begins with regeneration and continues in the hearts of believers by the presence and power of the Holy Spirit, the Sealer and Comforter. This progressive work requires several means; namely, repentance, prayer, the Word of God, self-examination, self-denial, and watchfulness.

Comments on the Definition to Clarify

This definition helps us to distinguish *sanctification* from *regeneration* in that the latter speaks of the beginning of the Christian life.

Sanctification is also distinguished from *glorification*, which focuses on the consummation of God's work in the believer.

To put it in simple words, *regeneration* refers to *the beginning*, *sanctification* to *the middle*, and *glorification* to *the end* of salvation.

The distinction between *sanctification* and *justification* requires more detailed attention.

- In the first place, *justification*, like *regeneration*, refers (though not exclusively) to the beginning of the Christian experience, whereas, *sanctification* is progressive in its nature.

- Second, *justification* refers to a judicial act of God by which believers are **at once** absolved of all their guilt and accounted legally righteous, whereas, *sanctification* draws our attention to the power of the Holy Spirit that transforms the character of God's children, and this is ***a process***.

We are made partakers of His holiness.[32] Therefore, the standard of holiness is complete conformity to Christ's image (Romans 8:29). Anything less than that standard is considered a lowering of the scriptural standard and is thus a dilution of the doctrine. However, the above definition implies that Christ is more than our pattern: He Himself provides His holiness for those united with Him; He is our sanctification (1 Corinthians 1:30).

Aspects of Sanctification

Sanctification has three aspects:

- *The positional aspect*

First, the believer has been set apart by his position in the family of God. This is usually called *positional sanctification.*

It means being set apart as a member of the household of God. It is true of every believer regardless of his spiritual condition, for this concerns his spiritual state.[33] This positional sanctification is based on the death of Christ as clear from Hebrews 10:10:

> By that will we have been sanctified through the offering of the body of Jesus Christ once for all.

- *The experiential aspect*

Of course, there is also the *experiential aspect of sanctification.* Because we have been set apart we ought to be increasingly set apart in our daily lives and conduct:

> But as He who called you is holy, you also be holy in all your conduct, because it is written, "Be holy, for I am holy" (1 Peter 1:15, 16).

---

[32] Hebrews 12:10

[33] Read 1 Corinthians 6:11 and remember the carnal condition of these believers.

In the positional aspect, no one is more sanctified than another. We are all equal in this positional sanctification because, in Christ, God has put us all in this level of sanctification. But in the experiential aspect, it is quite correct to speak of one believer as being more sanctified than another.

All the exhortations of the New Testament concerning spiritual growth are related to this progressive and experiential facet of sanctification. It is a life-long process.

- *The ultimate or future aspect*

We will not be fully set apart to God until our position and practice are brought into perfect accord, and this will happen only when we see Christ and become as He is:

> Behold what manner of love the Father has bestowed on us, that we should be called children of God! Therefore the world does not know us, because it did not know Him. Beloved, now we are children of God; and it has not yet been revealed what we shall be, but we know that when He is revealed, *we shall be like Him, for we shall see Him as He is. And everyone who has this hope in Him purifies himself, just as He is pure* (1 John 3:1–3).

Thus, there is an aspect to sanctification which is often called *ultimate* or *future sanctification* and which awaits our complete glorification with the resurrection of the bodies:

> That He might sanctify and cleanse her with the washing of water by the word, that He might present her to Himself a glorious church, not having spot or wrinkle or any such thing, but that she should be holy and without blemish (Ephesians 5:26, 27).

> Now to Him who is able to keep you from stumbling, and to present you fault-less before the presence of His glory with exceeding joy, to God our Saviour, who alone is wise, be glory and majesty, dominion and power, both now and forever. Amen (Jude 24, 25).

The Nature of Sanctification

In its nature, sanctification is a divine work:

> Now *may the God of peace Himself sanctify you completely*; and may your whole spirit, soul, and body be preserved blameless at the coming of our Lord Jesus Christ (1 Thessalonians 5:23).

> Elect according to the foreknowledge of God the Father, *in sanctification of the Spirit*, for obedience and sprinkling of the blood of Jesus Christ: Grace to you and peace be multiplied (1 Peter 1:2).

The Dynamics of Sanctification

- Sanctification is *already* ours

- *Yet*, we need to work out our salvation/our sanctification

- Sanctification is finally completed when we meet Christ

Now, let us look at each of these three points in some detail:

- **Sanctification is already ours in Christ**

Apostle Paul frequently refers to Christians as *saints*, meaning *holy people* (Romans 1:7; Ephesians 1:1).

Paul specifically says that the Christians of the church at Corinth *are sanctified*:

> To the church of God which is at Corinth, to those *who are sanctified in Christ Jesus, called to be saints*, with all who in every place call on the name of Jesus Christ our Lord, both theirs and ours' (1 Corinthians 1:2).

The sacrifice of Christ that was offered once for all, and which has been given to the believers from the very beginning of their walk with Christ, sanctifies them:

> But with His own blood He entered the Most Holy Place *once for all*, having obtained eternal redemption (Hebrews 9:12b).

For *by one offering He has perfected forever* those who are being sanctified (Hebrews 10:14).

It is thus clear that we have been sanctified by the offering of Christ and His blood.

- **Yet, we need to work out our salvation**

Sanctification is not merely a *gift* that we passively receive. Christians must live a holy life that reflects what they have received as the Scriptures highlight in many passages:

> Present your members as slaves of righteousness *for holiness* (Romans 6:19).

> For this is the will of God, your sanctification: that you should abstain from sexual immorality ... For God did not call us to uncleanness, but *in holiness* (1 Thessalonians 4:3, 4:7).

> Nevertheless she will be saved in childbearing if they continue in faith, love, and *holiness,* with self-control (1 Timothy 2:15).

> *Pursue* peace with all people, and *holiness,* without which no one will see the Lord (Hebrews 12:14).

The progressive nature of our sanctification is clear in many passages, particularly in Paul's statement that Christians are transformed *from glory to glory* into Christ's image (2 Corinthians 3:18; see also Romans 12:1–2; Philippians 3:14; Hebrews 6:1; 2 Peter 3:18). Moreover, the numerous commands found in the Scriptures imply that Christians ought to experience spiritual growth.

No passage of Scripture is more relevant to this issue than Philippians 2:12, 13, in which Apostle Paul puts the command for one to work out his own salvation side by side with the declaration that it is God who provides the spiritual strength necessary for the task.

Sometimes, we focus on the first part of the statement and ignore the fundamental significance of the second. Conversely, we may become so captivated by Paul's stress on divine grace that the weight of personal responsibility is overlooked. The apostle, however, appears to have deliberately and carefully preserved a fine balance between these two truths:

Therefore, my beloved, as you have always obeyed, not as in my presence only, but now much more in my absence, *work out your own salvation* with fear and trembling; for it is God who works in you both to will and to do for His good pleasure (Philippians 2:12, 13).

Working out our salvation is a commandment as the verse highlights. But it is also clear that God provides the spiritual strength necessary for this task.

Thus, we can say that it is a divine synergy between the Holy Spirit and the will of the believer:

God from the beginning chose you for salvation through sanctification by the Spirit and belief in the truth (2 Thessalonians 2:13).

Now may the God of peace Himself sanctify you completely; and may your whole spirit, soul, and body be preserved blameless at the coming of our Lord Jesus Christ (1 Thessalonians 5:23).

Sanctification requires discipline, focus, and effort, as is clear by the many exhortations of the Scriptures, especially in the passages where the Christian life is described with metaphors such as running and fighting (1 Corinthians 9:24–27; 2 Corinthians 6:14–7:1; Ephesians 6:10–17; 1 Timothy 6:12; 2 Timothy 2:3–5; Hebrews 4:11; 2 Peter 1:3–11).

It is important to keep this biblical truth in mind because some may think that sanctification has already been completed by grace and so nothing is required from us.

Yet, the real *secret of holiness* is learning to keep that balance: relying thoroughly on God as the true agent in sanctification, while faithfully performing one's personal responsibility.

Christ has completed everything. Therefore, our role is not to do something that merits receiving all that Christ has done for us because God's grace is given freely. But our role is to prepare ourselves to receive the grace. Inasmuch as we prepare ourselves, we will receive more and more of the grace, and hence we will be transformed more into Christlikeness. Grace is very near; it is around every person, visiting him. It searches for an available place inside the person to enter into, yet sometimes does not find one. We are so filled with worldly matters and fleshly desires to the extent that there is no room for the grace. Therefore, our role is to get rid of these things to prepare a place inside us for the grace to enter.

- **Sanctification is finally completed when we meet Christ**

Beloved, now we are children of God; and it has not yet been revealed what we shall be, but we know that *when He is revealed, we shall be like Him*, for we shall see Him as He is (1 John 3:2).

Perfect sanctification is not attainable in this life:

When they sin against You (for there is no one who does not sin) (1 Kings 8:46).

Who can say, "I have made my heart clean, I am pure from my sin"? (Proverbs 20:9).

For there is not a just man on earth who does good and does not sin (Ecclesiastes 7:20).

For we all stumble in many things. If anyone does not stumble in word, he is a perfect man, able also to bridle the whole body (James 3:2).

If we say that we have no sin, we deceive ourselves, and the truth is not in us (1 John 1:8).

Refer also to Philippians 3:12–14 and 1 Timothy 1:15.

See also the confessions of David (Psalms 19:12, 13; 51); of Moses (Psalm 90:8); of Job (42:5, 6); and of Daniel (9:3–20).

The more holy a man is, the more humble, self-renouncing, self-abhorring, and the more sensitive to every sin he becomes, and the more closely he clings to Christ. The moral imperfections which cling to him he feels to be sins, which he laments and strives to overcome.

Believers find that their life is a constant warfare, and they need to take the king-dom of heaven by storm, and watch while they pray. They are always subject to the constant chastisement of their Father's loving hand, which can only be de-signed to correct their imperfections and to confirm their graces.[34]

---

[34] Easton, M. G. (2015). *Easton's Bible Dictionary.*

IV. Practical Considerations

A. The Means of Sanctification

1. The Spirit of God

In the economy of redemption, the Holy Spirit performs this work of sanctification in us:

> But we are bound to give thanks to God always for you, brethren beloved by the Lord, because God from the beginning chose you for salvation *through sanctification by the Spirit* and belief in the truth (2 Thessalonians 2:13).

> And such were some of you. But you were washed, but *you were sanctified,* but you were justified in the name of the Lord Jesus and *by the Spirit of our God* (1 Corinthians 6:11).

> Elect according to the foreknowledge of God the Father, in *sanctification of the Spirit,* for obedience and sprinkling of the blood of Jesus Christ (1 Peter 1:2).

2. The Word of God

> *Sanctify them by Your truth.* Your word is truth (John 17:17).

> That He might *sanctify* and cleanse her with the washing of water *by the word* (Ephesians 5:26).

3. The Person of Christ, His Cross, and His Blood

> But of Him you are in Christ Jesus, who became for us wisdom from God— and righteousness and *sanctification* and redemption (1 Corinthians 1:30).

> And by Him to reconcile all things to Himself, by Him, whether things on earth or things in heaven, having made peace through the blood of His cross. And you, who once were alienated and enemies in your mind by wicked works, yet now *He has reconciled in the body of His flesh through death, to present you holy,* and blameless, and above reproach in His sight (Colossians 1:20–22).

For by one offering He has perfected forever those who are being sanctified ... Of how much worse punishment, do you suppose, will he be thought worthy who has trampled the Son of God underfoot, counted *the blood of the covenant by which he was sanctified* a common thing, and insulted the Spirit of grace? (Hebrews 10:14, 29).

Therefore Jesus also, that He might *sanctify the people with His own blood,* suffered outside the gate (Hebrews 13:12).

The cross and the blood of Christ are inseparable.

- In the Old Testament, there were two sacrifices that represented the work of the blood that cleanses from sins (the trespass offering) and the work of the cross that deals with the nature of sin (the sin offering). Both offerings refer to the work of the blood and the cross of Jesus. In fact, there are different views on this matter and scholars differ on it. But the point is that sin is the root, while trespasses are the branches. Therefore, the cross deals with the nature of sin, while the blood covers the trespasses.

- Jesus said, *Follow Me,* which in the original Greek language is *akoloutheō* and it means to be close and walk in the same direction as a disciple to a teacher because Jesus *became for us sanctification from God* (1 Corinthians 1:30).

- Being united with the Crucified Christ frees us from sin (Romans 6:5–13).

4. Faith

To open their eyes, in order to turn them from darkness to light, and from the power of Satan to God, that they may receive forgiveness of sins and an inheritance among those *who are sanctified by faith in Me* (Acts 26:18).

Faith is essential in the process of sanctification, exactly as it is essential in the believer's unity with Christ (Galatians 2:20) and in bringing the believer into living contact with the truth, whereby he obeys the commandments and embraces the promises of God for this life and the life to come.

5. The Altar

Fools and blind! For which is greater, the gift or *the altar that sanctifies* the gift (Matthew 23:19).

B. How Do All These Means or Tools Work Together to Bring About This Sanctification?

1. The *Holy Spirit* creates in us the desire and hunger for holiness.

2. The Holy Spirit directs the searchlight of the *Word of God* towards our conscience and urges us to hunger for holiness.

3. In response to His work, we bring every area in our lives into His light and put every hindering desire on the *Altar*.

4. Then, the work of the *Blood* cleanses us anew.

5. All this depends on exercising our *Faith*.

C. Two Aspects of Sanctification

Notice that there are always two aspects of sanctification. In one we deal with and get rid of negative matters, and in the other, we receive positive matters.

Some scriptural examples:

- Hebrews 12:1: *lay aside the sin which so easily ensnares us* (getting rid of negative matters)
  Hebrews 12:10: *that we may be partakers of His Holiness* (receiving a positive matter)

- Romans 12:2: *do not be conformed to this world* (negative aspect)
  Romans 8:29: *be conformed to His image* (positive aspect)

- Colossians 2:20–22 (negative aspect)
  2 Peter 1:3, 4 (positive or active aspect)

D. The Fruits of Sanctification

Sanctification is visible through its fruits and results:

> When he came and *had seen the grace of God*, he was glad, and encouraged them all that with purpose of heart they should continue with the Lord (Acts 11:23).

We ought to bear fruit to God:

> Therefore, my brethren, you also have become dead to the law through the body of Christ, that you may be married to another—to Him who was raised from the dead, *that we should bear fruit to God* (Romans 7:4).

Some of the fruits of sanctification:

• Love for God and watchfulness

> Search me, O God, and know my heart; try me, and know my anxieties; and see if there is any wicked way in me, and lead me in the way everlasting (Psalm 139:23, 24).

> "He who has My commandments and keeps them, it is he who loves Me. And he who loves Me will be loved by My Father, and I will love him and manifest Myself to him." ... "If anyone loves Me, he will keep My word; and My Father will love him, and We will come to him and make Our home with him" (John 14:21, 23).

> Therefore, as the elect of God, holy and beloved, put on tender mercies, kindness, humility, meekness, longsuffering; bearing with one another, and forgiving one another, if anyone has a complaint against another; even as Christ forgave you, so you also must do. But above all these things put on love, which is the bond of perfection (Colossians 3:12–14).

• Humility

> To me, who am less than the least of all the saints, this grace was given, that I should preach among the Gentiles the unsearchable riches of Christ (Ephesians 3:8).

> Let this mind be in you which was also in Christ Jesus (Philippians 2:5).

Not that I have already attained, or am already perfected; but I press on, that I may lay hold of that for which Christ Jesus has also laid hold of me (Philippians 3:12).

Likewise you younger people, submit yourselves to your elders. Yes, all of you be submissive to one another, and be clothed with humility, for "God resists the proud, but gives grace to the humble" (1 Peter 5:5).

- Dying to the world

Therefore put to death your members which are on the earth: fornication, uncleanness, passion, evil desire, and covetousness, which is idolatry (Colossians 3:5).

Do not love the world or the things in the world. If anyone loves the world, the love of the Father is not in him. For all that is in the world—the lust of the flesh, the lust of the eyes, and the pride of life—is not of the Father but is of the world. And the world is passing away, and the lust of it; but he who does the will of God abides forever (1 John 2:15–17).

Adulterers and adulteresses! Do you not know that friendship with the world is enmity with God? Whoever therefore wants to be a friend of the world makes himself an enemy of God (James 4:4).

- Patient submission to the will of God

Therefore humble yourselves under the mighty hand of God, that He may exalt you in due time (1 Peter 5:6).

- Having a growing desire for heaven

For we who are in this tent groan, being burdened, not because we want to be unclothed, but further clothed, that mortality may be swallowed up by life. Now He who has prepared us for this very thing is God, who also has given us the Spirit as a guarantee. So we are always confident, knowing that while we are at home in the body we are absent from the Lord. For we walk by faith, not by sight. We are confident, yes, well pleased rather to be absent from the body and to be present with the Lord (2 Corinthians 5:4–8).

For I am hard-pressed between the two, having a desire to depart and be with Christ, which is far better (Philippians 1:23).

Behold, I tell you a mystery: We shall not all sleep, but we shall all be changed—in a moment, in the twinkling of an eye, at the last trumpet. For the trumpet will sound, and the dead will be raised incorruptible, and we shall be changed. For this corruptible must put on incorruption, and this mortal must put on immortality. So when this corruptible has put on incorruption, and this mortal has put on immortality, then shall be brought to pass the saying that is written: "Death is swallowed up in victory." "O Death, where is your sting? O Hades, where is your victory?" The sting of death is sin, and the strength of sin is the law. But thanks be to God, who gives us the victory through our Lord Jesus Christ (1 Corinthians 15:51–57).

- Being ready for ministry

Holiness and ministry are inseparable. If one wants to serve God, one must live a holy life and be set apart for the Lord:

Depart! Depart! Go out from there, touch no unclean thing; go out from the midst of her, be clean, you who bear the vessels of the Lord (Isaiah 52:11).

Therefore if anyone cleanses himself from the latter, he will be a vessel for honour, sanctified and useful for the Master, prepared for every good work (2 Timothy 2:21).

V. Summary: Sanctification According to the Bible

1. Sanctification is separation to the service of God (Psalm 4:3; 2 Corinthians 6:17).

2. Sanctification is brought about by:

    a. God (Ezekiel 37:28; 1 Thessalonians 5:23; Jude 1:1).

    b. Christ (Hebrews 2:11; 13:12).

    c. The Holy Spirit (Romans 15:16; 1 Corinthians 6:11).

3. We are sanctified in Christ (1 Corinthians 1:2).

4. We are sanctified through the atonement of Christ (Hebrews 10:10; 13:12).

5. We are sanctified by the Word of God (John 17:17, 19; Ephesians 5:26).

6. Christ became for us sanctification from God (1 Corinthians 1:30).

7. Saints are elected to salvation through sanctification (2 Thessalonians 2:13; 1 Peter 1:2).

8. All saints are in a state of sanctification (Acts 20:32; 26:18; 1 Corinthians 6:11).

9. The Church is made glorious by sanctification (Ephesians 5:26, 27).

10. Sanctification should lead to:

    a. Dying to sin (1 Thessalonians 4:3, 4).

    b. Holiness (Romans 6:22; Ephesians 5:7–9).

11. The offering of the saints is acceptable through sanctification (Romans 15:16).

12. Saints are fit for the service of God by sanctification (2 Timothy 2:21).

13. Sanctification is the will of God for us (1 Thessalonians 4:3).

14. Ministers:

   a. are set apart to serve God through sanctification (Jeremiah 1:5).

   b. should pray that their people may enjoy complete sanctification (1 Thessalonians 5:23).

   c. should exhort their people to walk in sanctification (1 Thessalonians 4:1, 3).

15. No one can inherit the Kingdom of God without sanctification (1 Corinthians 6:9-11).

16. Sanctification is typified (Genesis 2:3; Exodus 13:2; 19:14; 40:9–15; Leviticus 27:14–16).

CHAPTER 9

THE BLOOD OF JESUS
CLEANSES MY CONSCIENCE
FROM ACTS THAT LEAD TO DEATH
SO THAT I MAY SERVE THE LIVING GOD

Readings

How much more shall *the blood of Christ*, who through the eternal Spirit offered Himself without spot to God, *cleanse your conscience from dead works to serve the living God*? (Hebrews 9:14).

For the worshipers, once purified, would have had no more consciousness of sins. ... Let us draw near with a true heart in full assurance of faith, having our hearts sprinkled from an evil *conscience* and our bodies washed with pure water (Hebrews 10:2, 22).

Introduction

The conscience exists deep within us and it must be cleansed. If it remains unclean, many hidden motives within us can direct us to wrong things.

We often pray saying, "Lord, I want to have a close fellowship with you." Many books, sermons, and prayers speak about intimacy with God. But the problem is that we ask for this intimacy with God without going through deep cleansing first. This can never happen because God knows the deep things in us. Thus, God urges us to take these matters out of our lives so that He can draw near us. For this reason, we ought to pay attention to our conscience, know what is in it, and allow the blood of Jesus to cleanse it deeply.

Deep cleansing is also essential because if one wants to build a house, he must first clean the land on which he wants to build the house. A process of spiritual building should take place in our inner life. God wants to build a house inside us for Him to dwell in. He wants to dwell in us and in our midst, as the Bible teaches.[35] Because of this, Apostle Paul calls himself a wise master builder.[36] He knew how to guide people to prepare a place for Christ to come and dwell in. He even said that believers ought to build or edify one another.[37] Therefore, cleansing is essential.

To study this topic and understand more about the power of the blood of Jesus in cleansing our conscience and the results of this cleansing, we need to examine the meaning of the words *conscience* and *guilt*, for guilt is the main problem related to the human conscience. We also need to discuss the effectiveness of Christ's sacrifice and its cleansing effect.

---

[35] John 14:23; Ephesians 2:22; Exodus 25:8; Zechariah 2:10
[36] 1 Corinthians 3:10
[37] 1 Thessalonians 5:11

I. Conscience[38]

A. The Meaning of the Word *Conscience*

- ### The Linguistic Meaning

   1a. The sense or consciousness of the moral goodness or blamewor-
   thiness of one's own conduct, intentions, or character together
   with a feeling of obligation to do right or be good

   1b. A faculty, power, or principle encouraging good acts

   2. Conformity to the dictates of conscience: being conscientious

   3. Sensitive regard for fairness or justice

- ### The Meaning of Conscience According to the Hebrew and Greek
   Languages of the Old and New Testaments

The Old Testament has no word for *conscience,* and the Greek term
syneidēsis is virtually absent from the Septuagint.

The Greek word translated as *conscience* in the New Testament literally
means *to be with knowledge* (συνείδησις /suneidēsis/ according to Thayer
definition[39]):

   1. The consciousness of anything

   2. The soul as distinguishing between what is morally good and bad,
       prompting to do the former and shun the latter; commending one
       and condemning the other

   3. The conscience

---

[38] There is another detailed study about the conscience that will be published later.

[39] Thayer, J. (2017b). *Thayer's Greek-English Lexicon of the New Testament: Coded With the
Numbering System from Strong's Exhaustive Concordance of the Bible.* PMA Publishing.

B. The Meaning of Conscience According to the Biblical Revelation

Conscience is the faculty by which the person understands the moral demands of God, and which causes him pain when he falls short of those demands.

> The spirit of a man is the lamp of the Lord, searching all the inner depths of his heart (Proverbs 20:27).

The conscience, therefore, is a gift of God that is granted to provide light in matters of good and evil.

It is common to all men. Like all our other faculties, it has been corrupted by the fall (John 16:2; Acts 26:9; Romans 2:15).

It is written about it that:

- It is defiled

To the pure all things are pure, but to those who are defiled and unbelieving nothing is pure; but even their mind and *conscience are defiled* (Titus 1:15).

- It is seared

Speaking lies in hypocrisy, *having their own conscience seared* with a hot iron (1 Timothy 4:2).

We ought to seek to have a conscience without offence (Acts 24:16; Romans 9:1; 2 Corinthians 1:12; 1 Timothy 1:5, 19; 1 Peter 3:21).

Thus, the conscience needs to be properly educated and informed by the Holy Spirit. Through repentance and faith, man will have a conscience without offence; thus, the conscience will no longer cause pain to the person; but faith is also the means whereby his conscience is quickened and instructed. To walk in the newness of life (Romans 6:4) implies having a living and growing faith, through which the Christian is open to the influence of the Spirit (Romans 8:14). This is the guarantee for having a good or a clear conscience (1 Peter 3:16; cf. Acts 23:1).

In the New Testament, the term occurs more than thirty times, mostly in Paul's letters. It also occurs twice in Acts (23:1; 24:16, mentioned by Paul on both occasions), five times in Hebrews (9:9, 14; 10:2, 22; 13:18), and three times in 1 Peter (2:19; 3:16, 21).

Apostle Paul gives us important clues regarding the function of the conscience for the Gentiles. The conscience for them is the main clue to distinguishing God's demands. Through it, God's character and will are actively appreciated:

> For when Gentiles, who do not have the law, by nature do the things in the law, these, although not having the law, are a law to themselves (Romans 2:14).

Thus, simply through their moral nature, unbelievers sense that they are ultimately responsible to God:

> Because what may be known of God is manifest in them, for God has shown it to them. For since the creation of the world His invisible attributes are clearly seen, being understood by the things that are made, even His eternal power and Godhead, so that they are without excuse, ... who, knowing the righteous judgement of God, that those who practise such things are deserving of death, not only do the same but also approve of those who practise them (Romans 1:19, 20, 32).

To sum up, we can say that the significance of the conscience in the New Testament is twofold:

- It is the means of moral judgement upon the actions of an individual whether completed or begun.

- It also acts as a witness and guide in all aspects of the believer's sanctification.

In other words, New Testament writers see man's conscience negatively as the *instrument of judgement* and positively as the *means of guidance*.

C. The Function of the Conscience According to Apostle Paul

- To approve or pronounce one *not guilty* is a function of the conscience.

This function is as important as self-condemnation.

In 1 Corinthians 4:4, Apostle Paul says, '*For I am conscious of nothing against myself*, *but not by this am I vindicated. But the one who judges me is the Lord'* (LEB).

Here, the apostle uses the same root word from which the word *conscience* is derived.

- However, the conscience is neither a final court of appeal nor an adequate guide.

In the same verse, Apostle Paul went on to say, '*but not by this am I vindicated. But the one who judges me is the Lord.'*

- In another passage, Apostle Paul calls on his conscience to verify his truthfulness, linking the verdict of the conscience with the Holy Spirit:

I tell the truth in Christ, I am not lying, my conscience also bearing me witness in the Holy Spirit (Romans 9:1).

Refer also to 2 Corinthians 1:12.

- Justifying his ministry to the Corinthians, Apostle Paul asks them to judge his conduct in the light of their own consciences:

Therefore, since we have this ministry, as we have received mercy, we do not lose heart. But we have renounced the hidden things of shame, not walking in craftiness nor handling the word of God deceitfully, *but by manifestation of the truth commending ourselves to every man's conscience in the sight of God* (2 Corinthians 4:1–2).

Insisting that God knew the motivation behind his conduct, which is *the fear of the Lord*, he hoped that the Corinthians' conscience would also recognise it:

Therefore, knowing the fear of the Lord, we persuade others. But what we are is known to God, and I hope it is known also to your conscience (2 Corinthians 5:11, ESV).

- When Paul wrote to Timothy, he linked a good conscience with sincere faith:

Now the purpose of the commandment is love from a pure heart, from *a good conscience*, and from *sincere faith* (1 Timothy 1:5).

When people depart from the faith, their consciences can become *seared* or *insensitive* due to their persistence in evil.

II. Guilt

The topics of *guilt* and the *conscience* are closely connected because guilt is sensed through the conscience. I believe that nobody is exempt from having experienced a sense of guilt at some point in their lives. However, a sense of guilt can greatly hinder spiritual growth; therefore, we must know how to deal with it correctly.

A. The Meaning of the Word *Guilt*

- **The Linguistic Meaning**

    1. The fact of having committed a breach of conduct, especially violating the law and involving a penalty broadly—guilt conduct

    2a. The state of one who has committed an offence especially consciously

    2b. Feelings of deserving blame, especially for imagined offences or from a sense of inadequacy—self-reproach

    3. A feeling of deserving blame for offences

- **The Meaning of Guilt in the Biblical Language**

In the Bible, guilt is not understood as an inward feeling of remorse or a bad conscience, but rather as involving a situation that has arisen because of sin[40] committed against God or one's neighbour.

Therefore, in the Bible, guilt exists because of two main factors:

---

[40] Sin being either of commission or of omission

1. Humans are responsible and accountable for their actions, thoughts, and attitudes.

2. These actions, thoughts, and attitudes constitute a state of guilt when relationships between humans and God or other humans have been broken because of sin.

There are two main Hebrew words that speak about sin: *chata* and *asham*.

Asham is translated as *guilt* or *trespass*. Some say that *chata* indicates a sin of commission, whereas *asham* indicates a sin of omission, meaning neglect. Others maintain that *chata* means sin in general and *asham* sin against the Mosaic Law.

An examination of all the passages in which the word *asham* occurs leads to the conclusion that *asham* is used where a sin has been committed through error, negligence, or ignorance. When such sin comes to one's knowledge, one ought to regard himself as having offended, even though it had been unintentional; and compensation must be made. An *asham* or guilt-offering ought to be offered in this case.

The following passages are the most notable in which the word occurs:

Leviticus 4:13, 22, 27; Leviticus 5:2, 3, 5, 6, 15, 17; Genesis 42:21; Numbers 5:6, 7; 2 Samuel 14:13; Judges 21:22; 1 Chronicles 21:3; 2 Chronicles 19:10, 28:10, 13; Ezra 10:19; Psalm 69:5; Proverbs 30:10; Jeremiah 2:3, 50:7; Ezekiel 22:4, 25:12; Hosea 4:15.

From these passages, we understand that while *chata* highlights the nature of sin as a missing of the mark, *asham* implies a breach of a commandment, done without due consideration, and which, when brought to the notice of the offender, requires amends or atonement.

B. Guilt in Relation to Grace: Guilt From the Perspective of Christian Psychology

A guilty conscience is the seasoning of our daily life. Deep inside every human being there is a conflict with people around him that makes him constantly worried about being criticised and hence he feels guilty.

Guilt, resulting from society's views and judgement, paralyses one's ability to be creative as he fears criticism.

The sense of guilt originates from childhood as children worry about losing their parents' love. This sense of guilt can extend to adulthood where adults may fear losing the love of others around them or the appreciation of their bosses, etcetera. When a person worries about the opinions of others, guilt appears.

Guilt could be false and it could be true. Quite often the two are mixed together and it is difficult to separate them.

C. What is Guilt?

Guilt is *a sin against oneself* (self-rejection), *a sin against others* (rejecting them), and *a sin against God* (when we blame God for bad circumstances).

D. What Makes Us Feel Guilty?

We feel guilty:

- When we waste time

- When we fail to achieve our goals

- When we haven't kept in touch with someone and we worry that they would criticise us for it

- Due to the constant comparisons that happen inside us

E. How Do We Usually Deal with Guilt?

- We cling to religious or moral principles to free ourselves from the sense of guilt.

- We sometimes over-express how we feel towards someone to cover up for not keeping in touch with them.

- Sometimes, we do outward things to relieve ourselves from the sense of guilt. An example of this is when Pilate washed his hands to relieve himself from the sense of guilt for crucifying Jesus. But he didn't feel relieved, so he ordered that the sign would read THIS IS JESUS THE KING OF THE JEWS.[41] Also, Jacob sent presents to his brother Esau to cover up for his sense of guilt.

Other Ways of Dealing With Guilt

Sometimes we deal with guilt by *repressing it, projecting it on others,* or *acknowledging it:*

- Sometimes we *repress guilt.*

The weight of guilt on the conscience is sometimes intolerable hence we tend to push it to the subconscious to get rid of it and justify ourselves. However, by doing so, we are actually *repressing the guilt* into the subconscious.

Repressing the guilt leads to anger, rebellion, fear, anxiety, and the death of the conscience.

An example of repressed guilt that produces anger is when Martha felt guilty because, unlike her sister Mary, she did not give enough care to spiritual matters. She expressed this guilt by being angry with her sister for not helping her with the housework.

- Sometimes we *project guilt on others.*

This reflects childishness and lack of responsibility as we tend to say, "It is not my fault."

---

[41] Matthew 27:37

Sometimes we also project it on God Himself as did Adam and Eve, as well as Job.

- Sometimes we *acknowledge guilt*.

Acknowledging guilt leads to repentance, peace, and refinement.

F. Consequences of Guilt

- Guilt makes us unable to express ourselves freely in front of others—unlike David who danced before the ark of the Lord[42] because he was free from guilt; he did not fear nor worry about the opinion of others.

- Any criticism causes us to justify ourselves. This, in turn, becomes an obstacle that prevents us from repenting.

- Guilt makes us angry and defensive.

G. How Should We React to Guilt?

- Jesus (at the age of 12) refused to yield to false guilt that could have resulted from his mother's reproach: "Where were you?" Yet, at the same time, he was totally submitting to her.[43]

- Some sins are apparent, and God forgives them by His grace, while others are hidden, and God has to reveal them to allow for repentance and forgiveness. This is obvious in the story of the woman who committed adultery.[44] Jesus forgave the woman but revealed the sins of the others who were blaming her. One of the psychologists said that there is guilt that ought to be alleviated, while another that ought to be awakened and recovered.

---

[42] 2 Samuel 6:14
[43] Luke 2:41–50
[44] John 8:3–11

H. The Solution to the Sense of Guilt

- The more we are freed from society's standards and people's views, and the more we submit to God's standards, we will be freed from a lot of the false guilt that weighs heavy on us. This can only happen by following Jesus and fully submitting to Him.

- A true, living, and loving relationship with God reveals the hidden sins that need repentance and this sets us free from guilt, for guilt may sometimes come as a result of sins that we are unaware of. Daily fellowship with the Lord reveals all the hidden sins and shows us how to repent of them, hence the power of the blood of Jesus cleanses our conscience and we become freed from guilt.

III. The Effectiveness of Christ's Sacrifice

How much more shall *the blood of Christ*, who through *the eternal Spirit offered Himself* without spot *to God*, cleanse your conscience from dead works to serve the living God? (Hebrews 9:14).

The *eternal redemption* that has been accomplished by the blood of Christ is of supreme value.

The writings of the early Church speak of Christ as *the priest, the altar, and the sacrifice*!

His sacrifice is of infinite value because, through the eternal Spirit, He offered Himself unblemished to God. Notice that this verse refers to the three Persons of the Trinity: the blood of Christ, the eternal Spirit, offering Himself to God. All three Persons of the Godhead are involved in the sacrifice of Christ, which magnifies the greatness of His redemptive sacrifice. Also, the sacrifice was unblemished, meaning His sacrifice was spotless. He also offered Himself voluntarily for our sake; no one forced Him to do it.

Thus, it was a sacrifice that was:

- Proclaimed by the three Persons of the Trinity

- Voluntary

- Spotless

There is another interesting point about the sacrifice of Christ, which is revealed in the Epistle to the Hebrews:

His offering began on the altar of the cross. Then, He entered the Holiest with His blood as our High Priest to continue His work as Intercessor on our behalf. This means that His redemptive work is still ongoing. On the cross, He completed the part that allows us to enter into a living fellowship with Him. But because He is preoccupied with His people who live in this world and who have many temptations around them, He continues to intercede on our behalf so that we may be protected from the world and our salvation may be worked out:

> Therefore He is also able to save to the uttermost those who come to God through Him, since *He always lives to make intercession for them* (Hebrews 7:25).

The Benefits of Christ's Sacrifice

1. It is sufficient to purge the conscience from dead works; it reaches to the very soul and conscience.

2. It is sufficient to enable us to serve the living God.

Now, let us look at these wonderful and great results one by one:

1. Cleansing the conscience

Christ's sacrifice goes to the centre of the moral and spiritual life and cleanses the original source of being. It purges away that guilt which separates between God and sinners. Thus, it purifies from fear, guilt, alienation from God, and selfishness, which are the source of *dead works*. It takes away anything that stands in the way between us and God, hence we can have continuous fellowship with Him.

Even more than that, it creates a *new spiritual conscience* in the inner man which is able to bear the witness of the Holy Spirit:

> I tell the truth in Christ, I am not lying, *my conscience also bearing me witness in the Holy Spirit* (Romans 9:1).

When our conscience is cleansed, we are no longer bound by guilt to our past. We are no longer overwhelmed with a sense of our inadequacy. This means that Christ's sacrifice gives the believer a perfect standing before God. We ought to hold fast to our confidence in the perfect efficacy of the cross and serve the living God according to the will of God.

2. Serving the living God

All works done in the natural state (carnal state), the state of sin, are considered *dead* works, because they do not come from a living faith in and love for the *living* God. The Bible highlights that we must be cleansed from dead works in order to serve the living God.

It is written:

> But without faith it is impossible to please Him, for he who comes to God must believe that He is, and that He is a rewarder of those who diligently seek Him (Hebrews 11:6).

Before receiving salvation, the sinner did the so-called *"good works"* in the strength of his own sinful nature.

Man's activities without the Holy Spirit are dead; therefore, they cannot be accepted before the living God. It is written:

> I beseech you therefore, brethren, by the mercies of God, that you present your bodies a living sacrifice, holy, acceptable to God, which is *your reasonable service* (Romans 12:1).

> God is Spirit, and those who worship Him must *worship in spirit and truth* (John 4:24).

> And there shall be no more curse, but the throne of God and of the Lamb shall be in it, and His servants *shall serve Him* (Revelation 22:3).

The effect of Christ's sacrifice upon the conscience is transmitted to the works, and hence fills them with the living energy of the eternal Spirit. It changes the character or the nature of the works by purging them of the element of death.

In simpler words, the blood of Jesus brings life to whatever we do. Christ's sacrifice brings divine energy to our natural and weak works. It changes the character and nature of what we do. It changes them from being dead, human, and weak works into being works that bear divine energy. Thus, these works can bring the stream of life to those we minister to.

God wants us to be life-bearers. In the early writings, the phrase *life-bearers* was the most common phrase used to describe Christians. Christians were called *life-bearers*. This description signifies that they have received life and that they also ought to transmit this life to others. However, if there is guilt in the conscience and the conscience is not cleansed, this process of receiving and transmitting life will be blocked. The person may still receive life but it will not be a continuous flowing stream, it will be interrupted, and hence the person will not be able to transmit life. In fact, we exist in this world in order to be channels of Christ's life to the dead world.

After salvation performs its mighty transformation within the individual, the good works are motivated, empowered, and produced by the Holy Spirit. They are, therefore, living works. Thus, the person serves the living God.

Note that the purpose of cleansing in the Old Testament was that the people might be consecrated again to God's service. Only the cleansing provided by Christ can set us free to *serve the living God*.

CHAPTER 10

THE BLOOD OF JESUS
MAKES ME ENTER THE MOST HOLY PLACE
TO SERVE THE HOLY GOD

Introduction

Therefore, brethren, *having boldness to enter the Holiest by the blood of Jesus, by a new and living way* which He consecrated for us, through the veil, that is, His flesh, and having a High Priest over the house of God, let us draw near with a true heart in full assurance of faith, having our hearts sprinkled from an evil conscience and our bodies washed with pure water. Let us hold fast the confession of our hope without wavering, for He who promised is faithful. And let us consider one another in order to stir up love and good works, not forsaking the assembling of ourselves together, as is the manner of some, but exhorting one another, and so much the more as you see the Day approaching (Hebrews 10:19–25).

This passage marks the beginning of the practical part of the Epistle to the Hebrews. This practical part comes after the apostle highlights the richness of Jesus, especially as a High Priest, in the first part of the epistle. The whole passage is closely connected; therefore, we need to understand it in detail to enter into the deep meaning of our topic.

This epistle was mainly written to believers coming to the Christian faith from a Jewish background. Therefore, in the first two verses of this passage, the apostle presents his invitation to faith in terms of the old covenant.

The exhortation to enter into the Holy of Holies by the blood of Jesus brings to the mind of the Jewish reader the picture of the high priest on the Day of Atonement. The high priest entered the Holy of Holies only once a year, on this day.

Every Israelite was represented in the person of the high priest when he entered the Holy of Holies. Thus, it is as though every Israelite entered the Holy of Holies with the high priest, and therefore had the privilege of being in the presence of God represented by the Ark.

This picture was presented to the Jews to refer to the day when a Saviour will come and remove the barrier (the veil) that stands in the way between God (His presence) and His people. This Saviour is Jesus Christ who was incarnated and tore the veil (Matthew 27:51).

The passage consists of two main parts that are closely linked. The first part is verses 19–21, and the second part is verses 22–25.

Part one highlights our privileges in Christ, especially as our High Priest. This is manifested in:

- A new and living way opened by the blood of Jesus

- A High Priest who continues to serve our salvation:

Therefore He is also able to save to the uttermost those who come to God through Him, since He always lives to make intercession for them (Hebrews 7:25).

Part two highlights our responsibility, which is presented in three exhortations:

- *Let us draw near*

- *Let us hold fast*

- *Let us consider one another*

We now want to study these verses in detail.

Part 1: Verses 19–21

Therefore, brethren, having boldness to enter the Holiest by the blood of Jesus, by a new and living way which He consecrated for us, through the veil, that is, His flesh, and having a High Priest over the house of God ...

- **Verse 19**

  Therefore, brethren, having boldness to enter the Holiest by the blood of Jesus ...

  - *Therefore, brethren*

How amazing the meaning reflected in this phrase! What was available only for the high priest—entering into the Holy of Holies once a year—became available for every believer, not only once a year, but at all times!

It became possible for us to enter into the presence of God and appear before God the Father because we belong to Christ, our High Priest: *'For through Him we both have access by one Spirit to the Father'* (Ephesians 2:18).

  - *Having boldness*

In the original Greek language, the word *boldness* is *parrhesia*, which means *freedom of speech*. St. John Chrysostom (4th–5th century) took it to mean *open boldness*.

Where did this boldness and freedom of speech come from?

As previously mentioned, this picture is taken from the Old Testament when the high priest entered once a year to the Holy of Holies by the blood of sacrifices. This was a time of trembling. It was known that when the Day of Atonement would come and the high priest was to enter the Holy of Holies, they would tie one end of a rope to his garment and the other end of the rope would be left outside the Holy of Holies. If something went wrong, causing the high priest to die, they would pull the body of the high priest out by the rope, as no one was allowed to enter the Holiest. In fact, this picture does not reflect any kind of boldness; it actually causes one to tremble.

But this verse in the Epistle to the Hebrews refers to the true High Priest, Jesus Christ. He Himself is the High Priest and the sacrifice at the same time. He entered the Holiest with His blood. Because He is perfect, He entered with boldness, making this entrance available for each of us—the believers—to the extent that any believer who enters the Holiest will be looked upon by the angels as if he were the High Priest Himself entering. Thus, every believer enters with the same honour of the High Priest, not once a year, but every day. This means that we must not be separated from Jesus Christ at any point because we, in ourselves, cannot be seen as a high priest, but when a believer enters, he must be seen as being clothed with Christ. In Galatians 3:27, the Bible says: *'For as many of you as were baptised into Christ have put on Christ.'* It is important to understand this truth to have true boldness. This is the only way to receive this boldness by which we can enter the Holiest.

Therefore, we receive the boldness from the blood of the High Priest! The High Priest Himself is the sacrifice, and it is He who also offers it!

The blood of Christ proclaims *the propitiation* and forgiveness of all our sins. It also proclaims the reconciliation with the Father, and even the adoption and the inheritance!

Apostle Paul uses the word *boldness* four times in this epistle. This shows its importance and its effectiveness. The word occurs in the following verses:

> But Christ as a Son over His own house, whose house we are if we hold fast *the confidence* and the rejoicing of the hope firm to the end (Hebrews 3:6).

> Let us therefore come *boldly* to the throne of grace, that we may obtain mercy and find grace to help in time of need (Hebrews 4:16).

> Therefore, brethren, having *boldness* to enter the Holiest by the blood of Jesus (Hebrews 10:19).

> Therefore do not cast away your *confidence*, which has great reward (Hebrews 10:35).

- *To enter the Holiest*

The reference here is not only to the act of entering itself but also to how we enter. We enter with the same honour of the High Priest! No one is able to enter the Holiest and appear before the Father apart from the High Priest; therefore, we enter in Christ and through Christ. He goes before us and presents us to the Father: '*In whom we have boldness and access with* **confidence** *through faith in Him*' (Ephesians 3:12).

The original Greek word translated as *boldness* in Hebrews 10:19 is the same word used in this verse in Ephesians.

- *By the blood of Jesus*

Our entrance to the Holies is based on the entrance of Christ as a forerunner for our sake:

> Seeing then that we have a great High Priest who has passed through the heavens, Jesus the Son of God, let us hold fast our confession. For we do not have a High Priest who cannot sympathise with our weaknesses, but was in all points tempted as we are, yet without sin. Let us therefore come boldly to the throne of grace, that we may obtain mercy and find grace to help in time of need (Hebrews 4:14–16).

> This hope we have as an anchor of the soul, both sure and steadfast, and which enters the Presence behind the veil, where the forerunner has entered for us, even Jesus, having become High Priest forever according to the order of Melchizedek (Hebrews 6:19–20).

Thus, the entrance of Christ by the blood of His complete atoning sacrifice has cleared the way, removing all the hindrances that had stood in the way and that had stopped man from entering the heavens into the presence of God.

What about the opposition of the evil powers that can hinder us from entering our heavenly places?

In Ephesians 6:12, we read:

> For we do not wrestle against flesh and blood, but against principalities, against powers, against the rulers of the darkness of this age, against spiritual hosts of wickedness in the heavenly places.

What about the flaming sword of the cherubim that guarded the way to the tree of life—the path to God (Genesis 3:24), after the fall of Adam?

What about the sentence of death that came upon Adam when he sinned and broke God's commandments?

The blood of Jesus has conquered all these hindrances, annulled every opposition, opened all the doors, and made it possible for us to enter into the presence of His Father!

Not only this, but He has also made us priests to God, His Father, ministering with Him in the Holies: *'And has made us kings and priests to His God and Father'* (Revelation 1:6).

- **Verse 20**

  > By a new and living way which He consecrated for us, through the veil, that is, His flesh.

  - *A way*

According to the original Greek language, *the entrance* and *the way* merge together. Thus, the verse reads: *having boldness regarding entering because it is a way which He consecrated for us.*

The verse thus means that Christ's entrance to the Holies with His broken flesh and His blood that was shed made this entrance *a way* or *a path* for others. According to the Greek language, the word translated as *the way* is *hodos* which means *a road*. Thus, the word *way* does not mean *a manner*, but it indicates an actual *road*.

Here, we see an analogy between what happened in the Old Testament, where the High Priest would sprinkle the blood seven times to enter the Holies, and what happens in the New Testament. In the Old Testament, the blood would quickly clot; thus, the entrance to the Holies would end, and no other entrance would be allowed until a year later. However, in the New Testament, entering the Holy of Holies is by a blood that never clots, as we shall shortly explain. Therefore, it is a continuous entrance; the door is open, and the way/road to the Holies is paved! Jesus said:

> I go to prepare a place for you ... I will come again and receive you to Myself ... I am the way, the truth, and the life (John 14:2–4, 6).

- *He consecrated for us*

The verb *to consecrate* according to the original Greek language is *engkainizo*. The same meaning is reflected in the Hebrew word. The word in both the Greek and Hebrew languages indicates *the anointing with oil for consecration*, whether the consecration of places or people.

- *New and living*

♦ New

The word *new* is the translation of the Greek word *prosphaton*, which indicates *being newly slain*.

If any person is wounded, his blood clots. But the Greek word used here indicates that the blood of Jesus never clots; it is always fresh.

This blood that is shed is not the blood of animals that clots, and hence when the day ends, the road to the Holies is closed, as was the case in the Old Testament. But, it is *a new fresh blood that never clots*.

Notice also that according to the biblical revelation, the blood speaks. In Genesis 4:10, God said to Esau:

> What have you done? *The voice of your brother's blood cries out* to Me from the ground.

Also, in Hebrews 12:24, we read:

> To Jesus the Mediator of the new covenant, and to *the blood of sprinkling that speaks* better things than that of Abel.

This fresh blood of Jesus speaks loudly, inviting everyone to come and receive forgiveness, cleansing, adoption, and a heavenly inheritance!

Thus, this part of the verse says that the blood of Jesus is fresh, as if Jesus is being crucified now. To apply this in our lives, whenever we pray, wherever we are, we ought to think that the Bible says that Christ and His cross are so near to us as if Jesus is being crucified now. His blood is still fresh. It has not clotted; therefore, it is as if the blood is speaking to us, inviting us, and saying, "Come close; you are most welcome."

This is the meaning of the Greek word that is used to refer to the fresh blood of Jesus that has opened the way for us.

♦ Living

It is also a living way because Christ offered His life so that His way (path) may bear life to everyone who enters it.

Jesus said, *'I am the way, the truth, and the life'* (John 14:6).

Notice that this way is *a new way, a living way, and* **the only way**:

> Nor is there salvation in any other, for there is *no other name* under heaven given among men by which we must be saved (Acts 4:12).

- *Through the veil, that is, His flesh*

In the Old Testament, the veils in the Tabernacle covered the Holies and covered God's glory that was inside the Tabernacle from the people who were outside. Similarly, Christ covered His divine glory by His flesh. The veil of the Tabernacle of old symbolised Christ's human body, for it covered the glory of God.

> And the Word became flesh and dwelt among us, and we beheld His glory, the glory as of the only begotten of the Father, full of grace and truth (John 1:14).

Then, when Jesus bore our sins in His flesh and completed redemption, His flesh was torn by crucifixion. Thus, the veil in the temple of Israel was also torn, as we read in Matthew 27:51 and Mark 15:38. This allowed for the appearance of God's glory to man, making man able to see and behold this glory:

> But we all, with unveiled face, beholding as in a mirror the glory of the Lord, are being transformed into the same image from glory to glory, just as by the Spirit of the Lord (2 Corinthians 3:18).

This is a great truth that invites us to practically experience it in our daily worship of God!

- **Verse 21**

  And having a High Priest over the house of God

  - *A High Priest*

According to the Greek origin, this term refers to the royal character of the Priest; He is a royal Priest or a priestly King; He is a Priest on His throne.

> Yes, He shall build the temple of the Lord. He shall bear the glory, and shall sit and rule on His throne; so *He shall be a priest on His throne*, and the counsel of peace shall be between them both (Zechariah 6:13).

Christ is the High Priest who is willing to dwell with men on earth and to have men dwell with Him in heaven.

  - *The House of God*

> But Christ as a Son *over His own house, whose house we are* if we hold fast the confidence and the rejoicing of the hope firm to the end (Hebrews 3:6).

We are God's house. God's household includes the redeemed creation on earth and in heaven with all their sectors. The angels are the guards and ministers of the house of God. The Church of the earth, represented in the redeemed, together with the Church of heaven, represented in the angels and saints, constitute this household, the house of God. Christ is a chief Priest over this house.

Thus, we see that when the body of Christ, the Church, is connected with the Head, Christ, she progressively grows towards her full stature and her description in Ephesians 4:13, is guarded by the angels, and awaits her proclamation as the bride of the Lamb. She is the heavenly Jerusalem coming down from heaven, filled with the glory of God.[45]

> For here we have no continuing city, but we seek the one to come (Hebrews 13:14).

---

[45] Revelation 21:2

Part 2: Verses 22–25

Let us draw near with a true heart in full assurance of faith, having our hearts sprinkled from an evil conscience and our bodies washed with pure water.

Let us hold fast the confession of our hope without wavering, for He who promised is faithful.

And let us consider one another in order to stir up love and good works, not forsaking the assembling of ourselves together, as is the manner of some, but exhorting one another, and so much the more as you see the Day approaching.

The second part contains three exhortations. In the original Greek language, they are written in the continuous tense which reflects our continuous responsibility in these respects.

The three exhortations are:

- *Let us draw near with a true heart*

- *Let us hold fast the confession*

- *Let us consider one another*

Notice that these three exhortations are based on faith, hope, and love.

We now want to understand in more detail the meaning of each phrase in these verses:

- **Verse 22**

  Let us draw near with a true heart in full assurance of faith, having our hearts sprinkled from an evil conscience and our bodies washed with pure water.

  - *Let us draw near with a true heart*

Apostle Paul begins with the heart because it is the centre of the whole life. In Proverbs 4:23, we read, '*Keep your heart with all diligence, for out of it spring **the issues of life**.*'

The word *true* in this phrase refers to *the truth*. According to the Greek origin, this word is derived from *alétheia,* which means *truth*. This signifies that the heart should side with the Truth, meaning with God. In this way, the heart is considered true.

We should not forget that God searches the hearts. It is written:

> All the churches shall know that *I am He who searches the minds and hearts* (Revelation 2:23).

> You desire *truth in the inward parts* (Psalm 51:6).

- *In full assurance of faith*

In the original language, the phrase *full assurance* means *fullness*. When faith grows to its fullness, we will have the assurance that when we come to God, He accepts us and listens to us. This, in turn, means that we will shake off any disbelief or lack of faith and repent because *'without faith it is impossible to please* [God]*'* (Hebrews 11:6).

The true sign of this assured faith is having absolute surrender to God and complete reliance on Him in every matter.

Thus, we can put this spiritual principle as follows:

True faith = full trust + full surrender

- *Having our hearts sprinkled from an evil conscience and our bodies washed with pure water*

In the Old Testament, blood and water were sprinkled for cleansing and purification (Exodus 24:8; Numbers 8:7).

In the New Testament, as believers who are considered to be priests in the Holies, we need to keep ourselves in a continuous state of purification and cleansing. The blood of Jesus cleanses us from within and cleanses our consciences.

An evil act initially begins in the conscience. If the conscience accepts it, the conscience becomes defiled and loses its effectiveness and function in convicting the person. Hence, the person goes ahead with committing the evil act. On the other hand, a cleansed and purified conscience preserves its spiritual sensitivity and hence alerts the person to any evil thought that may come. Thus, this purified conscience protects the person and keeps him from carrying out the evil act: *'The blood of Christ ... cleanse*[s] *your conscience'* (Hebrews 9:14).

Water, according to Bible scholars, refers to baptism. Refer to 1 Peter 3:21; Titus 3:5; and Ephesians 5:26.

Since we have both a material and a non-material nature, cleansing should be manifested both in the outer and inner man, meaning in the body and in the heart.

All this indicates that a holy life is essential for drawing close to God. We ought to have *'holiness, without which no one will see the Lord'* (Hebrews 12:14).

This highlights the necessity of being well-prepared in order to enter into the presence of the Holy God.

To conclude the meaning intended in this verse, we can say that:

+ Fellowship with God demands purity (2 Corinthians 7:1; 1 John 1:5–2:2).

+ The boldness and assurance we have in heaven ought to lead to spiritual growth and consecration to the Lord during our life on earth.

- **Verse 23**

  Let us hold fast the confession of our hope without wavering, for He who promised is faithful.

  - *Let us hold fast the confession of our hope*

Note here that according to the original language, the word used in this verse is *hope*, not *faith*, as some translations render it.

The phrase *hold fast* here means to adhere to or stick firmly to. This phrase is repeated in this epistle, and it has special significance.

> Whose house we are if we *hold fast* the confidence and the rejoicing of the hope firm to the end (Hebrews 3:6).

The verse indicates that holding fast the confidence is a condition for being considered the house of God.

It is also a condition for becoming partakers of Christ, as the following verse highlights:

> For we have become partakers of Christ if we hold the beginning of our confidence steadfast to the end (Hebrews 3:14).

The word *confession* in the above phrase is *homologia* in Greek. It means *to say the same thing as another* or *to agree with the statement of another*. When a person accepts the faith and is baptised, he has to repeat *the confession of faith* after another person (the person baptising him) phrase by phrase.

The confession of faith is a reminder that our salvation is yet to be fully realised:

> So Christ was offered once to bear the sins of many. To those who eagerly wait for Him He will appear a second time, apart from sin, for salvation (Hebrews 9:28).

> For yet a little while, and He who is coming will come and will not tarry. Now the just shall live by faith; but if anyone draws back, My soul has no pleasure in him. But we are not of those who draw back to perdition, but of those who believe to the saving of the soul (Hebrews 10:37–39).

> For here we have no continuing city, but we seek the one to come (Hebrews 13:14).

The confession of faith is also an emphasis on the glorious hope of the believer (Hebrews 2:10; Colossians 1:27c: *'Christ in you, the hope of glory'*).

- *Without wavering*

In the original Greek language, the word is *aklines* which means *not to bow* or *not to lean towards*. Thus, the focus is on warning of backsliding. We draw the strength that protects us from not wavering from the fact that God is faithful in His promises. It is written that *'He who promised is faithful.'* Refer also to 1 Corinthians 1:9; 1 Thessalonians 5:24.

- **Verses 24 and 25**

  And let us consider one another in order to stir up love and good works, not forsaking the assembling of ourselves together, as is the manner of some, but exhorting one another, and so much the more as you see the Day approaching.

  - *Let us consider one another in order to stir up love and good works*

    ♦ Love cannot be restrained, but it must always extend to others.

    ♦ The phrasal verb *stir up* signifies *triggering something.*

The purpose here is to stimulate, stir, or trigger the emotions in the direction of love towards one another. Jesus highlighted that love is a sign of true discipleship to Him. Further, love is the new commandment that He handed down to His disciples, as we read in John 13:34, 35.

    ♦ Good works

It is interesting to note that the emphasis here is not on what a believer gets from the spiritual community or the assembly of believers, but rather on what he can contribute to the assembly.

  - *Not forsaking the assembling of ourselves together, as is the manner of some, but exhorting one another*

According to the original language, the word *forsake* signifies *intentional negligence.*

The phrase *the assembling of ourselves together* means *gathering around Christ.*

The phrase *as is the manner of some* reflects a scenario of having a habit of attending a meeting without benefiting from it.

Exhorting one another means *comforting and encouraging one another.*

- *So much the more as you see the Day approaching*

This is a prophetic warning of the nearness of the desolation that Jesus referred to and warned of in Luke 21:20–24. It is the desolation that took place in the year AD 70 that was led by Titus, the Roman leader, where the temple was knocked down, Jerusalem was destroyed, and the Jews were dispersed throughout the whole world.

Ministering to God

This part constitutes the practical side of this biblical truth and study.

In this statement of the blood of Jesus, we proclaim that the blood of Jesus makes us enter the most holy place to serve the Holy God.

How can we serve the Holy God? What does it mean that we are called to serve the Holy God? In what way can we serve the Holy God?

This is actually one of the foundational truths of the Bible.

This is the role of our calling as priests serving with and under the leadership of our High Priest in the heavenly places.

To be able to understand this calling, we need to understand:

A. The Priestly role of Christ and its relation to our salvation

B. Our priestly calling as believers and how to minister to God

A. The Priestly Role of Christ: The Priesthood of Melchizedek

- **Was Christ's priesthood according to the order of Aaron or Melchizedek?**

According to the Book of Leviticus, Christ's priesthood must have been according to the order of Aaron since the whole Book of Leviticus refers to Jesus and also since Jesus Himself was a sacrifice for us. When Jesus was living on earth, He completed all the obligations of the Law, such as circumcision, attending the feasts, etc.

However, Psalm 110:4 shows that there was a prophecy during the time of David about a priest who was to come according to the order of Melchizedek.

The truth is that Christ represents both orders at the same time.

Until the crucifixion, He presented Himself as a sacrifice according to the order of Aaron but after His ascension to heaven, He became a priest according to the order of Melchizedek. This is because by His death on the cross, everything that was related to the Law died as well; He released us from the obligations of the Book of Leviticus and called us to be priests. Jesus could not have called us to be priests according to the order of Melchizedek until He ended Aaron's order by His death. So, on the cross, Christ was both a priest and a sacrifice according to the order of Aaron and He completed all the obligations of this order. Now, in heaven, He is a priest according to the order of Melchizedek.

> Now if perfection had been attainable through the Levitical priesthood (for under it the people received the law), what further need would there have been for another priest to arise after the order of Melchizedek, rather than one named after the order of Aaron? For when there is a change in the priesthood, there is necessarily a change in the law as well. For the one of whom these things are spoken belonged to another tribe, from which no one has ever served at the altar. For it is evident that our Lord was descended from Judah, and in connection with that tribe Moses said nothing about priests. This becomes even more evident when another priest arises in the likeness of Melchizedek, who has become a priest, not on the basis of a legal requirement concerning bodily descent, but by the power of an indestructible life. For it is witnessed of him, "You are a priest forever, after the order of Melchizedek" (Hebrews 7:11–17, ESV).

- **What is the benefit of Christ's ministry in heaven as a High Priest, according to the order of Melchizedek, interceding for our sake?**

Jesus intercedes for us so that our salvation may be worked out. There are many biblical references that confirm this truth. We will consider four of these references here:

- **Hebrews 7:25**

Therefore He is also able to save to the uttermost those who come to God through him, since He always *lives to make intercession* for them.

This verse highlights that Jesus helps us to work out our salvation through His intercession, which is according to the order of Melchizedek. Without this intercession, none of us would be able to work out our salvation.

- Hebrews 6:19, 20

This hope we have *as an anchor* of the soul, both sure and steadfast, and *which enters the Presence behind the veil*, where the forerunner has entered for us, *even Jesus, having become High Priest forever according to the order of Melchizedek.*

In these verses, Apostle Paul portrays Jesus in heaven as a priest according to the order of Melchizedek, looking upon the believers who accepted His salvation and seeing them as boats in a sea.

Jesus knows that the waves in the sea can capsize the boat. Therefore, He keeps hold of a rope, which is the anchor, and He throws the other end of this rope to the believers in the boats, asking them to keep it tied to their boats while He holds the other end. By doing so, He is reassuring them that no wave can capsize the boat, for He will pull the rope whenever a wave comes; consequently, the boat will float again on the water.

Not only this, but He also reassures them that if the boat goes astray, He will pull it back and correct its direction. Besides, if at any time, a boat stands still and is unable to move, He will pull it to enable it to move again, and He will persist and persevere in doing this with every single boat until it completes its journey on earth and arrives safely to Him.

- Romans 5:10

For if when we were enemies we were reconciled to God through the death of His Son, much more, having been reconciled, we shall be saved by His life.

This verse summarises the priesthood of Aaron and Melchizedek. It also sums up the epistles to the Romans and to the Hebrews. The verse consists of two parts and contains two truths.

The first part is the phrase, *'For if when we were enemies we were reconciled to God through the death of His Son'*. This refers to man's state until the crucifixion took place. We were enemies, non-believers. Through the death of Christ on the cross, we were reconciled to God and we became believers. Some may say that this is the end of the story of salvation as we were reconciled to God.

However, Apostle Paul says that this is not so, as there is still a continuation to this verse: *'much more, having been reconciled, we shall be saved by his life'*.

What does the phrase *shall be saved by His life* mean?

It refers to Christ's life in heaven, His intercession as High Priest according to the order of Melchizedek, and the rope that He extends to us to save us.

- **Philippians 2:12**

Work out your own salvation with fear and trembling.

Apostle Paul directly says to the believers to work out their own salvation. According to the Greek origin, the phrase *fear and trembling* indicates that every step taken has to be established, and the person needs to look with circumspection to his right and left, front and back, and make sure that the step is complete and well-established before taking the next step.

Unfortunately, we often do not work out our salvation because we lack the fear and trembling. This, in turn, makes our salvation weak and not manifested. The salvation we have received will surely allow us to go to heaven, but because it is not manifested, it will bear very little fruit while we are on earth and may hinder the Kingdom purposes in our lives.

B. The Priestly Role of the Believers and How to Minister to God

We have two main points in this section:

1. The Priestly Calling

2. Liturgical Prayer

1. The Priestly Calling

We are called to be kings and priests in Christ, as we read in Revelation 1:6: '[He] *has made us kings and priests to His God and Father, to Him be glory and dominion forever and ever. Amen.*'

Based on the biblical revelation, we all understand that we are called to be priests in Christ, but we may not understand what it means to be priests in Christ! We may think of it as an honour or something that gives us authority in prayer, and that is all. But this is not biblical! Actually, we are called to be priests because we are called to serve the Holy God. A priest is called to perform a duty. Therefore, our priesthood will be ineffective if we do not know our duty. Our main duty as priests is to minister to God.

We now ought to further understand the meaning of ministering to God.

When God described the role of the priest in the Old Testament, this reflected priesthood in general according to God's mind. In the Old Testament, this priesthood served the purpose of the people of Israel of old. In the New Testament, the priesthood has another purpose, but still contains the same idea because God's mind does not change, yet His economy and plans may change.

Reading the passages in Exodus 29 and 30 and Leviticus 8 and 9 helps us understand the ministry of the priests in the Old Testament, which, in turn, gives us an understanding of how to minister to God in the Holies as priests in Christ in the New Testament.

According to the books of Exodus and Leviticus, the priest in the Old Testament had two main roles:

- A role in the outer court
- A role in the inner court

The Tabernacle has an outer court where the priests serve the people. It also has an inner court, which is called the holy place, where the priests minister to the Lord every day. (There is also the Holy of Holies, which the high priest enters only once a year.)

The divine truth behind this arrangement still applies to the New Testament but in the New Testament language. As the priest in the Old Testament served the people in the outer court and served the Lord in the inner court, it is also our duty to serve the people of God (the believers) and, at the same time, not neglect our role of ministering to God the Holy. If we lose the balance between the two, we are no longer priests. What a great loss this would be!

We now want to understand more about these two types of ministries or roles.

We are all familiar with serving the people in the outer court. No believer is exempt from this service. It is not the duty of pastors only. It is the duty of every believer.

How did the priests minister to the people of God in the Old Testament? They helped people to offer sacrifices.

Thus, in the ministry of the New Testament in the outer court, the priest needs to minister to people the sacrifices of Christ and the mysteries of the cross, bringing them to people in many revelatory ways.

Also, in Romans 12:1, Apostle Paul says, *'Present your bodies **a living sacrifice**, holy, acceptable to God, which is your reasonable service.'* Therefore, our role in serving people is to live a holy life in order to help other believers to live a holy life as well. Presenting an example or a model should come before words. We still can help people by loving them, encouraging them, or offering any other kind of ministry, but primarily we must be a living example for them. Apostle Paul said more than once, "Imitate me as I imitate Christ."[46]

In the Old Testament, the priests were looked to as the example that the people of Israel had to follow. Similarly, in the New Testament, we look to pastors as an example that we ought to follow. Therefore, every believer has a responsibility to be an example if he understands his calling to be a priest.

---

[46] See 1 Corinthians 4:16; 11:1; Philippians 3:17; 2 Thessalonians 3:7, 9.

Ministering to the people in the outer court is only part of this calling. What about the inner court?

The Bible highlights that after the priest finishes his role with the people, he must enter the inner court to serve the Lord.

Ministering to the Lord is different from our usual prayers. If we use the biblical terms, there is also prayer in the outer court. We serve people in the outer court, and we can also pray, live, and do everything in the outer court.

Moses went up the mountain to meet the Lord. At the same time, there were others who met the Lord at the bottom of the mountain. Unfortunately, we quite often pray at the bottom of the mountain and do not ascend to the top of the mountain. However, we are called to ascend and go up to the top of the mountain. Encountering the Lord at the top of the mountain changes our faces, and thus we can reflect His glory. But at the bottom of the mountain, none of this happens!

Therefore, after we finish our role with the people, we minister to God. We ought to try to do this daily to activate our priestly calling.

Because the inner court is a holy place, the priest in the Old Testament had to do *two things* before entering it. He had to *wash* and *change his clothes*. This is an interesting point because it has a significance in the New Testament, which we will explain shortly as we look at the things that the priest does in the inner court.

What happens in the inner court?

- Incense

In ministering to God in the inner court, the priest brings incense.

Incense represents our prayer life before God. Many people rely on corporate prayer meetings for their prayer time. They go to prayer meetings and return home afterwards thinking that they do not need to do anything else. When they are on their own, their prayer life may be weak, interrupted, and not established. When they go to prayer meetings, they are refreshed, released, encouraged, and built up in the spirit. There is nothing wrong in this as this is what prayer meetings are for.

The priest, however, has to bring his incense before God when he is alone in the inner court. Incense is brought while we are alone; this pleases the Lord. God wants our incense every day. This prayer has a special character-istic according to the Word of God. We will come back to this point later.

Corporate prayer meetings have their role, but we should not neglect our inner altar or neglect bringing incense before the Lord because this pleases Him.

- Washing

The priest washes before he enters into the inner court. Washing means that the priest has to be completely separate from all that has happened ear-lier in his day and in his life; he has to be separate even from his ministry outside (in the outer court) and from those he has ministered to.

There is another dimension to this washing, which is forgetting every-thing since he is going into the priestly service with the High Priest before the throne.

- Clothes

The priest also has to change his clothes before entering the inner court.

What does this signify?

In the outer court, he serves the people as he is. Therefore, he ought to be dressed in normal clothes, which signify humility and weakness. He ought to minister to the people with meekness, not haughtily nor as being supe-rior to them. In Hebrews 5:1, 2, we read:

> For every high priest taken from among men is appointed for men in things pertaining to God, that he may offer both gifts and sacrifices for sins. He can have compassion on those who are ignorant and going astray, *since he himself is also subject to weakness.*

The priest is subject to weakness, as the verse says. We ought to pay attention to this point because what may happen is that when the Holy Spirit comes upon us, and hence we minister in power, we sometimes forget that we also have weaknesses and may tend to minister to people as if they are the only weak ones and we are not. This attitude does not bring forth any fruits! Therefore, we must acquire genuine humility. We must remember that we are subject to weakness. When one listens to people and their problems, one ought to be aware that he can be in the same place as them because he has the same humanity, the same clothes, and the same weaknesses.

However, when a priest goes into the inner court, he needs to change his clothes. He needs to forget about his weaknesses, at least for a while. He has to be dressed anew. He has to be clothed with Christ. God cannot see us except through Christ. In 2 Corinthians 5:4, we read:

> For we who are in this tent groan, being burdened, not because we want to be unclothed, but further clothed, *that mortality may be swallowed up by life.*

Thus, the priest needs to be further clothed with Christ to be able to enter the inner court so that mortality may be swallowed up by life!

Another related point:

If one ministers in true humility and through the Spirit of God, one may receive some of the death from the people while serving in the outer court. People come with their death and the dust of the world. Then, when they are ministered to, they shake off their dust and death; some of it may come upon the intercessor. However, all this is dealt with through washing, changing the clothes, and prayer. Apostle Paul says to the people of Corinth: *'So then death is working in us, but life in you'* (2 Corinthians 4:12).

Therefore, we need to be further clothed with Christ, not only to cover our own humanity, but also the death and dust that comes upon us, so that this death and dust may be swallowed up. After that, we can offer our incense.

- Light

The priest also lights the lampstand. He has to refresh the light of the lamps and remove the burnt parts.

What does this signify?

This is a special ministry that has great effects. The priests enter the inner court to offer their worship so that the world may be illumined and lit. We are the light of the world. The light illuminates the world. When we refresh the light, we actually break the power of darkness in the area we live in.

What darkens the world? The apostle explains this, saying:

> Whose minds *the god of this age has blinded,* who do not believe, lest the light of the gospel of the glory of Christ, who is the image of God, should shine on them (2 Corinthians 4:4).

The devil blinds the eyes of non-believers to keep them in darkness so as not to receive the light of the gospel. The gospel is light, yet the enemy does not want people to receive or comprehend the gospel. He fills the minds of people with darkness. He lets darkness prevail. His kingdom is the kingdom of darkness (Ephesians 6:12) and his activity is to spread darkness everywhere. Thus, darkness covers the minds of people, causing them to refuse to respond to the gospel.

How can we overcome this situation?

It should be through evangelism, for the work of an evangelist is to bring the gospel with the power of the Holy Spirit. However, many evangelists say, "We have been preaching the gospel for many years, yet we are unable to break the power of darkness."

If there are priests in Christ who have learned to enter the Holies to minister to the Holy God and who radiate the light of Christ in their lives—a light that results from their absolute obedience to the Lord and living a holy life—they will break the power of darkness in the area that they live in, and through this, the work of missionaries and evangelists will be augmented. As priests, we ought to push away the darkness from the minds of people, hence preparing the way for the gospel to be received.

This darkness is not the normal darkness or the inability to perceive, but it is like a veil that covers, causing total darkness; this is the activity of the evil one. As priests, ministering in the heavenly places, we ought to tear this veil of the enemy so that the minds may be released and opened to receive the light.

Because we are created in God's image, we feel drawn to God. However, the veil hinders this activity and paralyses this image and, hence, we no longer feel drawn to God, but rather drawn to the enemy.

Therefore, as priests in Christ, we ought to be in the heavenly places, offering incense to God and ministering light to the world from the heavenly places. It is the unseen mystical light that will break the veil of darkness over the minds of people.

Unfortunately, the veil does not only cover the minds of non-believers, but also the minds of believers. Even believers have lost the desire to go deeper in the Word of God and find the revelatory light hidden in God's Word, and have lost the hunger for the Word of God.

The minds of believers need this priestly ministry because they have a limited understanding of the Word of God. They deal with the Word of God so superficially. They also need the light that brings them deeper into the Word of God and closer to the Person and Source of light, the Father of lights,[47] so that everything may change in their lives and ministry.

It is the responsibility of those who are called to be priests to minister to God, offer incense to God, and work against the darkness on the minds of the non-believers as well as the limitation of light in the minds of believers which hinders them from receiving deep light. When we perform our role as intercessors in the heavenly places and minister to the Lord, we push away this darkness and the Holy Spirit brings a new anointing upon the believers to hunger for the Lord. This is the priestly calling and its intercessory role. It is written that 'the light shines in the darkness, and the darkness did not comprehend it' (John 1:5). As a general spiritual principle, everything begins in the heavenly places first and then is manifested in the physical/visible realm.

---

[47] James 1:17

How can we as priests experience light and send forth light that breaks the power of the dark veils coming from the devil on the minds of non-believers or the limitation of light in the minds of believers?

What is the cause of the limitation of light in the minds of believers? Why are believers not open to deeper light and not hungry for deeper revelations in the Word of God?

It is because the fallen nature controls every area in the person, the flesh is not dealt with, and the self is not crucified. We need Christ to be formed in us.

If we do not have the mind of Christ, we will have the mind of the first Adam, not the mind of the second Adam. The mind of the first Adam is the natural mind, the fallen wisdom.

The process of renewal means being changed from the first Adam into becoming like the second Adam. Sometimes we are wise in our own eyes, but we ought to take heed because the mind of the second Adam is vastly different (1 Corinthians 2:16).

In Titus 2:14, we read:

> Who gave Himself for us, that He might redeem us from every lawless deed and purify for Himself His own *special* people, zealous for good works.

We need to be different. Christ's mind is different. The natural wisdom of the mind is fallen. Christ's mind is revelatory, bringing light and life to the person.

- Place: Our place in the priestly service

In the Old Testament, a priest could never leave his place, otherwise a huge problem would occur to the people of Israel.

The Book of Exodus speaks about the fire that must always be burning on the altar. This fire must never be extinguished as it was a sign of God's presence in Israel. If the fire was extinguished, this meant that there was no longer protection, blessing, and guidance for the people of Israel. When the worship in the temple was neglected and the fire went out, the nations surrounding Israel defeated them and prevented them from entering into their calling to minister to God.

Reading the two books of Kings, we notice that whenever a devout king reigned, he would usually begin his reign by restoring the temple and the worship in the temple. The altar would be rebuilt and the fire would be lit to burn again day and night. The presence of God brought protection and direction for the kingdom of Israel.

It is so serious and dangerous for a priest to leave his place.

If one really wants to live out his priestly calling, he must be very consistent in his spiritual life. If you are familiar with the priestly calling, you will know that you have a place in the heavenly places and that you are not there alone, but you have a place among other priests from all over the world who represent the body of Christ and who come to serve with the High Priest Jesus. Everything in heaven is very orderly: 'Let all things be done decently and in order' (1 Corinthians 14:40). Therefore, you need to find your specific place before the throne and you are not supposed to leave your place even for a single day. Your heavenly place can even call upon you when you are absent: "Where are you? I am waiting for you. Do you really want to leave your place vacant? The service will start soon! Everybody is waiting for you!"

If you are absent for a day, the whole service is disrupted. The order in heaven cannot be disrupted. The angels will look for you, saying that the service has to begin. If you can no longer be trusted, you will be replaced. Heavenly matters cannot be taken lightly. We cannot deal with heavenly matters the way we deal with earthly matters. In the heavens, there is nothing called an absent priest. This happens only on earth where we take divine matters lightly. However, the situation is different in heaven; you cannot leave your place.

- Breastplate

The high priest in the Old Testament wore a breastplate on which the names of all the tribes were engraved.

What is the practical significance of this breastplate in the priestly calling?

The high priest wore this breastplate on his chest, meaning his heart, which signified that he was responsible for all the 12 tribes of Israel. When he entered before God on behalf of the people, he brought all the needs and requests of the people before God.

Aaron identified with the people of Israel, carrying their names on his chest and remembering the names of each tribe. He had to go through many rituals to be prepared to enter into the inner court (see Leviticus 16 as an example of what Aaron had to do on the Day of Atonement).

After offering many sacrifices and going through several steps of preparation, he would become completely tuned with God's heart and mind for His people. Only then could he enter into the inner court, putting on the breastplate, and having the same will that God had for the people. Therefore, when he would say: "God I bring these people to You!" God would respond: "The burden on your heart for them is an echo of what is on My heart towards them. I receive all your burdens and requests for the 12 tribes and I answer them; go home and be at peace."

Thus, the high priest would surrender all the burdens of the people to God, and then go outside and bless the nation:

> Then Aaron lifted his hand toward the people, blessed them, and came down from offering the sin offering, the burnt offering, and peace offerings. And Moses and Aaron went into the tabernacle of meeting, and *came out and blessed the people.* Then the glory of the Lord appeared to all the people, and fire came out from before the Lord and consumed the burnt offering and the fat on the altar. When all the people saw it, they shouted and fell on their faces (Leviticus 9:22–24).

If we spend enough time in prayer to be prepared and to practically be in the heavenly places, tuned with God and having one heart and will with God, everything that we bring into God's presence will already be on God's heart; consequently, a release of blessings and direction will go forth from God to the people He has entrusted to us.

If we live out our priestly calling, we will learn and witness the effective power of intercession. The names of the people we intercede for will be engraved on our hearts and we will enter before the Lord bearing them within us so that their needs may be brought before His throne, hence the Lord can answer their requests and fulfil their needs.

This is the full picture of the intercession of the priestly calling. It is a process that requires training.

Now the question that each person needs to ask himself is:

Am I keen on spending enough hours with God to be well prepared and tuned with Him so that I may be able to fulfil my intercessory responsibilities?

- Shoulder ephods

The priest also had shoulder ephods. We understand from Isaiah 9:6 that these shoulder ephods represent authority:

> For unto us a Child is born, unto us a Son is given; and *the government will be upon His shoulder*. And His name will be called Wonderful, Counsellor, Mighty God, Everlasting Father, Prince of Peace.

From this passage, we understand that authority rests on the shoulders. Soldiers have epaulettes or shoulder boards as a sign of their rank and degree of authority.

An intercessor in the priestly calling is also a soldier in God's army. There are different ranks for the soldiers. When one is committed to his spiritual life and calling, he moves to a higher rank. This grants him true authority over the enemy both in his life and ministry. The enemy understands the level of authority that each priest has. In Christ, we are victorious at different levels.

We ought to remember the great role of Christ as a High Priest interceding for us and that He invites us to partake in this great ministry as priests serving under His leadership.

What a mystery! What a blessing! What a responsibility!

Therefore He is also able to save to the uttermost those who come to God through Him, since He always lives to make intercession for them (Hebrews 7:25).

For if when we were enemies we were reconciled to God through the death of His Son, much more, having been reconciled, we shall be saved by His life (Romans 5:10).

2. Liturgical Prayer

This is the second point in relation to the priestly calling of the believers.

What is the type of prayer that we should pray in the holy place?

In the outer court, you can pray any prayer you want. But if you want to activate your priestly prayer, you must follow the biblical principle. The Bible instructs that those who minister to God must learn the liturgical prayer. In Hebrews 1:14, we read:

Are they not all *ministering* spirits sent forth *to minister* for those who will inherit salvation?

This verse speaks about the ministry of the angels. According to the original Greek language, two different words are used in this verse to refer to two different ministries of the angels. The two words are *liturgia* or *liturgy* in English and *diakonia* which comes from the word *deacon* in English. The difference in meaning between the two words is clear in the Greek language.

The writer of this epistle, Apostle Paul, uses the first word (*liturgia*) when he speaks about the ministry of the angels in the Holies as they minister to God, and uses the second word (*diakonia*) when he speaks about the ministry of the angels to human beings, as missionaries sent forth by God to bring a message to human beings or to aid them in certain matters.

The word *diakonia* signifies a continuous change in words or the kind of ministry according to the needs of human beings and God's message to those human beings. Therefore, when the angels are sent to speak to humans and minister to them, they speak a different message according to the purpose they are sent for.

However, the word *liturgia* means the opposite of that; it signifies that the words used in such ministry are always the same; they are repeated and do not change. We see evidence of this in the Book of Revelation where the Scripture speaks about the angels' worship to God. We notice that the angels use the same words and phrases of worship throughout the different chapters of the Book of Revelation. They do not change their words or prayers. They say, '*Holy, holy, holy*'.[48] They minister to God by repeating this phrase and bowing down before God.

In the Book of Isaiah, chapter 6, we also notice that the seraphim bowed before the Lord saying, '*Holy, holy, holy*,'[49] in the same way.

Learning the ministry of *diakonia* is based on knowing and serving the ministry of *liturgia*. The angels can serve the people through this inspired ministry of *diakonia* because they have first learned to minister their *liturgia* to God. In fact, the ministry of *liturgia* prepares the person in a special way because it is a continuous entrance into the presence of the Lord. This entrance into the presence of the Lord allows the mind of God, the heart of God, and the Spirit of God to flow to the person, changing his spirit and mind, directing them towards God.

> For as the heavens are higher than the earth, so are My ways higher than your ways, and My thoughts than your thoughts (Isaiah 55:9).

The ministry of the angels helps us understand God's mind regarding how He wants us to minister to Him. When the angels minister to God, they offer the same service daily. The Lord seems to be pleased with this ministry, despite being repeated. We may think that this repetition is boring, but God is interested in it and is pleased with it because God does not look at words but looks at the hearts.

He does not mind what words are used in worship but minds what the heart is like.

---

[48] Revelation 4:8

[49] Isaiah 6:3

We often think that the Lord wants us to use different words to express ourselves to Him, but this is actually our problem; we are the ones who like change and we think that routine is boring. However, God does not seek words, He seeks the heart.

We can say wonderful words to the Lord, but they will be rejected by God if the heart is divided or stained with sin. In the Book of Proverbs, it is written:

> The *sacrifice of the wicked is an abomination to the Lord*, but the prayer of the upright is His delight (Proverbs 15:8).

> One who turns away his ear from hearing the law, *even his prayer is an abomination* (Proverbs 28:9).

The Lord is pleased with words that come out of a pure heart that is full of love, no matter how simple these words may be.

A story to illustrate this point:

The events of this story took place in the desert of Egypt, in Wadi el Natroun, in the 4th century.

There was a person who desired to worship the Lord day and night. This man was illiterate and had limited knowledge. He left his village, and went to the worshippers in Wadi el Natroun because it was well-known that these worshippers were advanced in theology and in spiritual knowledge.

When he met the worshippers, he told them that he longed to worship the Lord day and night, but he was illiterate and didn't know what to do. At the same time, he was very poor and didn't have any money to buy any resources that could help him.

So they asked him: "What do you normally pray?"

The man said: "I have memorised the Lord's Prayer since my childhood and I pray it day and night."

The spiritual father, the worshipper, then told him: "I will teach you a short prayer; I want you to memorise it and keep repeating it and come back to me after one month."

The man agreed and this spiritual father taught him this short prayer and helped him to memorise it.

After the man memorised the prayer and repeated it several times, the spiritual father said to him: "Now you can go back to your village and come back after one month. When you come back, I will teach you another prayer."

So the man left, but after two or three hours he came back to this spiritual father and said: "I am sorry, father, I forgot one or two words of the prayer. Could you please tell me the prayer again?"

This spiritual father was a man of God and had spiritual insight; thus, he was able to sense that there was a secret or a mystery in the life of this man. So, he asked the man a direct question saying: "Are you poor? Do you have any money?" The man was very surprised by this question. The father continued to say: "There is a river between your village and this place so you need to take a boat in order to cross the river; this means that you must have the fare for the boat."

The man said: "I don't have the fare for the boat and I have not used the boat."

The father said: "But how did you cross the river and come back?"

The man had a heavy cloak on his shoulder, and he said: "I put the cloak on the surface of the river and I walked on it; it is my means of transport, and it is my boat."

The spiritual father then said: "If so, continue as you are with the Lord's Prayer and don't learn anything else; you do not need any other prayer. Continue to do what you are already doing."

Of course, the spiritual father had a purpose for saying this. He understood that this man was actually given the Lord's Prayer as his *liturgy* to use to minister in the presence of God day and night.

After the spiritual father blessed the man and sent him home, he went to his spiritual disciples and told them the story. His comment on this story was as follows:

"There is a mystery in the life of this man. This man has a very pure heart and it is filled completely with the Spirit of God. He lives in the realm of miracles and wonders. He reached this level by repeating only one prayer all his life. We pray different kinds of prayers and we have not yet reached this purity of heart or this degree of infilling of the Spirit. Our prayers ought to be a means of cleansing and purifying us in order to attain a pure heart."

This spiritual father then started to remind his disciples of various verses in this context:

> But the Lord said to Samuel, "Do not look at his appearance or at his physical stature, because I have refused him. For the Lord does not see as man sees; for man looks at the outward appearance, but *the Lord looks at the heart*" (1 Samuel 16:7).

> Blessed are *the pure in heart*, for they shall see God (Matthew 5:8).

The great focus on the mind and the intellect in our modern age has estranged us from preliminary truths such as purity of heart and simplicity of heart while using simple and honest words in prayer.

God wants His children to minister to Him in the heavenly places because this is actually their prime calling according to God's mind. God created us to minister to Him and worship Him.

> Everyone who is called by My Name, whom I have created for My glory; I have formed him, yes, I have made him ... This people I have formed for Myself; they shall declare My praise (Isaiah 43:7, 21).

We are created for the glory of God (verse 7) and we are also created to proclaim praises to God (verse 21).

> You are worthy, O Lord, to receive glory and honour and power; for You created all things, and *by Your will they exist and were created* (Revelation 4:11).

In some translations, the phrase *'by Your will they exist and were created'* reads: *'for Your pleasure they exist and were created'*.[50] We were created for the pleasure of God. This is not because God is selfish or wants us for Himself; on the contrary, it is because He is a giver of love and wants us to partake in His love.

In the early Church, liturgical prayers meant praying the Book of Psalms because they believed that the Book of Psalms was inspired mainly to teach the people of God how to pray.

If you want to learn how to minister to God as a priest, you need to use the Book of Psalms because God wants to hear His own words, inspired by the Holy Spirit, prayed before Him. The Book of Ecclesiastes alerts us that when we come before God, we must be careful what words we use.[51] God does not want to hear casual words because this disturbs the symphony of heaven. He has a purpose and He has given us a specific book to use when we pray and minister to Him.

To pray these liturgical prayers, the worshippers would stand and recite the Psalms prayerfully, singing them before the Lord. Then, they would prostrate (bow down) as described in the Book of Revelation about the worship of the angels before the Lord. The Greek word means to bow down with the forehead touching the ground (prostrate). This reflects a humble attitude and giving the glory to God.

The early fathers explain the significance and practical benefit of this kind of worship as follows:

Due to human weakness, one may find his mind distracted or preoccupied with many activities. Similarly, one may struggle with sleepiness or be unable to understand the Bible or receive any new revelations. If this person prays the Psalms and prostrates, he engages his mind, spirit, and his whole being. As a result, he will experience the following:

---

[50] Refer to Revelation 4:11, KJV.

[51] Ecclesiastes 5:2

For the mind, it will be like taking a shower that washes away all the dirt. The living water of the Word of God will wash your mind. Bowing down and rising up again girdles the inner man. Then, you stand as a priest—a soldier in the army of God—and minister to the Holy God. Since you are ministering before the Lord as a priest, when you come out from the presence of the Lord, you will come out with a different authority. When any evil power sees you, it will flee away; it cannot come near you. But if you do not do this, the evil powers will come on your face like flies. The Bible speaks about the evil powers as Beelzebub, meaning *lord of flies*.

Ministering to God in the early Church

> Now in the church that was at Antioch there were certain prophets and teachers: Barnabas, Simeon who was called Niger, Lucius of Cyrene, Manaen who had been brought up with Herod the tetrarch, and Saul. *As they ministered to the Lord and fasted,* the Holy Spirit said, "Now separate to Me Barnabas and Saul for the work to which I have called them." Then, having fasted and prayed, and laid hands on them, they sent them away (Acts 13:1–3).

The Greek origin of the phrase *ministered to the Lord* is *liturgia*.

What is the liturgia that we should use in our prayers?

The Holy Spirit can teach each one his own special *liturgia*.

This can only happen after the person is trained to worship God regularly and consistently with commitment and with a sense of partaking in the ministry of the angels in heaven.

In the first chapters of the Book of Acts, the word *continually* is repeated frequently. In its Greek origin, this word means *to do something continuously without any interruption.* This word is also mentioned in more than one place in the epistles.

Some of these references:

> And they *continued* steadfastly in the apostles' doctrine and fellowship, in the breaking of bread, and in prayers (Acts 2:42).

But we will give ourselves *continually* to prayer and to the ministry of the word (Acts 6:4).

Rejoicing in hope, patient in tribulation, *continuing* steadfastly in prayer (Romans 12:12).

Praying *always* with all prayer and supplication in the Spirit, being watchful to this end with all perseverance and supplication for all the saints (Ephesians 6:18).

Continue earnestly in prayer, being vigilant in it with thanksgiving (Colossians 4:2).

Night and day praying exceedingly that we may see your face and perfect what is lacking in your faith (1 Thessalonians 3:10).

Now she who is really a widow, and left alone, trusts in God and continues in supplications and prayers *night and day* (1 Timothy 5:5).

When the person continues to worship regularly and consistently before the Lord for a sufficient period of time, he goes through a special experience that cannot occur if the person's worship is interrupted and irregular. Therefore, we need to learn to worship continuously and regularly every day, even for a short time, but we should never miss a day without worship. The worshipper starts to feel that a specific place in the heavenly places is assigned for him, and that this place can never be left vacant. So, for example, if at any point this person feels that he is unable to pray as he used to, it becomes clear to him that this place as if calls him in the language of the spirit saying: "Don't leave your place; your place is vacant now. You are counted as a worshipper and a priest before the Lord and there is a place assigned for you." This is actually the meaning of being priests in Christ. The ministry of priesthood calls you saying: "You cannot leave your place as a priest. The High Priest, Jesus Christ, looks around to see who is absent and is not in his place because this can disturb the service and it is not allowed at all in heaven."

Being priests in Christ is a great authority that can change the form of heaven and earth. Yet, it has to be released. It is hidden inside us and needs to be released.

This can be practically achieved through the ministry of *liturgia*, by taking our place among the spiritual priests of Christ, and serving with the High Priest in the heavens. The High Priest will then speak to us about what is on His heart and mind.

I want to conclude with a story that took place in the early centuries about the fruits of the ministry of *liturgia*:

One of the well-known worshippers in the south of Egypt, St. Shenouda the Archimandrite, had a special spiritual gift, which was a fruit of the ministry of *liturgia*. This gift was having spiritual eyes that were able to see everything that happened in the world. He would stand the whole night praying his *liturgia*, and then in the morning, he would go out of his cell and stand up, raising his hands to see what was happening in the world and would begin to intercede for all the events that were happening in the world. The Holy Spirit allowed him to see particular events that were taking place in different places in the world and then he would start to intercede for these events. Due to the power of prayer by which he was filled while praying all night, his intercessions bore very clear fruits. Though he was a hermit, this did not prevent him from going on some journeys in the world when it was necessary to do so.

CHAPTER 11

THE BLOOD OF JESUS
GRANTS ME VICTORY OVER SATAN
AND ALL HIS PRINCIPALITIES

Introduction

A nd they overcame him by the blood of the Lamb and by the word of their testimony, and they did not love their lives to the death (Revelation 12:11).

We will study this topic in five main titles:

I. A Comment on the Main Verse

II. God's Promise of Old of Victory Over Satan

III. Overcoming the Enemy in Christ's Life and Ministry

IV. The Teaching of the New Testament About Overcoming Satan (From the Epistles)

V. Final Points (Conclusion)

I. A Comment on the Main Verse

The verse states three factors that lead to victory and overcoming the enemy:

A. The blood of Jesus

B. The word of their testimony

C. They did not love their life to the death

A. The Blood of Jesus

It is clear that the blood of Jesus is not only the means to overcome the enemy, but it is much more than that; it is the basis and the grounds upon which we can overcome the enemy. Why?

This is because Satan can overcome us when there is sin in our lives. Sin is the main weapon by which Satan overcomes the believers. Therefore, the blood of Jesus is not only a weapon or a means to overcome Satan, but it actually annuls sin. The Bible tells us that the blood of Jesus has dealt with sin from different aspects. He took away sin and annulled its power completely. Accordingly, Satan lost his main weapon—sin, which is the cause or the grounds of the enemy's continuous accusations against the children of God. The enemy is described as *'the accuser of our brethren, who accused them before our God day and night'* (Revelation 12:10).

Some references that highlight that Christ has taken away sin:

The next day John saw Jesus coming toward him, and said, "Behold! The Lamb of God who *takes away the sin* of the world!" (John 1:29).

He then would have had to suffer often since the foundation of the world; but now, once at the end of the ages, He has appeared to *put away sin* by the sacrifice of Himself (Hebrews 9:26).

And you know that He was manifested *to take away our sins*, and in Him there is no sin ... He who sins is of the devil, for the devil has sinned from the beginning. For this purpose the Son of God was manifested, that He might *destroy the works of the devil* (1 John 3:5, 8).

Therefore, if we deal with sin daily by the blood of Jesus (1 John 2:2), we will continuously overcome the enemy (1 John 2:14b):

> If we confess our sins, He is faithful and just to forgive us our sins and to cleanse us from all unrighteousness. If we say that we have not sinned, we make Him a liar, and His word is not in us. My little children, these things I write to you, so that you may not sin. And if anyone sins, we have an Advocate with the Father, Jesus Christ the righteous. And He Himself is the propitiation for our sins, and not for ours only but also for the whole world (1 John 1:9–2:2).

> I have written to you, young men, because you are strong, and the word of God abides in you, *and you have overcome the wicked one* (1 John 2:14b).

B. The Word of Their Testimony

Again, the word of their testimony is not only the means of victory but the grounds on which they are victorious.

What does this mean practically?

There are two ways by which the Word of God becomes a testimony:

- One way is by sharing it with others through evangelism and preaching. In this case, it cannot be one of the facets of victory.

- But the other aspect, which is intended here, is that their life itself became a testimony of the work of Christ's grace in them, without them speaking or saying any words. It is not about the words we share but the life we present or the life manifested in us. In other words, if we meet someone whose life is a testimony, we will immediately sense that the gospel is personified in his life and that his life speaks of or portrays a truth that is lived out.

The Word of God is the sword of the Spirit as written in Ephesians 6:17. When we obey the Word of God and give it its due place in our life through reading it, meditating on it, studying it, proclaiming it, and obeying it, it becomes a sword of the Spirit by which we overcome Satan. When he attacks us with various thoughts and temptations, we overcome him with this sword of the Spirit. Also, when we serve others, we find that the Word of God breaks the authority of Satan over them.

C. They Did Not Love Their Life to the Death

According to the original Greek language, this phrase signifies that they continued not to love their lives until the very end, even unto death or as far as death.

They had absolute and unwavering surrender to Christ and to the purposes of His Kingdom.

When the love of their life stood in the way of their loyalty to Christ, they were ready to lay down their lives for the sake of Christ.

This attitude helped them overcome the enemy and encouraged others to be faithful unto death. Thus, this greatly contributed to the purposes of God's Kingdom.

This was the same attitude of Apostle Paul when he heard from Agabus about the possibility of facing suffering in Jerusalem. He said:

> What do you mean by weeping and breaking my heart? For I am ready not only to be bound, but *also to die* at Jerusalem for the name of the Lord Jesus (Acts 21:13).

It is also the same attitude of Christ the Son of God who obeyed to the point of death:

> And being found in appearance as a man, He humbled Himself and became obedient to the point of death, even the death of the cross (Philippians 2:8).

In the same way, we ought to acquire absolute obedience to Christ. This happens when Christ reigns in our hearts, and when serving His Kingdom becomes the purpose of our lives: 'For to me, to live is Christ, and to die is gain' (Philippians 1:21).

Thus, this verse (Revelation 12:11) outlines the basis or the grounds to overcome the enemy and his unceasing confrontations.

From this perspective, we need to look at the ways of victory over the enemy as revealed in the Bible.

From the very beginning, in Genesis 3:15, God gave man a promise of victory over the enemy.

II. God's Promise of Old of Victory Over Satan

Because God is merciful—as the Psalmist says, *'He is good! His mercy endures forever'* (Psalm 136:1)—immediately after the fall, He gave man a promise of overcoming the enemy:

> And I will put enmity between you and the woman, and between your seed and her Seed; he shall bruise your head, and *you shall bruise His heel* (Genesis 3:15).

Throughout the whole of the Old Testament, we find many promises of victory and overcoming the enemy, especially in the Book of Psalms. This is another confirmation that the Book of Psalms is a book of prayer because as we pray it, we are encouraged by the promises of victory:

> You shall tread upon the lion and the cobra, the young lion and the serpent you shall trample underfoot (Psalm 91:13).

The lion, the cobra, and the serpent refer to the devil and his evil plans. This was well-known to the Jewish person.

> Endless ruin has overtaken [the enemy] (Psalm 9:6, NIV).

> [You] have not shut me up into the hand of the enemy; You have set my feet in a wide place (Psalm 31:8).

> For You have been a shelter for me, a strong tower from the enemy (Psalm 61:3).

> He saved them from the hand of him who hated them, and redeemed them from the hand of the enemy (Psalm 106:10).

> Oh, give thanks to the Lord, for He is good! For His mercy endures forever. Let the redeemed of the Lord say so, whom He has redeemed from the hand of the enemy (Psalm 107:1, 2).

All these references highlight our redemption from the hand of the enemy and his authority. This redemption was completed for us in Christ through His cross and resurrection.

III. Overcoming the Enemy in Christ's Life and Ministry

Christ Himself taught us to be victorious.

A. When the devil came to Christ with the three temptations while He was fasting in the wilderness, Christ conquered him by the authority of the Word (Matthew 4:1–11).

Notice the following:

- Christ used the Word of God to resist the devil.

- The devil did not succeed and eventually Christ sent him away saying, *'Away with you, Satan!'* (Matthew 4:10).

- Despite this, the devil did not cease to oppose and resist Christ in various ways because the Bible says that *'he departed from Him until an opportune time'* (Luke 4:13), indicating that he would come back. This means that the conflict with the enemy is a long-life conflict, but there is always victory.

B. From the beginning of His ministry, Christ had absolute authority over the devils and He freed many demon-possessed people.

To quote just a few references:

Then they were all amazed, so that they questioned among themselves, saying, "What is this? What new doctrine is this? For with authority He commands even the unclean spirits, and they obey Him" (Mark 1:27).

And the unclean spirits, whenever they saw Him, fell down before Him and cried out, saying, "You are the Son of God" (Mark 3:11).

Also, when Jesus sent forth His disciples for ministry, He gave them authority over the evil powers:

And He called the twelve to Himself, and began to send them out two by two, and gave them power over unclean spirits (Mark 6:7).

Then the seventy returned with joy, saying, "Lord, even the demons are subject to us in Your name" (Luke 10:17).

C. Some of Christ's discourses that refer to overcoming Satan:

- Luke 10:18, 19

And He said to them, "*I saw Satan fall like lightning* from heaven. Behold, I give you the authority to trample on serpents and scorpions, and over all the power of the enemy, and nothing shall by any means hurt you."

This verse refers to breaking the authority of the enemy due to the coming of Christ into the world (His incarnation). This is what Isaiah prophetically saw and recorded, saying:

How you are fallen from heaven, O Lucifer, son of the morning! How you are cut down to the ground, you who weakened the nations! (Isaiah 14:12).

It is also what John the Seer prophetically recorded saying:

So the great dragon *was cast out*, that serpent of old, called the Devil and Satan, who deceives the whole world; he was cast to the earth, and his angels were cast out with him (Revelation 12:9).

Lightning signifies speed. The authority of the devil may sometimes seem sweeping or frightening, but the presence of Christ exposes him, causing him to dissolve quickly and annulling his influence.

Therefore, we ought to be keen on and vigilant over the presence of Christ in our lives through our continuous, uninterrupted, and living relationship with Him. This can be achieved through repentance, worship, and fellowship with the Lord.

Even more than this, Christ proclaims His authority over the activity of the enemy's kingdom. The serpents and scorpions also refer to human beings who have wicked plans against God's children.

- Luke 11:21, 22

When a strong man, fully armed, guards his own palace, his goods are in peace. But when a stronger than he comes upon him and overcomes him, he takes from him all his armour in which he trusted, and divides his spoils.

The scribes and the Pharisees accused Jesus of casting out demons by Beelzebub.[52]

Jesus answered their accusation by clarifying the important truths highlighted in this verse. The enemy seems strong because he is armed and uses his weapons to guard the souls whom he takes captive. The weapons of the enemy are sin and its authority over man as well as deceiving man so that he may remain captive to sin, withdrawn from God, and not repent. Christ is the *stronger* who came to conquer the enemy and annul the effect of his weapons. The blood of Jesus and His cross take away sin and break its authority. Thus, the captives are set free: *'To set at liberty those who are oppressed'* (Luke 4:18).

- John 12:31

Now is the judgement of this world; *now the ruler of this world will be cast out.*

Casting out the enemy signifies that the enemy has lost his authority over the children of God. This refers to a continuous act that started with the ministry of Christ and His crucifixion and which continues until the devil is finally cast into the lake of fire at the very end, as we read in Revelation 20:10:

The devil, who deceived them, *was cast into the lake of fire* and brimstone where the beast and the false prophet are. And they will be tormented day and night forever and ever.

Casting out the enemy is practically achieved in the life of God's children from now (Jesus said *now* in John 12:31) by coming out of the sphere of Satan's authority, which is the world, for it is written that *'the whole world lies under the sway of the wicked one'* (1 John 5:19), and entering into the sphere of the Kingdom of God—God's authority:

---

[52] Beelzebub, *prince of devils,* from Latin; from Greek *Beelzeboub;* from Hebrew *Ba 'al zĕbhūbh,* a Philistine god, literally, *lord of flies.*

He has delivered us from the power of darkness and conveyed us into the Kingdom of the Son of His love (Colossians 1:13).

It is also achieved by coming out from being under the effect of the devil's work, meaning the captivity of sin, corruption, and death, and entering into the life of the liberty of the children of God, meaning holiness and eternal life, which are the fruits of redemption.

D. The ministry of the disciples as reflected in the Book of Acts:

After the day of Pentecost, we witness the authority of the disciples in freeing people from Satan:

> Also a multitude gathered from the surrounding cities to Jerusalem, bringing sick people and those who were tormented by unclean spirits, and they were all healed (Acts 5:16).

> For unclean spirits, crying with a loud voice came out of many who were possessed; and many who were paralysed and lame were healed (Acts 8:7).

> And [Paul] said, "O full of all deceit and all fraud, you son of the devil, you enemy of all righteousness, will you not cease perverting the straight ways of the Lord? And now, indeed, the hand of the Lord is upon you, and you shall be blind, not seeing the sun for a time." And immediately a dark mist fell on him, and he went around seeking someone to lead him by the hand (Acts 13:10–11).

> And this she did for many days. But Paul, greatly annoyed, turned and said to the spirit, "I command you in the name of Jesus Christ to come out of her." And he came out that very hour (Acts 16:18).

IV. The Teaching of the New Testament About Overcoming Satan (From the Epistles)

The teachings of the apostles also help us understand how to overcome the enemy.

A. The Epistles of Apostle Paul

- Romans 16:20

And *the God of peace will crush Satan* under your feet shortly.

The word *crush* reminds us of the promise of old in Genesis 3:15. The verse proclaims *victory* (crushing Satan) and *honour* (under your feet). *The God of peace* restores to us the peace that the enemy wants to take away; victory preserves our peace.

- 2 Corinthians 10:4

For the weapons of our warfare are *not carnal* but *mighty in God* for pulling down strongholds.

Carnal weapons do not refer to the usual weapons of war but to the moral weapons of the world such as philosophy and debates, meaning the wisdom of the world:

And I, brethren, when I came to you, *did not come with excellence of speech or of wisdom* declaring to you the testimony of God ... And my speech and my preaching were *not with persuasive words of human wisdom*, but in demonstration of the Spirit and of power (1 Corinthians 2:1, 4).

The phrase *mighty in God* here means that God is the source of the weapons of our warfare, hence signifying that they are according to God's mind.

The phrase *pulling down strongholds* here means annulling all that gives the enemy a chance to conquer us; consequently, our complete victory over him is achieved.

- Ephesians 1:22

And He put all things under His feet, and gave Him to be head over all things *to the church.*

The two verses before this verse (Ephesians 1:19, 20) highlight that the resurrection of Christ has revealed His supreme power, and that His resurrection and ascension have put all things under His feet. Then, the apostle clarifies that this was done for the sake of the Church. According to the Greek origin, the phrase *to the church* means *for the sake of the church.*

This signifies that the authority of Christ's victory and putting all things under His feet has been transferred to us and accredited to us as members of His body. Hence, resurrection has become a new spring given to us, the believers, by which we overcome the enemy.

- Ephesians 6:10–20

Finally, my brethren, be strong in the Lord and in the power of His might. Put on the whole armour of God, that you may be able to stand against the wiles of the devil. For we do not wrestle against flesh and blood, but against principalities, against powers, against the rulers of the darkness of this age, against spiritual hosts of wickedness in the heavenly places (verses 10–12).

- *Be strong in the Lord*

This phrase is used in the passive form in the original Greek language, hence indicating that God's power is available for us and has been granted to us in Christ, but we need to give it an opportunity to be practically released in our lives. This happens through prayer and obeying God and His commandments.

- *Put on the armour*

The armour, as Apostle Paul clarifies, is truth, righteousness, the gospel, faith, prayer, vigilance, and the Word of God. We need to be trained in these matters in order to be in a state of readiness to overcome the enemy.

- *The devil's wiles/schemes*

This phrase draws our attention to the devil's cunning devices by which he wants to destroy humans. Therefore, it is necessary to be armoured and to use all that has been granted to us in Christ because Christ has overcome the enemy for our sake, as written in John 16:33:

> These things I have spoken to you, that in Me you may have peace. In the world you will have tribulation; but be of good cheer, *I have overcome the world* ...

- Colossians 2:15

> Having disarmed principalities and powers, He made a public spectacle of them, triumphing over them *in it*.

In it means *in the cross*.

From this verse, we understand that three elements of victory against the kingdom of darkness were accomplished for us in the cross:

- *Disarmed principalities and powers*

This means that Christ has put an end to their authority over us.

- *Made a public spectacle of them*

The word used here is the same word used in Matthew 1:19: *'did not want to expose her to public disgrace'* (NIV). Therefore, the phrase signifies that Christ has publicly exposed the evil powers. It became possible to expose the devil's devices and evil plans through the work of the Holy Spirit in us.

- *Triumphing over them*

This phrase means that Christ made this victory similar to the Roman procession of victory. The word used here is the same word used in 2 Corinthians 2:14: *triumphal procession* (NIV). In these processions, the emperors would lead the defeated kings in processions that would proclaim their own victory and expose the defeated kings before everyone. The victory that Christ completed for us is public and is shameful for the enemy.

- Hebrews 2:14

Inasmuch then as the children have partaken of flesh and blood, He Himself likewise shared in the same, that through death He might *destroy* him who had the power of death, that is, the devil.

The enemy has the power of death through sin (Romans 6:23). Thus, Jesus called him *'a murderer from the beginning'* (John 8:44).

The word *destroy* used in this verse is mentioned 27 times in the New Testament and it indicates putting a complete end to the enemy's power of death on God's redeemed children because death is not God's economy. This has been rightfully accomplished by the death of Christ and has been credited to us:

But also for us, to whom God will credit righteousness—for us who believe in him who raised Jesus our Lord from the dead. He was delivered over to death for our sins and was raised to life for our justification (Romans 4:24–25, NIV).

B. Other Writings of the Apostles

- Apostle James

Therefore submit to God. *Resist* the devil and he will flee from you (James 4:7).

- *Submit*

Here we notice the importance of submitting to God. According to the original Greek language, the word *submit* is used in a military context. Here, the word indicates that we should come under the banner of God, meaning to keep ourselves in God's military camp, and hence, God fights for us while we are silent.[53]

---

[53] Exodus 14:14

    - *Resist the devil and he will flee*

The devil no longer has authority, yet if we resist him, meaning if we reject his counsel and temptations, he flees.

> But each one is tempted when he is drawn away by his own desires and enticed (James 1:14).

- Apostle Peter

Be sober, be vigilant; because your adversary the devil walks about like a roaring lion, seeking whom he may devour. *Resist* him, *steadfast* in the faith, knowing that the same sufferings are experienced by your brotherhood in the world (1 Peter 5:8, 9).

    - *Be sober; be vigilant*

This is our responsibility. God has accomplished a great victory for us in Christ, and we need to be vigilant over this great victory.

    - *Resist*

The same point that Apostle James emphasised is repeated here. When the Scriptures repeat something this means that the Holy Spirit wants to emphasise its importance.

    - *Steadfast in the faith*

A steadfast faith is an expression used to describe strong and solid foundations that are practically laid through prayer, searching oneself in the light of God's Word, and growing in grace. Refer to Colossians 1:23.

    - *Knowing*

Simply knowing that others go through the same sufferings as us encourages us, especially that the whole body of Christ is knit together through the head—Christ. We are strengthened through the unity of the body of Christ.

- Apostle John

I have written to you … because you are strong, and *the word of God abides in you,* and you have overcome the wicked one. Do not love the world or the things in the world. If anyone loves the world, the love of the Father is not in him (1 John 2:14b, 15).

Here Apostle John links overcoming the wicked one to the Word of God abiding in the believers. This reveals to us another dimension of overcoming the enemy, and that is through the Word of God abiding in us.

Apostle John also warns of the love of the world because the devil is the ruler of this world, as Jesus said in John 14:30. Therefore, if we are involved in worldly matters, we can easily be trapped.

In verses 15–17 of this chapter, the apostle clarifies that we ought to avoid the love of the world, highlighting that the world perishes and passes away:

Do not love the world or the things in the world. If anyone loves the world, the love of the Father is not in him. For all that is in the world—the lust of the flesh, the lust of the eyes, and the pride of life—is not of the Father but is of the world. And the world is passing away, and the lust of it; but he who does the will of God abides forever (1 John 2:15–17).

V. Final Points (Conclusion)

1. Our weapons are:

a. The blood of Jesus

b. The name of Jesus

c. Our place in Christ

d. Christ's intercession

Christ intercedes for our sake that we may be protected from the plans of the devil:

> And the Lord said, "Simon, Simon! Indeed, Satan has asked for you, that he may sift you as wheat. But I have prayed for you; that your faith should not fail; and when you have returned to Me, strengthen your brethren" (Luke 22:31, 32).

e. The Holy Spirit as the Parakletos

One of the names of the Holy Spirit, according to the Greek language is Parakletos, meaning the Comforter and the One who stands beside us; He is always on our side, defending our case against the enemy. The meaning according to the Greek language clearly highlights that the Holy Spirit defends us against our enemy—the accuser.

2. Our responsibilities are:

a. Keeping our place in Christ through a continuous, living fellowship with Christ by prayer, repentance, and the Word of God

b. Learning how to put on and keep our spiritual armour (Ephesians 6:10–19)

c. Faith through obedience and the Word of God

d. Resistance when the enemy tempts us

e. Vigilance through searching oneself and repenting

CHAPTER 12

THE BLOOD OF JESUS IS THE REASON FOR MY EVERLASTING REJOICING

Introduction

L et us be glad and rejoice and give Him glory, for the marriage of the Lamb has come, and His wife has made herself ready (Revelation 19:7).

We will study this topic in five main titles:

   I. The Meaning of the Word *Joy/Rejoicing*[54]

  II. The Biblical Revelation About Spiritual Joy/Rejoicing

 III. Is Joy a Feeling or an Action?

 IV. The Fruits of a Life of Rejoicing

  V. Summary: References About Joy/Rejoicing Throughout the Bible

---

[54] We will use both words interchangeably throughout this study as they both have similar meanings and both occur in the biblical references.

I. The Meaning of the Word *Joy*/*Rejoicing*

A. The Linguistic Meaning

Joy/*rejoicing* as a noun:

1a. The emotion evoked by well-being, success, or good fortune or by the prospect of possessing what one desires: delight

1b. The expression of such emotion

2. A state of perfect happiness

3. A source or cause of delight

Joy/*rejoice* as a verb:

To experience great pleasure or delight: rejoice (verb)

B. The Meaning According to the Hebrew and Greek Languages of the Old and New Testaments

The biblical words are:

- Hebrew: *simha* which also implies the outward expression of joy

- Greek: *chara* [verb *chairō*, frequently used in the Septuagint and corresponds to the Hebrew word *simha*] means intense joy

In both the Old Testament and the New Testament, joy is consistently the mark of the believer and of the Church. It is a quality, and not simply an emotion, based on God Himself and is indeed derived from Him:

You will show me the path of life; in *Your presence is fullness of joy*; at Your right hand are pleasures forevermore (Psalm 16:11).

Rejoice in the Lord always. Again I will say, rejoice! (Philippians 4:4).

Now may *the God of hope fill you with all joy* and peace in believing, that you may abound in hope by the power of the Holy Spirit (Romans 15:13).

It characterises the Christian's life on earth:

Though now you do not see Him, yet believing, you rejoice with joy inexpressible and full of glory (1 Peter 1:8).

It also foretells eschatologically the joy of being with Christ forever in the Kingdom of heaven:

Let us be glad and rejoice and give Him glory, for the marriage of the Lamb has come, and His wife has made herself ready (Revelation 19:7).

II. The Biblical Revelation About Spiritual Joy/Rejoicing

A. In the Old Testament

- God rejoices in His people.

  Then I was beside Him as a master craftsman; and I was daily His delight, rejoicing always before Him, rejoicing in His inhabited world, and *my delight was with the sons of men* (Proverbs 8:30, 31).

  The Lord your God in your midst, the Mighty One, will save; *He will rejoice over you with gladness,* He will quiet you with His love, *He will rejoice over you with singing* (Zephaniah 3:17).

- God wants His people to be always rejoicing.

  And there you shall eat before the Lord your God, and *you shall rejoice in all to which you have put your hand,* you and your households, in which the Lord your God has blessed you ... *And you shall rejoice before the Lord your God,* you and your sons and your daughters, your male and female servants, and the Levite who is within your gates, since he has no portion nor inheritance with you (Deuteronomy 12:7, 12).

  Seven days you shall keep a sacred feast to the Lord your God in the place which the Lord chooses, because the Lord your God will bless you in all your produce and in all the work of your hands, *so that you surely rejoice* (Deuteronomy 16:15).

  So *you shall rejoice in every good thing which the Lord your God has given to you* and your house, you and the Levite and the stranger who is among you (Deuteronomy 26:11).

  You shall offer peace offerings, and shall eat there, and *rejoice before the Lord your God* (Deuteronomy 27:7).

- God's people rejoice in their God and worship Him.

  But let all those rejoice who put their trust in You; let them ever shout for joy, because You defend them; let those also who love Your name be joyful in You (Psalm 5:11).

I will be glad and rejoice in Your mercy, for You have considered my trouble; You have known my soul in adversities (Psalm 31:7).

And my soul shall be joyful in the Lord; it shall rejoice in His salvation (Psalm 35:9).

For You, Lord, have made me glad through Your work; I will triumph in the works of Your hands (Psalm 92:4).

Serve the Lord with gladness; come before His presence with singing (Psalm 100:2).

Glory in His holy name; let the hearts of those rejoice who seek the Lord! (Psalm 105:3).

This is the day the Lord has made; we will rejoice and be glad in it (Psalm 118:24).

- God's people rejoice in their God because He dwells among them.

"Sing and rejoice, O daughter of Zion! For behold, I am coming and I will dwell in your midst," says the Lord (Zechariah 2:10).

There is a river whose streams shall make glad the city of God, the holy place of the tabernacle of the Most High (Psalm 46:4).

I was glad when they said to me, "Let us go into the house of the Lord" (Psalm 122:1).

- God's people rejoice in His salvation.

Therefore with joy you will draw water from the wells of salvation (Isaiah 12:3).

I will greatly rejoice in the Lord, my soul shall be joyful in my God; for He has clothed me with the garments of salvation, He has covered me with the robe of righteousness, as a bridegroom decks himself with ornaments, and as a bride adorns herself with her jewels (Isaiah 61:10).

Sing, O daughter of Zion! Shout, O Israel! Be glad and rejoice with all your heart, O daughter of Jerusalem! (Zephaniah 3:14).

- God's people rejoice in God's Word.

  Your words were found, and I ate them, and Your word was to me the joy and rejoicing of my heart; for I am called by Your name, O Lord God of hosts (Jeremiah 15:16).

- God's people rejoice in all circumstances because they trust their God.

  Though the fig tree may not blossom, nor fruit be on the vines; though the labour of the olive may fail, and the fields yield no food; though the flock may be cut off from the fold, and there be no herd in the stalls—*Yet I will rejoice in the Lord*, I will joy in the God of my salvation (Habakkuk 3:17, 18).

- God always provides His people with joyous events.

  - Consecrating the temple (1 Kings 8:66; 1 Chronicles 29:9)

  - Rebuilding the ruined temple and the walls of Jerusalem (Ezra 3:13; Nehemiah 12:27, 43)

  - Events of victory over their enemies (2 Chronicles 20:27)

B. In the New Testament

1. The Synoptic Gospels

- Joy is centred on events related to Jesus:

  - His birth: *'Then the angel said to them, "Do not be afraid, for behold, **I bring you good tidings of great joy** which will be to all people"'* (Luke 2:10).

  - His ministry: *'Then the seventy returned with joy, saying, "Lord, even the demons are subject to us in Your name"'* (Luke 10:17).

  - His triumphal entry: *'Then, as He was now drawing near the descent of the Mount of Olives, the whole multitude of the disciples began to rejoice and praise God with a loud voice for all the mighty works they had seen'* (Luke 19:37).

  - His resurrection: *'So they went out quickly from the tomb with fear and great joy, and ran to bring His disciples word'* (Matthew 28:8).

- Joy in relation to Jesus' teachings:

  - Joy in heaven when a sinner repents: *'Likewise, I say to you, there is joy in the presence of the angels of God over one sinner who repents'* (Luke 15:10).

  - Joy even when accused with false sayings: *'Rejoice and be exceedingly glad, for great is your reward in heaven, for so they persecuted the prophets who were before you'* (Matthew 5:12).

2. The Gospel of John

- Jesus Himself speaks about this joy:

These things I have spoken to you, that My joy may remain in you, and that your joy may be full (John 15:11).

Until now you have asked nothing in My name. Ask, and you will receive, *that your joy may be full'* (John 16:24).

But now I come to You, and these things I speak in the world, that they may have My joy fulfilled in themselves (John 17:13).

- Seeing the resurrected Lord brings joy:

When He had said this, He showed them His hands and His side. Then *the disciples were glad when they saw the Lord* (John 20:20).

- Proclaiming and sharing the news of eternal life makes our joy full:

The life was manifested, and we have seen, and bear witness, and declare to you that eternal life which was with the Father and was manifested to us— that which we have seen and heard we declare to you, that you also may have fellowship with us; and truly our fellowship is with the Father and with His Son Jesus Christ. And these things we write to you *that your joy may be full* (1 John 1:2–4).

3. The Book of Acts

- Joy spreads as a result of the good news of the gospel:

And there was *great joy* in that city (Acts 8:8).

- Rejoicing in the midst of persecution:

So they departed from the presence of the council, *rejoicing* that they were counted worthy to suffer shame for His name (Acts 5:41).

- Joy characterised the life of the early church:

And the disciples were filled with joy and with the Holy Spirit (Acts 13:52).

- It also characterised the Eucharistic meal:

So continuing daily with one accord in the temple, and breaking bread from house to house, they ate their food with gladness and simplicity of heart (Acts 2:46).

4. The Epistles

Paul's letters

- Apostle Paul speaks of joy as a commandment:

Rejoice in the Lord always. Again I will say, rejoice! (Philippians 4:4).

Rejoice always (1 Thessalonians 5:16).

Finally, brothers, *rejoice*, be restored, be encouraged, be in agreement, be at peace, and the God of love and peace will be with you (2 Corinthians 13:11, LEB).

- Believers need to train themselves to exercise joy always, even in paradoxical circumstances:

As *sorrowful, yet always rejoicing*; as poor, yet making many rich; as having nothing, and yet possessing all things (2 Corinthians 6:10).

I am filled with comfort. *I am exceedingly joyful in all our tribulation* (2 Corinthians 7:4b).

And you became followers of us and of the Lord, *having received the word in much affliction, with joy of the Holy Spirit* (1 Thessalonians 1:6).

For you had compassion on me in my chains, and *joyfully accepted the plundering of your goods,* knowing that you have a better and an enduring possession for yourselves in heaven (Hebrews 10:34).

Rejoicing in such circumstances can be attained:

- Because of the Holy Spirit: *'But the fruit of the Spirit is love,* **joy,** *peace, longsuffering, kindness, goodness, faithfulness'* (Galatians 5:22).

- Because of our hope: *'**Rejoicing in hope,** patient in tribulation, continuing steadfastly in prayer'* (Romans 12:12).

- Because of being Kingdom people: *'For the Kingdom of God is not eating and drinking, but righteousness and peace **and joy in the Holy Spirit'*** (Romans 14:17).

- Because of God's grace that enables us: *'And He said to me, "My grace is sufficient for you, for My strength is made perfect in weakness." Therefore most gladly I will rather boast in my infirmities, that the power of Christ may rest upon me. Therefore I take pleasure in infirmities, in reproaches, in needs, in persecutions, in distresses, for Christ's sake. For when I am weak, then I am strong'* (2 Corinthians 12:9, 10).

- Because of God's power that is working in us: *'Strengthened with all might, according to His glorious power, for all patience and longsuffering with joy'* (Colossians 1:11).

• Rejoicing with others as an expression of fellowship with them in all their circumstances:

Rejoice with those who rejoice, and weep with those who weep (Romans 12:15).

And if one member suffers, all the members suffer with it; or if one member is honoured, all the members rejoice with it (1 Corinthians 12:26).

- Joy in suffering for the sake of the Body of Christ:

I now rejoice in my sufferings for you, and fill up in my flesh what is lacking in the afflictions of Christ, for the sake of His body, which is the church (Colossians 1:24).

- Joy in the fruits of ministry:

For what is our hope, or joy, or crown of rejoicing? Is it not even you in the presence of our Lord Jesus Christ at His coming? For you are our glory and joy (1 Thessalonians 2:19, 20).

- Joy for the leaders and superiors when they are obeyed:

Remember those who rule over you, who have spoken the word of God to you, whose faith follow, considering the outcome of their conduct (Hebrews 13:7).

Other Epistles (James' and Peter's)

- Joy in trials and temptations:

My brethren, count it all joy when you fall into various trials (James 1:2).

- Joy in knowing Christ and in the fellowship of Christ's sufferings:

Whom having not seen you love. Though now you do not see Him, yet believing, you rejoice with joy inexpressible and full of glory (1 Peter 1:8).

But rejoice to the extent that you partake of Christ's sufferings, that when His glory is revealed, you may also be glad with exceeding joy (1 Peter 4:13).

5. The Book of Revelation

- Bridal joy in the wedding of the Lamb:

Let us be glad and rejoice and give Him glory, for the marriage of the Lamb has come, and His wife has made herself ready (Revelation 19:7).

III. Is Joy a Feeling or an Action?

Actually, it is both a feeling and an action.

A. Joy as a Feeling

- Psalm 137:1–6 shows that the emotion of joy cannot be commanded. The captors of the Jews wanted them to sing in the land of their exile—something they were unable to do. Far away, Jerusalem was their chief joy.

By the rivers of Babylon, there we sat down, yea, we wept when we remembered Zion. We hung our harps upon the willows in the midst of it. For there those who carried us away captive asked of us a song, and those who plundered us requested mirth, saying, "Sing us one of the songs of Zion!" How shall we sing the Lord's song in a foreign land? If I forget you, O Jerusalem, let my right hand forget its skill! If I do not remember you, let my tongue cling to the roof of my mouth—if I do not exalt Jerusalem above my chief joy (Psalm 137:1–6).

- A person automatically experiences joy because of certain favourable circumstances:

  - The shepherd experienced joy when he found his lost sheep:

And if he should find it, assuredly, I say to you, *he rejoices* more over that sheep than over the ninety-nine that did not go astray (Matthew 18:13).

  - The multitude felt this joy when Jesus healed a Jewish woman whom Satan had bound for 18 years:

And when He said these things, all His adversaries were put to shame; and all *the multitude rejoiced* for all the glorious things that were done by Him (Luke 13:17).

  - The disciples returned to Jerusalem rejoicing after Jesus' ascension:

And they worshipped Him, and *returned to Jerusalem with great joy* (Luke 24:52).

- Joy was also the feeling of the church at Antioch when its members heard the Jerusalem Council's decision that they did not have to be circumcised to keep God's law:

When they had read it, they rejoiced over its encouragement (Acts 15:31).

- Paul mentioned his joy in hearing about the obedience of the Roman Christians:

For your obedience has become known to all. Therefore I am glad on your behalf (Romans 16:19a).

He wrote to the Corinthians that love does not rejoice in wrong but rejoices in the right: '[Love] *does not rejoice in iniquity, but rejoices in the truth'* (1 Corinthians 13:6).

Thus, joy as a feeling can occur as a result of good events. But at other times, we cannot have the feeling of joy because of sad situations. Yet, there is another type of joy that the Scriptures command!

B. Joy as an Action

Joy is an action that the person can participate in regardless of how he feels.

• Christ instructed his disciples to rejoice when they were persecuted and slandered:

Blessed are you when they revile and persecute you, and say all kinds of evil against you falsely for My sake. *Rejoice and be exceedingly glad,* for great is your reward in heaven, for so they persecuted the prophets who were before you (Matthew 5:11–12).

• Apostle Paul commanded continuous rejoicing:

Rejoice in the Lord always. Again I will say, rejoice! (Philippians 4:4).

Rejoice always (1 Thessalonians 5:16).

- Apostle James said that Christians ought to consider it all joy when they fall into various testing because such testing produces endurance:

  My brethren, count it all joy when you fall into various trials (James 1:2).

Joy in adverse circumstances is possible only as a fruit of the Holy Spirit, who is present in every Christian (Galatians 5:22).

IV. The Fruits of a Life of Rejoicing

1. Strength

Do not sorrow, for the joy of the Lord is your strength (Nehemiah 8:10c).

2. Joy arises from sadness

To clarify this point, Jesus mentioned the example of a woman in labour pain. At first, the woman is sad because of the pain involved, but when the child is born, she rejoices:

> A woman, when she is in labour, has sorrow because her hour has come; but as soon as she has given birth to the child, she no longer remembers the anguish, for joy that a human being has been born into the world (John 16:21).

3. Speedy spiritual growth

St. Anthony the Great (4th century) said that divine joy aids spiritual growth. It provides the believer with unseen spiritual wings that carry him, allowing him to move on speedily in his walk with Christ.

V. Summary: References About Joy/Rejoicing Throughout the Bible

A. A Suggested Formula for Joy

Joy = J for Jesus

    O for Others

    Y for Yourself

When I make Jesus, others, and myself a source of joy, joy springs up. In other words, I need to remind myself that Jesus is the source of joy, others are a source of joy when I serve them, and being a servant in Christ is a source of joy.

B. The Joy of God Over His People

1. The greatness of this joy is described in Zephaniah 3:17.

2. The joy of God over His people on account of their:

    a. Repentance (Luke 15:7, 10).

    b. Faith (Hebrews 11:5, 6).

    c. Fear of God (Psalm 147:11).

    d. Praying to God (Proverbs 15:8).

    e. Hope in God's mercy (Psalm 147:11).

    f. Meekness (Psalm 149:4).

    g. Uprightness (1 Chronicles 29:17; Proverbs 11:20).

3. The joy of God over His people leads to Him:

    a. Prospering them (Deuteronomy 30:9).

    b. Doing them good (Deuteronomy 28:63; Jeremiah 32:41).

    c. Delivering them (2 Samuel 22:20).

    d. Comforting them (Isaiah 65:19).

    e. Giving them their inheritance (Numbers 14:8).

4. The joy of God over His people is illustrated:

For as a young man marries a virgin, so shall your sons marry you; and as the bridegroom rejoices over the bride, so shall your God rejoice over you (Isaiah 62:5).

"And bring the fatted calf here and kill it, and let us eat and be merry; for this my son was dead and is alive again; he was lost and is found." And they began to be merry (Luke 15:23, 24).

5. The joy of God over His people is exemplified:

    ♦ Solomon

Blessed be the Lord your God, who delighted in you, setting you on the throne of Israel! Because the Lord has loved Israel forever, therefore He made you king, to do justice and righteousness (1 Kings 10:9).

C. Biblical References About Joy/Rejoicing

1. God gives joy (Ecclesiastes 2:26; Psalm 4:7).

2. Christ has been appointed to give joy (Isaiah 61:3).

3. Joy is a fruit of the Spirit (Galatians 5:22).

4. The gospel is the good tidings of joy (Luke 2:10, 11).

5. God's Word provides joy and rejoicing (Nehemiah 8:12; Jeremiah 15:16).

6. The gospel ought to be received with joy (1 Thessalonians 1:6).

7. Joy is promised to the saints (Psalms 132:16; Isaiah 35:10; 55:12; 56:7).

8. Joy is prepared for the saints (Psalms 97:11).

9. Joy is enjoyed by the saints (Psalms 32:11; Philippians 3:1).

10. There is fullness of joy in God's presence (Psalm 16:11).

11. Vanity of seeking joy from earthly things (Ecclesiastes 2:10, 11; 11:8).

12. Joy is experienced by:

   a. Believers (Luke 24:52; Acts 16:34).

   b. Peacemakers (Proverbs 12:20).

   c. The just (Proverbs 21:15).

   d. The wise and the discreet (Proverbs 15:23).

   e. Parents of good children (Proverbs 23:24).

13. Joy shall increase to the humble (Isaiah 29:19).

14. The joy of the saints is:

   a. In God (Psalm 89:16; 149:2; Habakkuk 3:18; Romans 5:11).

   b. In Christ (Luke 1:47; Philippians 3:3).

   c. In the Holy Spirit (Romans 14:17).

   d. That their names are written in heaven (Luke 10:20).

   e. In the Lord's salvation (Psalm 21:1; Isaiah 61:10).

   f. For being delivered from bondage (Psalm 105:43; Jeremiah 31:10–13).

   g. Because of the manifestation of God's goodness (2 Chronicles 7:10).

   h. For temporal (material) blessings (Joel 2:23, 24).

   i. For supplies of grace (Isaiah 12:3).

   j. For divine protection (Psalm 5:11; 16:8, 9).

   k. For divine support (Psalm 28:7; 63:7).

    l. For the victory of Christ (John 16:33).

    m. For the hope of glory (Romans 5:2).

    n. For the success of the gospel (Acts 15:3).

15. The joy of the saints should be:

    a. Great (Zechariah 9:9; Acts 8:8).

    b. Abundant (2 Corinthians 8:2).

    c. Exceeding (Psalm 21:6; 68:3).

    d. Full of life/lively (Psalm 32:11; Luke 6:23).

    e. Inexpressible (1 Peter 1:8).

    f. Full of glory (1 Peter 1:8).

    g. Constant (2 Corinthians 6:10; Philippians 4:4).

    h. Forevermore (1 Thessalonians 5:16).

    i. With awe (Psalm 2:11).

    j. In hope (Romans 12:12).

    k. In sorrow (2 Corinthians 6:10).

    l. Under trials (James 1:2; 1 Peter 1:6).

    m. Under persecutions (Matthew 5:11, 12; Luke 6:22, 23; Hebrews 10:34).

    n. Under calamities (Habakkuk 3:17, 18).

    o. Expressed in hymns (Ephesians 5:19; James 5:13).

16. The afflictions of the saints are followed by joy (Psalm 30:5; 126:5; Isaiah 35:10; John 16:20).

17. We ought to pray for the restoration of joy (Psalm 51:8, 12; 85:6).

18. We ought to promote joy in the afflicted (Job 29:13).

19. The joy of the saints is made full by:

    a. The favour of God (Acts 2:28).

    b. Faith in Christ (Romans 15:13).

    c. Abiding in Christ (John 15:10, 11).

    d. The Word of Christ (John 17:13).

    e. Answers to prayer (John 16:24).

    f. The communion of saints (2 Timothy 1:4; 1 John 1:3, 4; 2 John 1:12).

20. Saints should provide joy to their ministers (Philippians 2:2; Philemon 1:20).

21. Ministers should:

    a. Consider their people as their joy (Philippians 4:1; 1 Thessalonians 2:20).

    b. Promote joy in their people (2 Corinthians 1:24; Philippians 1:25).

    c. Pray for joy for their people (Romans 15:13).

    d. Have joy in the faith and holiness of their people (2 Corinthians 7:4; 1 Thessalonians 3:9; 3 John 1:4).

    e. Come to their people with joy (Romans 15:32).

    f. Finish their course with joy (Acts 20:24).

    g. Desire to render an account with joy (Philippians 2:16; Hebrews 13:17).

    h. Serve God with joy (Psalm 100:2).

22. Serving God willingly brings us joy (1 Chronicles 29:9, 17).

23. Joy strengthens the saints (Nehemiah 8:10).

24. Saints should engage in all feasts and services with joy (Ezra 6:22; Psalm 42:4).

25. Saints should have joy in all their undertakings (Deuteronomy 12:18).

26. Saints shall be presented before God with exceeding joy (1 Peter 4:13; Jude 1:24).

27. The coming of Christ will give saints exceeding joy (1 Peter 4:13).

28. Joy will be the final reward of saints on judgement day (Matthew 25:21).

29. The joy of the wicked:

    a. Is derived from earthly pleasures (Ecclesiastes 2:10; 11:9).

    b. Is derived from folly (Proverbs 15:21).

    c. Is delusive and false (Proverbs 14:13).

    d. Is short-lived (Job 20:5; Ecclesiastes 7:6).

    e. Will be turned into mourning (James 4:9).

    f. Will be taken away (Isaiah 16:10).

30. Joy is illustrated (Isaiah 9:3; Matthew 13:44).

31. Joy is exemplified:

    a. Hannah (1 Samuel 2:1).

    b. David (1 Chronicles 29:9).

    c. Wise men (Matthew 2:10).

    d. The Virgin Mary (Luke 1:47).

    e. Zacchaeus (Luke 19:6).

    f. Converts to the Christian faith (Acts 2:46; 13:52).

    g. Peter and the other apostles (Acts 5:41).

    h. The Samaritans (Acts 8:8).

    i. The Philippian jailer (Acts 16:34).

APPENDIX

Practical Steps for Releasing Oneself from Curses

Releasing oneself from a curse is a spiritual battle. Therefore, begin by proclaiming the 12 statements of the blood of Jesus[55] to protect yourself from any counterattack from the enemy, for breaking the curse means breaking the enemy.

As you take this time of prayer in the Lord's presence, be sensitive to His voice and respond to it. If the Holy Spirit convicts you of something or reminds you of a sin that you need to repent of, respond to Him because this will help release you from any curse.

Therefore, the first step is to proclaim the 12 statements of the blood of Jesus followed by a time of silent prayer to extend the power of the blood of Jesus on your household, your job, your possessions, your relationship and everything in your life.

This is a spiritual battle, so it is serious.

Afterwards, follow the following steps:

1. Establish a clear scriptural basis and understanding about the power of the Word of God

- In the spirit of prayer, repeat the following verses, specifying them to yourself:

Christ has redeemed us from the curse of the law, having become a curse for us (for it is written, "Cursed is everyone who hangs on a tree"), that the blessing of Abraham might come upon the Gentiles in Christ Jesus, that we might receive the promise of the Spirit through faith (Galatians 3:13, 14).

---

[55] See p.4 for the 12 statements of the blood of Jesus.

In Him we have redemption through His blood, the forgiveness of sins, according to the riches of His grace (Ephesians 1:7).

He has delivered us from the power of darkness and conveyed us into the Kingdom of the Son of His love, in whom we have redemption through His blood, the forgiveness of sins (Colossians 1:13, 14).

He who sins is of the devil, for the devil has sinned from the beginning. *For this purpose the Son of God was manifested, that He might destroy the works of the devil* (1 John 3:8).

Behold, I give you the authority to trample on serpents and scorpions, and over all the power of the enemy, and nothing shall by any means hurt you (Luke 10:19).

- Ask the Holy Spirit to let these words settle deep in your inner man and perform their work in you.

- Now, proclaim Jesus Christ as your Saviour, Lord, King, and High Priest. Say:

"I proclaim Jesus Christ as my Saviour, my Lord, my King, and my High Priest" (repeat 3 times).

2. Confess sins

- Ask the Holy Spirit to reveal any hidden sin so that you may confess it.

- After taking some time of prayer and confessing your sins, proclaim:

"The blood of Jesus has granted me forgiveness of all my sins."

- Continue to ask the Holy Spirit to reveal any hidden sin.

Now proclaim:

"The blood of Jesus, the Son of God, cleanses me from all sin."

- Continue to ask the Holy Spirit to search your heart and reveal any hidden sin.

Now proclaim:

"The blood of Jesus has granted me forgiveness of all my sins."

"The blood of Jesus, the Son of God, cleanses me from all sin."

3. Forgive

Remember that without forgiveness, you cannot be released from curses. Sometimes there are situations that are so difficult to forgive. But it all depends on your heart. If deep within you truly want to let go of everything and forgive, the Holy Spirit will enable you and give you the grace to forgive.

Forgiveness is a decision and not a feeling.

Forgive your friends.

Forgive your parents.

Forgive your pastors.

Forgive anyone who has hurt you.

Remember that all these matters are trivial. Be free in the spirit; let go; forgive; ask the Holy Spirit to help you.

4. Renounce all contact with the occult

Renounce all occult, known and unknown, what you are aware of and what you are unaware of.

Now proclaim:

"Jesus I love You. I submit myself to You. I adore You.

Jesus, You are the Saviour. My past, present, and future belong to You. I belong to You. I unite myself with You.

In the power of Your redemptive work, I renounce all contact with any occult. Amen."

5. Release yourself from any curse

Take a few minutes of silent prayer.

Now, pray the following prayer to release yourself:

- "Lord, Jesus Christ, I believe that you are the Son of God and the only way to God, and that you died on the cross for my sins and rose again from the dead. I proclaim Jesus is Risen.

- I renounce all my sins and I turn to You, Lord Jesus, for mercy and for forgiveness. I believe that you do forgive. From now on, I want to live for You; I want to hear Your voice and I want to obey You.

- In order to receive Your blessing, Lord, and to be released from any curse on my life, I have confessed the known sins committed by me, by my ancestors, or by other people related to me.

- Lord, I thank You because I believe that You have forgiven everything that I have confessed. Now, I want to say that I also forgive all the people who have harmed or wronged me. I forgive them all now as God has forgiven me.

- Also, Lord, I renounce any contact (whether through myself or anyone related to me) with Satan, any occult power in any form, or any kind of secret society. I also commit myself, Lord, to renounce from my house any kind of occult objects that honour Satan and dishonour Jesus Christ. With Your help, Lord, I will remove them all.

- And now, Lord Jesus, I thank you further that You were made a curse on the cross so that I may be redeemed from curse and may receive blessings. Because of what You did for me on the cross, I now release myself from every curse, every evil influence, and every dark shadow over me or my family from whatever source.

- I release myself now, in the name of Jesus. Amen."

Now take quiet prayer time to reflect on Jesus and be filled with thanksgiving and gratefulness to Him.

Conclusion: A prayer said by the Lord's servant

- "Now, Lord, because of this person's prayer, I break every curse that has been over his/her life. I revoke these curses now and I release him/her from them in the name of Jesus, the Son of God. In His all-prevailing name, I declare this person released.

- Satan, I declare to you that you no longer have any claim or any access to this person's life, his/her family, or his/her business. They have all been lifted out of the domain of darkness and transferred into the Kingdom of God's love.

- Thank You, Lord Jesus. I praise You. I give You the glory. I give You thanks. Amen."

Now, conclude with a time of worship and praise.

Made in the USA
Las Vegas, NV
08 January 2025

16038836R00215